Action Now!

A Citizen's Guide to Better Communities

RICHARD W. POSTON

SOUTHERN ILLINOIS UNIVERSITY PRESS
Carbondale and Edwardsville

Feffer & Simons, Inc.
London and Amsterdam

Library of Congress Cataloging in Publication Data

Poston, Richard Waverly.
  Action now!

  Includes index.
  1. Community development—United States.   2. Regional planning—United
States—Citizen participation.
1. Title.
HN90.C6P67   309.2'6'0973   76–949
ISBN 0–8093–0760–X
ISBN 0–8093–0763–4 pbk.

To
Marjorie
my wife

Contents

Preface

IN 1953 Harper & Row published *Democracy Is You: A Guide to Citizen Action*, which I prepared to help small communities develop increased civic initiative for the purpose of making themselves better places in which to live. The procedures suggested in that guide were drawn from extensive experimentation in Montana and Washington during the late 1940s and early 1950s, and have provided a point of departure which over the years has proved highly useful in effecting numerous social and physical improvements, including many millions of dollars worth of new and relocated industry. In principle, the basic concepts outlined in that book are still applicable. However, in recent years vast changes have occurred in America which have created many new community problems and greatly intensified many of yesterday's, thus bringing an enormous new surge of public interest in community development.

This public interest is reflected in the host of governmental aids—both technical and financial—which have been assembled at federal, state, and regional levels, and in the policy of using the federal government as an instrument for local problem-solving to an infinitely greater extent than at any previous time in American history. This national policy, which grew rapidly during the 1960s and will likely continue to grow in varied forms into the foreseeable future, has in itself created many practical and complex problems, not the least of which is how the small community can get itself into a position to make effective use of the enormous reservoir of aids the bureaucracy is attempting to deliver.

As this new surge of interest continues to spread, heavy emphasis is being placed on *area development*, for which local officials are being urged to organize formal agencies at county and multicounty levels. These agencies are expected to comply with federal requirements, and in accordance with these requirements, area development programs are commonly conducted by a paid staff using considerable amounts of financial assistance from the higher levels of government. Citizen participation is almost always one of the eligibility requirements for federal money. From the standpoint of effective development this is technically sound, but unfortunately this requirement usually receives little more than lip service.

The area approach to community problem-solving has come about in part because in ever-increasing numbers our small communities are finding it impossible to supply many of the advantages of modern living people desire. Not every small town can, for example, support the hospital facilities it needs. The obstacles to acquiring even a local doctor are often overwhelming. Many small communities are unable to develop enough economic activity to offer their people an adequate means of earning an income. These and numerous other attributes of modern living are feasible in much of small-town America only if they can be developed within a geographical area that contains one or more "growth centers" capable of supplying certain services to the entire area. For reasons such as these it is becoming increasingly clear that unless ways can be found to accomplish certain essential developments on an area-wide scale, it is not realistic to hope that the continuing decay of countless numbers of small communities can be reversed or even substantially checked—a condition which is contributing in significant ways to multiplying today's urban and suburban problems. Thus, the validity of area development must be recognized. But in the mass of new guidelines constantly being put out by the bureaucracy and in the push to make area development occur, there is a basic flaw that all too often is overlooked.

Comprehensive development at the area level requires not only a broad area outlook, it also requires the formation of cooperative arrangements among all individual communities in the area, and the need for citizen participation calls for a far more realistic effort than it usually receives. Despite mandates from the higher levels of government, these cooperative arrangements among local communities are not easily achieved, and with enough money it is much easier to set up a formal agency with a paid staff putting plans on paper that few people ever read or even know exist, than it is to generate real in-depth citizen participation—the principal ingredient of successful community and area development.

This brings us to the important fact that regardless of how much federal or state money is pumped into area planning and development, these programs are not likely to succeed to the degree expected of them unless effective development is also organized and carried out by the citizenry itself within each local community of which the area is comprised. For unless each individual community in the area develops an inner solidarity of its own, it will not be able to relate effectively and cooperatively to its neighboring communities or to the area as a whole, and the chances of building a firm foundation of real citizen participation will steadily decrease. Moreover, even in the social and economic complexities of today there are many community problems that can be handled only on a strictly local basis by determined local citizens. These principles have been proved over and over again, yet in case after case they continue to be ignored.

The fact is that development efforts are essential at *both* local and area levels, and only as such efforts are organized and set in motion —community by community—throughout the area will it be possible to build the coordinated and mutually supportive operations which are the basic underpinnings of effective area development.

Because of these fundamental principles, together with the enormous changes in American life we are now witnessing, I have decided to write this new guide tailored to the current scene as a textbook for citizens who are willing to take the initiative which is necessary to make local and area development actually work. This guide may also be used as a student text at the graduate level and by professional community development practitioners.

Action Now! A Citizen's Guide to Better Communities will focus first on individual communities as social units of the area in which they exist, then move to the area level. If maximum success is to be achieved each community in the area will organize a development effort of its own, which as I have indicated, is essential to successful area development. The guide will offer material that each individual community can use, either in whole or in part according to its local situation, and will point the way to an effective area-wide effort. With appropriate adaptations, the guide may be used in suburban areas and in local neighborhoods of the large urban complex. But primarily it is written for small towns and cities in rural America.

No arbitrary limits are set on the size of communities in which it may be used. What people regard as a small community differs from one part of the nation to another, and specific operational procedures will necessarily vary in accordance with local conditions, including among other factors the size and distribution of the population. This is simply to say that because all communities are unique, as are all human beings, no development guide can be devised that will fit without alteration every local and area situation.

For this reason the guide should be treated as a working tool to be used with flexibility, not as a blueprint or magic formula. It makes no attempt to say if you do this, then this, then this, your community and area problems will, *ipso facto*, be resolved. One of the hard facts of life is that no community or area can achieve real improvements beyond the willingness and determination of its own citizens. The guide will offer principles, recommendations, and suggested ways of organizing and generating effective action. It will begin with a statement of philosophy concerning the need for community and area development in America today. From that background it will move into the crucial matter of goal setting, then present specific strategies and procedures for putting your development effort into operation.

Richard W. Poston

Carbondale, Illinois
July 1975

Action Now!

1

The Need

FOR nearly two hundred years American democracy—a design for living that shaped a nation, altered the course of history, and conditioned the thinking of generations—has struggled for survival. Today that struggle continues. This, then, is one of the urgent questions we must ask: Can our American dream, with its traditions of freedom and equality of opportunity, be fully realized?

The answer to this question will depend upon many actions and events—national and worldwide—but in the final analysis it will depend upon how much effort we Americans are willing to make inside our own cities and towns and neighborhoods. For unless there is a continued exercise of civic responsibility by the people themselves in the places where they live, no democratic society can exist. No matter what actions we may take at the upper reaches of our national life—administrative, legislative, or judicial—it is here, at the local level, that democracy must work and have meaning if it is to work and have meaning anywhere. No institution or bureaucracy, no national organization or association —private or public, political or religious, professional or academic—can substitute for the qualities of local initiative and civic performance that are needed to make democracy a living method of human society. Democracy cannot be set in motion or made real through actions super-imposed from above. It cannot be manufactured and projected nationally in the form of mass movements. It can come only from within, from the people in their local communities. But today the local community is being overwhelmed.

With our science and technology we have created an age of bigness, of corporate structures and giant agencies that have brought achievements our country's founders could not have imagined. We have mastered new principles of physics and chemistry and electricity, pushed outward the frontiers of medicine, synthesized the gene, unlocked the atom, and extended our explorations from the mysteries of the ocean depths to the secrets of outer space. We have fashioned tools of engineering and planning that have enabled us to add new riches to our store of wealth and set ourselves free from the drudgery of yesterday.

In arriving at this state of advancement we have developed a business and financial enterprise that has increased our potential for productivity and given us a system of credit that makes it unnecessary to wait even until tomorrow for much of what we want. We can now enjoy next year's income this year while we are still paying for what we enjoyed last year, and we need not fret over items that wear out or become obsolete. We can merely throw them away, clutter our landscape, and acquire new ones.

We have built our schools and universities into great factories of learning where graduates are mass produced, where knowledge is sorted and classified into carefully prescribed compartments, and where information is fed to our children that only a few years ago was unknown even to their teachers. Our research has become so extensive we have had to invent the microfilm because we no longer have even space enough to store our recorded product. We have created computers with which to expand the capacity of the human brain. We have developed systems of specialization that make it possible to devote a lifetime to becoming an expert in the most minute particle of human endeavor without caring or knowing much of anything about anything else, and from a maze of academic curricula we are turning out more holders of advanced degrees than we know what to do with—many of whom are virtually out of touch with the world as it is.

With these instruments of mass learning and productivity we have succeeded spectacularly in creating the social and cultural fabric of modern America. Yet with all our intelligence our society grows more frustrated and more bizarre, its internal stresses grow deeper and more destructive, and the threat to our republic and to our American dream grows more severe.

This is the age in which we are living, an age in which forces more frightening and more powerful than ever before are gnawing at the sinews of our democracy. These forces have not come from democratic processes. They are a side effect of the very technology and growth from which we have derived our modern advantages. This is not to condemn technology, or to renounce the inevitability of bigness. Nor is it to attack private enterprise which is increasingly accepting social responsibilities, as well as the business responsibilities that are essential to a sound economy.

It is merely to acknowledge the fact that along with the enormous advantages our technology and our massive growth have brought, we are sacrificing at a steadily increasing pace the qualities of local self-determination that are essential to democracy. We are losing much of the richness of community life. We are allowing our democracy to be smothered by gigantism. We are forgetting that if most Americans are to apply themselves in any personal or satisfying way to the pressing needs of our age they will have to do it, not as bits and pieces of mass movements or as statistical abstractions of nationwide programs, but as fully accredited human beings in their home towns and neighborhoods. Amidst the clamor of bigness and the demands for institutional change we must find ways to focus on the community, for this is the one institution that must work if any other democratic institution is to work.

Within the framework of modern times we must organize and develop patterns of community life that will permit us to work on our problems, at least in part, by practicing democracy in a direct, personal way in accordance with responsible insights and concerns we develop on our own in concert with our fellow townsmen and neighbors without waiting for directives from a government office. Within the context of the present we must continuously renew and reapply those qualities of our national heritage expressed by that famous Frenchman, Alexis de Tocqueville, who in reporting his observations of American democracy in the 1830s, wrote these words:

"These Americans are the most peculiar people in the world. You'll not believe it when I tell you how they behave. In a local community in their country a citizen may conceive of some need which is not being met. What does he do? He goes across the street and discusses it with his neighbor. Then what happens? A committee comes into existence and then the committee begins functioning on behalf of that need. And you won't believe this but it is true. All of this is done without reference to any bureaucrat. All of this is done by the private citizens on their own initiative."

It was this civic behavior which Tocqueville described as "peculiar," emerging as it did out of a long period of colonialism, that led America into the path of democracy from its earliest beginnings. For more than a century and a half before the Declaration of Independence, villages and towns were organized and developed by the people who lived in them. Frequently, these early communities became disorganized, riddled by factions, and hampered internally. Many of them failed. Others almost failed.

But little by little, the colonists were moved by experience to deal with their differences, to exercise responsibility in civic affairs, to help each other when help was needed, and—in the course of taking action to cope with adversity—civic effort, neighborliness, and mutual respect gradually emerged as integral parts of American community life.

And so a new nation was born—unlike any other the world had seen—a nation in which principles of freedom, equal rights, local responsibility, and representative government were for the first time in history proclaimed as a practical way of life; a concept that startled the then civilized world. It was a set of ideals yet to be fully realized, but from the experience gained in developing their communities in accordance with their self-determined goals, then building upward from that local base, the American people had made a substantial beginning.

Today, two centuries later, life has grown more complicated, our society more complex, and our troubles infinitely more aggravated and resistant to solution. Yet there is one basic fact that has not changed one iota: We still cannot handle our community problems by any less effort at the local level than was required in the earliest years of our nation's history.

If in our time we are to continue the task of translating our democratic faith into democratic action, it is imperative that we not forget the parallel task of organizing and developing communities in which that peculiar brand of civic behavior noted by Tocqueville in nineteenth-century America can still occur. In our small towns and in infinite numbers of neighborhoods in our urban areas, we must develop for today local settings in which a viable, humane, personalized, self-renewing community life can flourish. These two fundamental tasks—the continuing development of democracy, and the continuing development of communities in which there is an atmosphere of civic responsibility, informal social control, neighborly good will, and mutual concern with the common good—must go hand in hand. For the failure of either will mean the failure of both. If in this age of bigness, in this day of the megalopolis, we cannot find either the time or the means to accomplish these interlocking tasks, our American dream will become a nightmare.

With our science and technology, our material wealth, and our massive public service, we now have an array of tools for community problem-solving that was not available to our forebears. But the possession of these modern tools—impressive though they may be—does not guarantee that democracy will continue to be built. Only vigorous localities and areas inhabited by courageous men and women, using these tools for the common good can do that.

We cannot bring back the small community of our American past, and would not do so if we could. The good old days weren't that good, and undue romanticism about an earlier and simpler time would be an illusion, an escape from the stringent needs of the present. But if in the age in which we are living we are to achieve in actual practice the national ideals proclaimed by our founding fathers, it is imperative that we develop units of community life that will enable us to exert at least as much determination from the bottom up as is now being exerted from the top down.

In a community where there is vigorous community life—whether it is a small town or a neighborhood in a city or suburb—there is a spirit of local pride, an interpersonal network of relationships, that make it possible for the people who live there to act with unity and resolution. There is a pervading climate of civic vitality that makes cooperation the rule—not the exception, enough organizational machinery to provide open access to decision making, enough acceptance of differences to allow for healthy debate, and enough active friendship, mutual respect, and internal cohesiveness to maintain the community's integrity as an organic whole. There is a pattern of living that makes it possible for all local residents to feel—and in fact be—important. Vigorous community life is intangible, exceedingly difficult to define, perhaps impossible to measure. But it is this social quality that more than any other single factor can make our democracy real.

We have such communities in America today, but there aren't nearly enough of them, and in the swirl of current social change even many of those we have are barely managing to hold on. High-speed transportation, the mass media, the continuous shifting of population and markets, the centralization of economic and political power—the whole complex of forces which has marked the advent of modern times—is exerting a national impact that is causing our rural areas and small towns to become increasingly unattractive as places in which to live, and our cities increasingly unbearable and more hostile to the basic tenets of democracy. The human attributes that flow from a viable community life are being eaten away because community life itself is being eaten away. Nationally, we are taking on the character of a fabulous mansion in which the residents are very busy with their affairs, but which has termites in the supporting timbers. The local community, an essential unit in the foundation of any democratic society, is badly in need of repair.

A new age of excitement, variety, and opportunity has come into being, and the displacement of the old by the new is relentless and inevitable. As the metropolitan complex spills over the landscape in great extensions of steel and concrete, increasing millions take up residence without knowing or caring about each other, without being conscious of themselves as communities. Neighbors rarely speak. Men, women, and children go their daily separate ways to be swallowed in the anonymous crowd, and the family loses much of the significance it must have to remain intact.

Increasingly, the urban inner core becomes a cesspool of racial enclaves, the urban extremities an assortment of mortgaged dwellings and a fractured and impersonal mass of population globs. Human interaction and individuality are lost to batteries of punch cards, computer tapes, and programmed systems devoid of flesh and blood. Steadily and systematically we are moved toward uniformity and compliance, as scores of millions are reduced to spectators of the passing scene. Easy virtue gains acceptance. Moral and spiritual values grow sterile. Uncounted numbers wander aimlessly in a social void. Crime, delinquency, a fear of something we cannot define take increasing hold, and in the ceaseless struggle between rival groups acts and threats of violence are commonplace. These are some of the symptoms of our failure to build into modern times a social climate capable of nurturing the basic social qualities to which we as a nation are historically committed.

Gradually, we are putting aside ancient prejudices that have violated our belief in democracy, and have risen to a level of sophistication that has led to vast national programs dedicated to long needed reforms. With these massive programs we are making powerful nationwide onslaughts against virtually all forms of social injustice and are attempting to remake our environment. But in our haste to capitalize on our new enlightenment and to smash by mighty blows all obstacles in our path, we are unwittingly losing ground. The very magnitude of our national programs, coupled as they are with the continued erosion of community life, is making it increasingly difficult for most Americans to identify personally with the reforms that are being organized, or to acquire any real significance in the planning that is being done.

Guiding policies and decisions come not from enlightened communities, but from remote centers of control that have little regard for the community as a viable social unit as long as nationally determined objectives are pursued. Local compliance—not local initiative—is the overriding concern. Protest—not discussion; demand—not persuasion; confrontation—not exchange are the encouraged modes. Exercised reason is replaced by exercised power. Cooperation is forced out of date. Community programs become not functions of the community, but of splinter elements within the community supported by benevolent outside powers in accordance with whatever national policies are currently in fashion. National bureaucracies, free of restraint from the local base of the society, range at will over the country, cut across local boundaries, form alliances with selected clientele, search out and heighten existing hostilities, and set diverse segments within the community against each other. Progress toward desired ends is sometimes achieved, at least temporarily, but new fissures are opened, and the potential for united local effort is wrecked.

In our rural areas, our small towns, and our urban neighborhoods —democratic living and community self-reliance are being reduced. Top-level strategists and high-level combinations riding the crest of mass-media publicity are preempting the field, and in the community there is a rising trend toward abdication of responsibility. Perhaps this is merely to recognize life as it is. The mass society is, after all, a reality, and for many of our problems there are no solutions other than mass solutions. But the gap between our capacity to develop within our communities a social and physical environment favorable to our well-being, and our actual level of performance is not being closed. Instead, it is being widened to an awesome crevasse.

In summary, then, this is today's challenge for community development: To reawaken within the framework of modern times community settings and conditions that will make it possible for those social and spiritual values which are a part of our national heritage—values such as neighborliness and human understanding, such as community consciousness, local initiative, and civic competence—to be fully expressed. This is not a challenge for more social action of the mass-pressure variety that makes daily headlines. It is not a challenge for action that focuses on a specific issue or reform as an end in itself, however worthwhile the cause. The challenge for community development in America today is much broader and far more difficult to define. It is a matter of discovering and putting to work practical methods of creating a force for community problem-solving—rooted in the community itself, generated from the local level upward—that will enable us to use our modern technology and our mass public services to make good our national concern for social progress. It is a matter of recognizing that regardless of what public agencies, mass movements, or programs of reform may be established at the national level, democratic self-determination can be kept alive only to the extent that we are able to maintain and continuously renew a vigorous community life at the local base of our society.

This book is addressed to those of you who wish to bring about this kind of development.

2

The Goal

ONE of the most crucial elements that will determine the success or failure of your community development effort is the ultimate goal you have in mind from the moment you begin making plans to get started. Just what, in the long run, should a successful development effort enable your community and area to accomplish?

Let's first take a look at the broad meaning of the term "community development" as it is used in this guide. Usually, people think of community development in relation to new industry, more jobs, more and better housing, needed school construction, a better water or sewer system, a cleaner and more attractive environment, a new library, a recreation center, or virtually any other physical improvement. It may be thought of as the development of almost any new public service, or as the promotion of what may be regarded as an important issue or reform. Certainly, goals such as these are necessary parts of community development, and if you carefully determine your community's needs and limitations, then work out a definite plan of action, using whatever local resources you have and can afford, plus whatever additional resources you may be able to generate on an area-wide scale or bring in from the outside, you can obtain the improvement you wish to go after. Usually, that is. Though you may have to put up a considerable fight to get it done.

In this guide, however, I am going to suggest—indeed, urge—that in getting ready to start a development effort in your community, you avoid stirring up fights and begin thinking in a much larger context than that of any single issue or project or improvement. First, do some serious thinking about the basic makeup of your community, about its physical and social composition. Think of it in its entirety. Envision it as a physical unit in which there are buildings and grounds and streets that can be plotted on a map. Let your mind wander through all its physical features until you have formed a mental picture of its total structure. Then, envision it as a maze of human activity, as a body of people in which there are many diverse attitudes, interests, aspirations, characteristics, and internal forces and pressures, all of which contribute to the special flavor and conditions that distinguish your community from others. These varied ingredients—social, economic, cultural, political—form numerous crosscurrents which exert a powerful influence on the direction your community is moving, affect profoundly its ability for civic achievement, and largely determine its way of life—either for better or for worse. It is this whole complex pattern of social attributes woven into a living mosaic of human behavior that provides the essential grist to be taken into account if a truly effective development effort is to be launched and carried out.

Now, with this wide-ranging perception of your community, tick off the projects you would like to initiate—a campaign for new industry, the development of better housing, a drive against environmental pollution, whatever they might be. Then—and this is the critical element in your deliberations—consider a point of view which says that *none* of these projects you have listed, no matter how important, comprises the ultimate goal of the community effort you are about to start. Look upon these specific projects, not as ends in themselves, but merely as intermediate actions in a series of actions, which if accomplished within the frame-work of widespread citizen participation and informed public discussion and decision-making, instead of being pushed through by a small hand-picked group ready to do battle with all comers, can become instrumental in achieving the most important goal of all: *The development of your community into an effective problem-solving citizenry.*

At first glance this goal may seem somewhat nebulous. It is. And those who are accustomed to deciding behind closed doors what improvements the community should have, then moving ahead, whether the community as a whole likes it or not, may even tend to discount such a goal. Others who believe the application of sheer power is the only way anything of significance ever gets done may say such a goal is impossible. But in a democracy this is the most practical and important goal toward which any community can strive. This is the heart of what real community development is all about, for what it means is simply this: That democracy itself, when fully activated and put to work, is the single most powerful human force a community can muster for the satisfaction of its physical and social needs; that once your community begins to realize *this* goal, then *every* needed improvement will be more easily accomplished, and the very act of each achievement will contribute still further to the cultivation of an effective citizenry.

This is a concept of community development that regards the *ability* to achieve needed projects even more important than the projects them-selves. Indeed, in getting ready to start the development effort in your community, this concept is so important it cannot be overstated. For even if you succeed in accomplishing what appears to be an extremely valuable project, unless in doing so the community moves substantially in the direction of this underlying goal, the civic ignorance and indifference, the internal jealousies and hostilities—all these intangible human factors that comprise the major obstacles to virtually every community improvement, that tend to undermine a town's desirability as a place in which to live—will remain intact, perhaps even increase.

To make this seemingly nebulous goal, your stated objective is simply to say that although certain facilities and services are needed in all communities, community development is concerned fundamentally, not with *things*, but with *people*—their relationships and interactions with each other and with their institutions, including their agencies of government. It is to see community development as a many-faceted exercise in civic organization and action carried out by the whole community in such a way as to make it possible for the people to generate among themselves a deeper sense of community, to make themselves more adept as a body politic. It is to say that what is most important is not the tangible improvements that may be accomplished, but the degree of civic spirit, the level of social cohesion and solidarity, the skill in cooperative action which the community as a whole may acquire in the course of planning and carrying out those improvements.

Obviously, these intangible civic attributes cannot be expected to just come about all of a sudden. Their development will be an open-ended journey, never fully completed. But as these attributes take form and become increasingly a part of the community's way of life, your town will grow into an ever-richer environment in which to live. It will become increasingly able to provide the facilities and services it must have. It will grow in its power to get things done.

By proceeding with this goal firmly in mind you will initiate an operation that can grow into a deliberate effort by the whole citizenry to lift its overall level of civic performance, thereby strengthening its position as a self-determining unit of society. In most local improvement programs this nebulous goal—just because it is nebulous and in many respects difficult to grasp—is seldom recognized as the ultimate objective. Yet the realization of this goal is imperative to the well-being of all human communities. Why then not recognize from the outset that this is the basic goal, and organize the development effort accordingly!

It means: A growing in civic quality; a way of doing things that makes it possible for the local citizenry to mold itself into a community more capable of sustaining its social and economic health; an increasing desire by the whole community to instill within itself those qualities of goodwill that cause apathy, resentment, and needless conflict to give way to positive thinking. This is the *development of community*, the gradually unfolding process of creating a social climate in which the most priceless resource of every community—its people—will not be wasted. This, in the long run, is the only kind of development that will enable your community to rise to its real potential for achievement.

This, then, is the central purpose of this development guide: The effort itself, a concerted civic endeavor that can make the difference between a town in which democracy is really practiced and one in which it is just talked about. To accomplish this purpose, the development effort must be conceived and planned not as just another promotion by a particular interest group but as a community-wide operation encompassing a broad range of interrelated actions that will penetrate all aspects of local need. It must be structured in a way that will make it possible for all elements in the community—rich and poor and all in between—to have a voice in determining the varied projects and actions it produces as it goes along.

Planned and organized in this manner, fruitful new avenues will be opened to responsible citizenship. An ongoing flow of interesting and significant community doings may be set in motion through which all local residents will gain increased respect toward themselves and each other; become increasingly adept at replacing suspicion with trust, hostility with understanding; and at finding practical opportunities to turn their social discontent into moods and attitudes that will enable them to eliminate the causes of discontent. In the course of building and carrying out such a development effort, realistic adjustments to both internal and external limitations will be discovered, and the people will learn how to preserve those values they wish to retain while at the same time gaining whatever new values they must have to continuously renew their integrity as a viable community.

Thus, in preparing for your development effort, give careful attention to the importance of providing openings for the talents and resources that all citizens, groups, and existing organizations in your community have to offer. Devise ways of putting the effort together so that its very structure will create easily accessible roles for all who may become interested. Make it possible for all persons to have a personal stake in its success. Set it up so that it will provide a definite means by which people may discover for themselves the nature and causes of their community problems and make themselves aware of what they can do to help solve those problems. Remember that what you are starting is much more important than just another improvement project. Be conscious of the fact that you are setting in motion a process of experience and self-discovery; an operation through which local incentive for self-help can grow and assert itself; a ferment of democratic action that can engender a local will for constructive action for whatever purpose action is needed.

With these principles in mind, we are now in a position to define the concept of community development to which this guide is committed: A democratic process of community self-discovery and problem-solving organized to deal comprehensively with the community in its entirety and with all the varied functions of community life, recognizing that all of these functions are interrelated and are integral parts of the whole. The ultimate goal is to evolve through cooperative study, planning, and action an increasingly higher level of civic performance, and a physical and social environment best suited to the maximum growth of all the community's residents—as individuals, as productive members of their society, as a self-determined civic body.

If this kind of effort is built in each individual community in a given area, then a firm foundation will have been established for an effective area development effort. The term "area" as used here refers to whatever the residents of your community and of your neighboring communities regard as your area. This may be your county, two or more counties, or depending on terrain and various geographical features it may not coincide entirely with any official political boundaries. But whatever is determined locally to be the area of which your community is a part, it is that area and the individual communities it includes with which this development guide is concerned.

3

Strategy

HAVING discussed the broad meaning of community development, we must now consider a strategy by which it can be put into practice. We must allow a certain leeway for bold and imaginative thinking and accept the importance of doing some things that may seem a bit unusual, perhaps even startling. But above all we must be realistic. We must take into account the fact that a comprehensive effort in community development will require a great deal of voluntary civic energy, which even under the best of circumstances can be sustained at peak levels of productivity for only limited periods of time.

Bearing both these considerations in mind—the need for boldness and the need to be practical—I am going to suggest that we approach the important matter of strategy by thinking of the development effort in two distinct phases of operation: The first phase to be short range in nature and organized in a fairly informal way; the second phase to be long range in nature and organized on a more formal basis. The first phase will in essence be aimed at breaking through certain intangible obstacles to which we have already alluded—apathy, negative thinking, and the many other attributes that make effective civic performance impossible. The first phase of operations therefore requires an organizational structure wherein people can come to grips with these basic obstacles in unthreatening ways and begin to eliminate them.

To create this framework within which to function, it is extremely important during phase one to avoid insofar as possible the typical bureaucratic entanglements that almost inevitably accompany financial aid for special projects from the higher levels of government, either federal or state. This does not mean that phase one should be so informal that nothing definite can be accomplished, but it does mean a citizens operation open to everyone in the community, and which is conducive to a kind of fun as well as work.

This calls for setting aside a clear-cut period of time which the community consciously and deliberately carves out of its business-as-usual existence for the specific purpose of taking a new and intensive look at itself; a period during which all elements of the community's population may join together in a fresh start toward local problem-solving through their own efforts, thereby treating themselves to an exciting experience in grass-roots democracy without getting bogged down in the complexities of officialdom. Setting aside this special period of time is not always easy to accomplish on a community-wide scale. But it can be done. It has been done in other communities, and it is essential if maximum success is to be achieved.

For the duration of this special period of commitment, the development effort must be organized in a manner that will enable the community as a whole to examine realistically and objectively all aspects of its total-life situation, formulate plans, and carry out actions that can be completed quickly without large expenditures of money. This should make it unnecessary to go outside the community for financial assistance, and provide the citizenry with an immediate sense of accomplishment, thus generating a high degree of civic unity and determination with which to proceed into the second phase of operations during which the development effort will continue on a more formal but less intensive basis. The length of time to be set aside for the first operational phase should cover an uninterrupted period of at least six to seven months, depending on the scope of program planning and development the community wishes to undertake.

As frequently as once a week during this initial period, special public meetings—procedures for which will be suggested in succeeding sections—should be held for the purpose of discussing local problems and deciding what to do about them. This may mean that some of the community's organizations may temporarily need to rearrange their customary meeting times in order to clear this one night a week for these special community development meetings. If such rearranging is needed it may cause a bit of grumbling here and there, but think about it. Actually, this is a pretty small short-term sacrifice for a substantial long-term gain.

If a weekly schedule is too much for your community, a less demanding schedule may be adopted, but again weekly public meetings over a period of six or seven months are no great price to pay for this important phase of the development effort. However, whatever schedule is adopted these special public meetings should be held at sufficiently frequent intervals to maintain close continuity from each meeting to the next, and every effort should be made to develop the activity and the resulting action at as high a level of intensity as the community can muster. *Under no circumstances should these special public meetings be left merely to an "on-call" basis.*

Also, the public meeting schedule should be regular, clearly understood, and agreed to in advance, and unless there is a compelling reason to change the dates of one or two meetings, this schedule, once established, should be religiously adhered to. I have worked with communities in which the people refused to postpone one of these scheduled meetings even during the Christmas holiday season.

For added emphasis we should now make more explicit two other steps already mentioned briefly that *should not* be taken during this initial period, but postponed until the development effort is well under way and moving into the second phase of operations.

First, *do not* inject into the phase-one organizational structure any political overtones or legal formalities that could detract from broad citizen participation and local self-determination. Specifically, do not get the phase-one organizational structure incorporated—either on a non-profit or for-profit basis. Second, keep the phase-one organizational structure strictly a community affair by avoiding any special-project grant or loan from state or federal sources.

To refrain from these two steps during the initial period of operations may seem very much out of the ordinary. But either of these steps if taken during the early stages of the development effort could be disastrous. Either would require some kind of a formally organized entity, an official charter, official bylaws, official board of directors, and in all probability would result in a paid staff to do the work. This formal entity could be either public or private, but in either case it would not be a true community effort. Instead, eager, well-meaning individuals, anxious to move on a particular project or line of action they are convinced the community needs, jump out in front, set up a formal corporate entity eligible to receive special government grants or loans, then talk themselves into believing they will have the community's backing. Repeatedly, this assumed backing fails to materialize; the promoters find themselves out struggling alone, trying desperately to plow their way through waves of opposition, resenting the community's lack of support, and wondering why the people can't seem to understand. Gestures may be made toward obtaining community representation, such as appointing a citizens advisory council. But very few people will know what the council is supposed to do. Even fewer will care.

As a result of these formal actions which in recent years have become virtually routine, important services and improvements are floundering in communities across the country while conflicting groups jockey for control of programs most of the people know nothing about. Delay piles on delay, local tempers flare, charges and countercharges are hurled, paid staff members become so preoccupied guarding their positions and writing reports they have little time for anything else, and endless numbers of projects bearing the label "community development" are in reality no more than payroll operations that have the effect of suppressing—instead of aiding—community development.

Even worse, many communities have been stricken by what could aptly be called the "waiting-for-the-government-disease," a civic malady from which there is no promise of recovery. It works like an opiate on local initiative, tending to put the citizenry to sleep. Old problems go unsolved. New ones are added. The community becomes increasingly inept, and state and federal agencies—even municipal and county governments—are confronted by situations they are not equipped to handle. With only the barest minimum of effort by the citizenry itself, government at all levels is left with just that: A minimum effort to assist.

Such pitfalls will not be easy to avoid in starting your development operation, for attitudes and practices which lead to these problems have become ingrained in the national scene. These are powerful forces, which coupled with the continuing breakdown of vigorous community life, are conditioning local leaders to think of outside financial aid by whatever name may be in vogue at the moment as an exceedingly glittering lure. Thus, largely by default, responsibility for the resolution of community problems is being transferred away from the community itself and placed in the hands of formal agencies whose directions come from outside the community.

Considering the nature of modern times, this is to a large extent inevitable. But as this transfer has accelerated without sufficient attention being given to the fact that local civic responsibility is still essential to local development, it has become next to impossible for many communities to engage in almost any independent action to deal with local needs. Indeed, it has become extremely difficult to maintain enough independence of action to make it possible for democratic problem-solving to function effectively at any level. More and more, local communities are beginning to feel that because many of their problems have become too heavy to handle by their own efforts, local self-reliance is no longer relevant. As a weekly newspaper editor put it: "There is nothing that can't be done in this town if God and the federal government will do it."

Today this state of dependency is assuming the proportions of a national epidemic from which almost no community is immune. Government at the higher levels has become so widely accepted as the principal instrument for dealing with local problems that when local leaders begin thinking of an effort in community development it is virtually automatic to look first, not to the community itself, but to

Washington or the state capital. It is simply the fashionable thing to do.

Thus, a fantasy image is built of what government is able to accomplish. Caught up in this fantasy, civic leaders are willing to expend endless amounts of energy pursuing state or federal deliverymen long before the community is organized or prepared to receive, digest, and make effective use of the deliveries. This is not to ignore the practical value of a formal corporate entity or of federal and state aids as tools for community development. Current state and national tax structures, corporate development organizations, and the mechanisms of the bureaucracy are some of the realities of modern America. And if most communities are to meet their social and economic needs, they must learn to deal with these realities.

But for purposes of effective community development a crucial part of the strategy is timing, of doing first things first. It is a matter of exercising enough patience and civic effort to build solidly from the bottom up by going through what we have designated as the first phase of operations—a period during which the community establishes informally and on its own initiative a system that enables it to chart its own course of action. It is a matter of staying away from legalistic formalities which tend to create the illusion that a community development effort is being mounted, when in reality it is not.

As development tools, the formalities we have been discussing should be treated as exactly that and nothing more—development tools. For these tools, however alluring they may seem, will be of little value unless they are used *only* as a means of supplementing and strengthening the local effort *after* that effort has been firmly established.

The importance of going through the first phase of operations in order to actually build this local effort without allowing it to be sidetracked by outside forces or premature formalities may seem a demanding route to successful community development. And it is. But if you and your community are really serious there is no shortcut. In summary, then, let us reiterate the two-phase strategy we are recommending.

1. That it would be impossible to sustain over more than a relatively short period of time the high level of intensity the development effort should attain during the first phase of operations.

2. Without having first gone through phase one, it would be equally impossible to achieve the depth of civic initiative and cooperation necessary to maintain in effective working order the more formal development

entities the community effort will require during the second phase of operations.

Later in the guide we will discuss steps that may be taken to effect an orderly transition between these two operational phases and deal with the important matter of area organization. However, for now we must focus on the details of organization and procedure for phase one of the operation to be accomplished by each community in the area.

4

The General Assembly

IN this section we will describe one of the major parts of the organizational machinery that will make it possible to activate and carry out the first phase of the development effort. Sections 5 through 7 will deal with other component parts of this machinery, and in sections 8 through 13 we will deal with the preliminary groundwork that will be needed to actually create this machinery and put it into operation.

The composition of this organizational machinery has been carefully worked out from extensive experience and research in widely separated geographical areas, and is based on certain principles that may be applied in virtually all communities in rural America. However, it should again be pointed out that this organizational machinery should not be regarded as a rigid blueprint to be used without alteration, but as a practical and flexible design to be used in whole or in part along with whatever additions may be deemed appropriate to fit your particular local situation. This organizational machinery consists of three basic parts:

1. A community-wide citizens group to function as a general assembly. This will provide the vehicle for the special public meetings to which we referred in Section 3, and serve as both a public forum and civic action body.

2. A series of fact-finding committees to prepare reports and recom-

mendations for action in all major aspects of community life. These reports will supply the necessary material for orderly and purposeful deliberations in the general assembly. The work of these committees coupled with the discussions in the general assembly will provide the community with a practical means of conducting the self-examination, to which we referred in section 3, and will build into the first phase of the operation a definite thrust toward specific planning and action.

3. A series of administrative committees to perform promotional, coordinating, and special service tasks that will be required to facilitate the workings of the general assembly and its fact-finding committees.

The community-wide citizens group which forms the general assembly should be exactly that—community-wide. It must not in any sense become an exclusive organization. It should include people from all existing organizations and institutions, plus all residents who may be interested but are not identified with any existing organization. It may grow in number to any size. The more the better; people from all occupations, including homemaking; people from all religious affiliations, all creeds, all races, and all shades of political opinion; people from all levels of income and all levels of education—male and female, young and old—everybody and anybody who cares about the community and is willing to help make it a better and more satisfying place in which to live. To function with maximum productivity the general assembly will need at least four elective positions, the holders of which should serve throughout the first phase of the development effort.

1. A *general chairman*, or president if that title is preferred, to function as the chief coordinator of the overall operation and chair the general assembly meetings. This should be a person who is widely respected throughout the community, favorably accepted in all segments of the population, keenly sensitive to the community's needs, and deeply understanding of its varied interests and peculiarities. This job will call for a good organizer, a person who has considerable vision and common sense, knows how to get things done, can be depended upon to follow through on essential details, and who has the ability to motivate and inspire others.

2. An *assistant general chairman*, or vice-president, to share the duties of the general chairman. This person should have the same community-wide acceptance as the chairman, but it would be desirable to look for people to fill these two positions whose personal qualities will

enable them to supplement each other, who can work well together, and who can be counted on to divide their responsibilities in ways that will avoid ambiguities or doubts as to who is responsible for what—a stiuation that could cause critical matters to be left unattended by both of them.

3. A *secretary*, to keep minutes of the meetings, maintain a master file of program reports, and develop a detailed history of the operation as it goes along.

As has already been pointed out, the development effort—especially during the first operational phase—will be a process of cultivating new insights and understandings that will lead to a stronger community. One of the important functions in this process will be the keeping of a running account of proceedings, recommendations, and actions that can be used for periodic review and evaluation of the thinking, the discussions, the problems, the plans, and the numerous activities that grow out of the effort. This record will help the community keep tabs on itself—to see with clarity where the effort is going right or going wrong and the direction it is moving—thus providing a means by which performance and productivity may be continuously sharpened.

To serve this purpose, the secretary's records should convey as fully as possible what actually is taking place. Completeness, not brevity, is the objective to be sought after. The more comprehensive the better. Direct quotes of what people are saying, anecdotes, items of humor, interesting situations and events, points of view, agreements and disagreements, problems cited, solutions recommended, decisions reached and decisions left dangling, actions completed and actions started but left unfinished —this is the kind of information the secretary's report on each meeting of the general assembly should contain. This report should be typed and duplicated, and copies should be handed out to all persons as they arrive for the following assembly meeting. All participants in the operation should be encouraged to keep their own personal files of these reports for periodic reference, review, and evaluation of the development work as it goes along.

In addition to these written accounts, the files maintained by the secretary may also include photographs, newspaper clippings, or any other form of information that will help document the workings and activities of the community effort. As will be pointed out in section 7, the secretary also serves as chairman of a secretarial committee which will be needed to produce the various typewritten materials the operation will require. Thus, the secretary should be a person who not only has writing and record-keeping skills, but also has organizational and administrative ability.

4. A *treasurer*, to keep financial records and handle necessary funds for whatever items of expense may be incurred. The treasurer should be a person who is skilled in fiscal management, and who is in a position to help spearhead any fund-raising drives that may be needed. This person will need to work closely with the general chairman, assistant general chairman, and secretary, as well as with other persons engaged in the operation, and should therefore be well qualified to function in a key leadership role.

5. In addition to these four positions to which persons should be elected, a number of people should be appointed to serve as *discussion leaders* at meetings of the general assembly, and a like number appointed to serve as *recorders*.

We have said the general assembly may grow to any size. But in a large assembly, effective in-depth discussion by all persons present is impossible, and for that reason special techniques must be employed to make certain that all persons who attend the assembly meetings may enter freely into the discussions and decisions these meetings are designed to produce. Otherwise, active participation will be seriously limited. Indeed, most individuals who attend the assembly meetings will feel virtually no opportunity to make any contribution to the deliberations.

Therefore, in order to enable everybody who attends to have a personal say in whatever questions or recommendations are brought up, and to participate actively with the least possible restraint, a portion of each assembly meeting should be conducted with the assembly divided into small workshop or discussion groups. The size of these groups should be no larger than fifteen or twenty each. A dozen would be preferable.

During this period of discussion the general assembly—broken into these small subgroups — should move out of the auditorium in which it convenes, each group going into a separate room or place in the building where its deliberations will not be disturbed by the other groups. In each group, one person should serve as the discussion leader, another as the recorder or note-keeper.

The mechanics of dividing the assembly into these small discussion groups may be handled by any device that will effect the division quickly and without confusion. For example, numbered cards may be distributed which designate the group each person is to go into, along with the room or location in which that group is to meet. These cards may be handed out at the entrance to the auditorium as people arrive for the general assembly meeting, along with copies of the secretary's report on the previous meeting and the report of the fact-finding committee which is to be discussed that evening. There are, of course, other methods that could be used to get the assembly divided into these small groups for the discussion period, but whatever method is adopted, it should be simple. And it should be one that will soon become so routine as to require no more than three or four minutes to accomplish.

Another important point is that these discussion groups should be formed by a process of random selection that will produce varying mixes of people at each assembly meeting, thus facilitating a broadening of personal contacts and acquaintances as the development effort progresses. Inasmuch as each group will be discussing the same subject at each assembly meeting—the report of the fact-finding committee scheduled for that evening—this random mixing of persons for the discussion groups will not detract from the continuity from one meeting to the next.

However, even though the composition of the discussion groups will change from meeting to meeting, the people appointed to act as discussion leaders and recorders should serve in these capacities for the entire series of assembly meetings during the first phase of operations, thus allowing them to develop as much skill as possible for the performance of these important leadership functions. If special training in the art of stimulating and leading group discussions, and of recording the salient points, can be provided, so much the better. For the success of the assembly meetings will largely depend upon the personal skill of the discussion leaders and recorders. In section 16 we will deal specifically with some of the leadership techniques the discussion leaders and recorders may employ in carrying out their respective tasks.

The number of discussion leaders and recorders needed will depend upon how many people attend the assembly meeting and on the size of each discussion group. As attendance grows, the number of persons required for these functions will increase. If there is an off night, and attendance is less than expected, two or more pairs of discussion leaders and recorders may team up and work together, with the number of discussion groups being reduced accordingly. Details such as these are some of the mechanics that will need to be worked out by the general chairman or assistant general chairman for each assembly meeting.

Another question of mechanics is the matter of space—that is a suitable building in which to hold the assembly meetings. Ideally, this should be a building in which there is an auditorium or gymnasium or a room large enough to accommodate the general assembly, plus additional rooms or spaces to accommodate the small-group discussion sessions. In most communities this will probably be a public school building. If there is a community college, it will undoubtedly have these facilities. But it could be any building, including a church. Not all small communities will have a building that fits these specifications as well as might be desired, but with a bit of ingenuity various arrangements can be used to make do.

There may be some evenings when it will be desirable to go through the entire assembly meeting without making use of the small-group discussion period. This could arise, for example, if it were determined that an outside guest speaker would be the best means of providing certain important information concerning a specific aspect of the development effort, followed by questions and answers. Indeed, it may be a good idea to occasionally make use of such an arrangement as a means of varying the pace. However, meetings of this kind should be the exception, not the rule, for it will soon be found that the period during which the assembly breaks into small discussion groups will not only become a stimulating and enjoyable experience, but a highly productive means of exploring varying points of view and reaching conclusions that contribute to constructive decision-making.

Now, a quick review: At regular intervals—once every week if at all possible, but often enough to ensure the continuity we have stressed and generate momentum—for the initial period of six or seven months which is set aside for the first phase of operations, the general assembly will convene in the spirit of an old-fashioned American town meeting to provide an opportunity for the citizenry to study systematically the life and problems of its community and determine what actions or projects are needed for improvement. If the frequency of these meetings is less than once a week, it may be necessary to extend the duration of the first phase of the operation in order to provide enough time to cover all the material that will come from the fact-finding committees with which we will be dealing in subsequent sections.

Informality, self-discovery, and the idea of self-help should be the

keynotes of each assembly meeting, with all participants being encouraged to get acquainted on as personal a basis as possible. If the wearing of
name tags is helpful for this purpose, they should be provided. Parlia-
mentary procedure should be used only when needed to reach definite
decisions. Every effort should be made to create an atmosphere in which
all persons in attendance feel free to raise questions or speak out as they
see fit. Frankness, objectivity, and simple courtesy should be the practice, with open expression of ideas and opinions being encouraged by
every possible means.

Another rule that should be strictly adhered to concerns the matter of
attendance. As we have repeatedly emphasized, it is extremely important
to develop continuity from each meeting to the next. This continuity will
depend not only upon the frequency and regularity of the assembly
meetings, but also upon a reasonably unbroken chain of attendance. Each
participant, upon entering into the operation, should therefore make
every effort to attend every assembly meeting thereafter.

Another cardinal principle is that all meetings of the general assembly
should open and close on time, meaning that punctuality should be
standard practice. Otherwise the meetings will begin to drag, and many
people will not want to keep coming if they find they can't get home by a
reasonable hour. Others won't mind staying up late. Some will want to
hang around or go out for refreshments after the meetings adjourn. These
differences among individuals are, of course, normal, and much of the
value of the general assembly will be in the conversation and socializing
it stimulates outside the meetings themselves. Prompt adjournment,
however, will serve the desires of those who wish to get home early,
while at the same time not inhibiting those who are in no hurry to get
home. Moreover, it is usually better to stop while interest and attention
are high than to go on until people become restless and exhausted.

Taken as a series, the meetings of the general assembly are designed to
generate a deeper and more comprehensive understanding of community
problems and make clear the intricate relationships that exist between
them, thus creating an orderly progression of learning that will provide a
sound basis for action, and for moving into the second phase of operations. Within this framework of local self-analysis, each meeting should
build on what has occurred in the previous meetings and pave the way for
those yet to follow. This means that steps should be taken to reach
definite decisions and to avoid aimless wandering. Ordinarily, each

assembly meeting should focus on only one committee report or subject matter. In all cases, each meeting should be limited to an agenda that can be covered in a single evening so that people don't go home feeling they didn't have enough time to finish their discussion, or that nothing was accomplished. Each meeting should be carefully planned to stimulate a high level of interest, and the subject of the evening should be well publicized in advance. The agenda for a typical general assembly meeting may be somewhat as follows:

1. The general chairman calls the assembly to order.

2. A member of the local clergy gives a brief invocation.

3. The secretary presents a brief summary of the previous meeting —not the usual dull reading of minutes, but a quick highlighting of major points, along with conclusions that were reached and actions and recommendations that were adopted, then allows opportunity for questions or comments. As this oral highlight summary is being presented, each person in the assembly will be able to follow the secretary's full written report, copies of which, as has been pointed out, will have been distributed as people arrive for the meeting.

4. The general chairman calls for whatever announcements may be necessary, then introduces the subject of the evening.

5. The fact-finding committee scheduled to supply the report for discussion at this assembly meeting, is called upon to make an oral or visual presentation that will set the stage for the small-group discussion period. The nature of this presentation will be discussed more fully in section 6.

6. After this presentation, followed by questions or comments anyone may wish to raise, the assembly then breaks into the small discussion groups, each with its own discussion leader and recorder, each moving out into a separate location in the building to discuss the problems and recommendations for action being submitted by the reporting committee.

7. After a sufficient period for these deliberations the general assembly then reconvenes.

8. The recorders form a panel at the front of the auditorium or meeting room, with the general chairman serving as the panel leader and report to the assembly the conclusions reached in their respective discussion groups. When this reporting session is completed, the recorders then turn over their notes to the secretary for use in preparing the overall minutes of the meeting.

9. The general chairman invites comments from the floor, summarizes

the conclusions concerning the problems and recommendations that have been discussed, points out areas of agreement and disagreement, notes the decisions that have been reached, pulls together any loose ends that may need clarification, and if necessary calls for a vote on recommendations for action. The committee that made the report upon which the discussion was based is now charged with whatever follow-up planning or arrangements may be required to actually carry out the action which has been approved.

10. The general chairman announces the subject for the next meeting of the assembly and alerts the appropriate committee, which may wish to make a brief announcement concerning the report it will be presenting.

11. A member of the local clergy pronounces a brief benediction.

12. The general chairman declares the meeting adjourned. *Total elapsed time: Not more than two hours.*

In section 15, additional suggestions will be provided for the detailed planning that will be necessary for each assembly meeting, and the functions and responsibilities of those in leadership positions will be discussed at further length. We will also discuss later in the guide how the general assembly, after it becomes firmly established, can provide the necessary vehicle for moving into the second phase of operations. Specific suggestions will also be offered as to how the assembly can enable the community to form workable partnerships, with its neighboring communities, with development operations at the area level, and with whatever outside aid programs may be needed from regional agencies or from the state or federal government.

5

Choosing the Fact-Finding Committees

THE fact-finding committees which are to comprise the second part of our phase-one organizational machinery will occupy a crucial position in the workings of that machinery, and some of them will continue—perhaps with certain alterations—into phase two of the development effort. As we have seen, these committees will supply essential material for the meetings of the assembly and will perform key roles in planning and carrying out specific action projects. In section 6 we will discuss in further detail the operations of these committees, but first we must deal with the critically important question: What fact-finding committees should we establish?

This decision may vary from one community to another depending upon local desires and conditions. However, recognizing this need for flexibility, certain fundamental principles should be carefully observed in making this decision. As a means of getting into these principles another note of caution should be raised against a possible pitfall that could prove disastrous. This concerns the common tendency—to which we referred in section 2 in discussing the ultimate goal of community development—of choosing these committees on the basis of specific projects or reforms that certain well-meaning groups have already decided would be good for the community even before the fact-finding and discussion of the first phase of the effort has had a chance to begin.

For example: An air pollution committee, a sewage disposal committee, a golf course committee, a swimming pool committee, or a committee based on any other pre-determined project. These projects may be eminently worthwhile and urgently needed, but to begin the community development effort on strictly a narrow project basis is to run the unnecessary risk of prejudicing and handicapping the effort even before it starts, and as a practical matter, may actually work against the success of the projects. Even if by sheer pressure such projects are finally pushed through, the pressure used to accomplish them is likely to leave scars that will create other community problems even more serious than those the pre-determined projects were designed to solve.

If this project approach to committee selection is employed during the first operational phase, the development effort will in all likelihood attract support from only limited elements in the population, while at the same time attracting unremitting opposition from other elements. In most instances this will arouse needless emotion and controversy, and instead of uniting the community is likely to split it even further apart. What you would have under these conditions would not be an effort in *community* development, but merely an effort in *project* development. This piecemeal approach to committee selection, which may also become a "steamroller" approach, will tend to create a kind of "projectitis" that would violate in almost every detail the entire concept of community development we have been talking about; a concept that can be put into practice only if there is an organizational machinery that makes it possible for the community as a whole to look at itself objectively and comprehensively, and improve its performance as a problem-solving unit of society. This means—to state the principle again—*community self-discovery,* a process in which the community, operating as an organic whole, formulates and carries out actions it determines for itself are essential to its well-being in *all* aspects of need.

In keeping with the ultimate goal we discussed in section 2, the question of what fact-finding committees to establish should therefore be determined, not on the basis of certain preconceived projects, but on a basis that is so inclusive in scope as to make it clear that no major aspect of community life is to be overlooked; that all possible actions which may contribute to the community's total well-being are to come in for careful attention.

If the fact-finding committees are chosen in accordance with this approach, the work they perform in combination with the proceedings of the general assembly, will open practical opportunities for all segments of interest within the population to express their special concerns without resorting to the type of pressure tactics that divide communities into bitter opposing camps, coerce people into silence, and thus become counter-productive.

This comprehensive manner of deciding what fact-finding committees to establish will have the effect of generating community-wide acceptance and support for the entire development effort, and as this acceptance builds, a climate of local unity will emerge in which each project undertaken will not only help solve the problems for which that project is intended, but will add momentum to all other facets of the effort as well, thus increasing the community's will and capacity for still more action.

Because this matter of determining what fact-finding committees to establish is so important, we should once again remind ourselves that in this development effort we are looking at the community, not as an assortment of disconnected parts and pieces, but as a living whole; that just as a doctor looks at a man, not as an arm or a leg or a kidney, but as a whole human being, we are looking at the community as a whole social being. As in man himself, just as in all other living forms, each component part and function that goes into the total makeup of the community,is dependent upon every other part and function. All are interrelated. And if any one part is defective, the whole community is affected—just as in the human body, if a lung breaks down, the whole body is damaged.

If, therefore, the development effort is to grow into the most effective possible operation, the fact-finding committees must be chosen and put together in a way that will enable the people to examine cooperatively, without bickering, every facet of their local situation, ferret out every weakness, every problem, inventory carefully and systematically their resources and potentialities, and in this way decide what changes or improvements are in order. This process of development can be achieved only if the effort begins at the point of inquiry, self-analysis, self-evaluation, self-discovery—meaning, a search for facts and insights in all vital areas of activity so that all projects and actions may grow in response to legitimate recognitions of need by the whole community. A community effort such as this doesn't just happen. It isn't just slapped together piecemeal. And it is not likely to occur if it is initiated merely as a means of satisfying certain pressure groups—either internal or external—out to promote their pet projects or reforms, regardless of possible adverse side effects.

This is not to close the door to controversy, or to emotional outbursts and heated debate. Controversy is a part of democracy. Emotional expression is an ingredient of human behavior. But an effective effort in community development must be so organized as to provide a framework of operations within which controversy and emotion may be expressed and in which any project any group feels is important may be proposed without forcing local residents to needlessly choose up sides and thereby paralyze the overall effort.

With these principles as a point of departure, we are now in a position to decide what fact-finding committees to establish—first, by considering as we indicated in section 2 the varied aspects of the community's physical and social makeup, then by devising a list of committees that will ensure a systematic coverage of this makeup in its entirety. Because of the differences that prevail from one community to another—including such factors as size of population, location in relation to other communities, economic potential, and the like—the guide will not attempt to suggest a complete list of fact-finding committees for all communities, but will set forth a variety of committee possibilities, together with the rationale for choosing them.

We can begin by considering the fact that all communities, irrespective of individual differences, have a certain spatial dimension, or geographical territory, within which there is a complex of man-made facilities along with various natural features, as we mentioned in section 2, which we may call the community's *physical structure*. In some instances the man-made portion of this structure is a result of imaginative thought and careful planning, but in most cases it simply grows up by chance and takes on whatever design circumstances happen to dictate. This aspect of the community's makeup may be crowded or uncrowded, clean or dirty, attractive or unattractive, well kept or run-down, wisely used or unwisely used, suitable or unsuitable for people to inhabit. Or it may be a mixture of these attributes. But whatever its quality or state of repair—good, bad, or a combination of both—this physical structure will have an important bearing on the desirability of your community as a place in which to live, in which to work, conduct a business or industry, go shopping, go to school, attend church, spend leisure time, associate with other people, find entertainment and recreation, raise a family, enjoy life. And this is just for starters. You can go as far as you wish listing the varied features of your community's physical structure.

But as you look at your community in this way it will soon become apparent that interlaced in this physical structure, shaping it and being shaped by it, there is also a *social structure*—the composition and configuration of the community as a civic body, as an infinite maze of human activity. This aspect of your community's makeup may be looked at in terms of the total number of residents; whether the population is increasing, decreasing, or staying about the same. It may be looked at in terms of the distribution of the population according to age, sex, race, occupation, martial status, and family units. It has to do with the way the people are organized into groups—formal and informal. It concerns the people's likes and dislikes, their attitudes toward themselves, toward each other, toward the community itself. It includes such qualities as political and religious beliefs, the varied levels of schooling and economic attainment, and what the people regard as important or unimportant as life goals and ambitions. The community's business, industrial, and agricultural activities are a part of this social structure. So too are its recreational and entertainment activities, its health services, its library services, its school system, its local government, and all other functions and services in its makeup.

All of these component parts and functions—physical and social —plus many others that could be mentioned, are interwoven threads in the total fabric of community life. Each exerts its influence on the well-being or lack of well-being of the people—as individuals, as families, as a community. Each helps determine the direction your community is moving—toward improvement and a better life, or toward deterioration and decay. By thinking of your community in this manner, considering the vast multitude of its varied activities and structural forms, we can devise a list of categories that will suggest needed fact-finding committees for a comprehensive effort in community development.

For example: We have noted that the community has a certain geographical territory. If, therefore, the development effort is to be community-wide in scope, a decision has to be made as to just what is the extent of your community—geographically speaking. This important decision will call for a *Boundary Committee.*

Another aspect of the community's internal structure that we have noted, and will call for careful fact-finding, is the composition of the local population—or, what we have referred to as the civic body, the people themselves. Information about the makeup of your community's population will provide a statistical basis for essential planning in virtually all aspects of the development effort and will point up sharply and specifically many community problems that might otherwise be overlooked. For this part of the fact-finding we suggest a *Census Committee.*

We have noted that another vital aspect of the community's internal structure is the whole complex of attitudes which the people—both individually and collectively—hold toward themselves and each other. These varied attitudes, along with the differing life styles and patterns of human behavior that accompany them, largely determine the community's ability to deal with its problems—indeed, are the source of many of its problems—and for these reasons exert a major influence on its progress and its whole future destiny. By careful and objective analysis, an overall picture of this critical aspect of your community's makeup can be drawn for all to see. But this picture of your community's internal structure will provide another ingredient that will be even more important to the success of the development effort than the picture itself. The very act of collecting and assembling the information that will be needed to put this picture together—which will involve the entire community—followed by interpretations of what this information says about local conditions, will become a powerful instrument in the process of self-discovery that will generate increased awareness of needed improvements, give the community an enlightening new perspective of itself, and add in substantial ways to the people's desire for constructive planning and action. This part of the fact-finding will call for a *Community Attitudes Committee*.

The network of voluntary associations—social clubs, service groups, and other private membership organizations—is another vital part of the community's internal structure to which we have referred, and should therefore come in for attention in a comprehensive development effort. These organizations may provide some of the community's most important assets for problem solving, or they may themselves become a part of the community's problems. But in either case they will have significant bearing on the level of local civic performance, and much of the leadership that will be needed to carry out the development operation will necessarily come from this network of voluntary membership associations. The fact-finding needed to examine this important element of community life calls for a *Community Organizations Committee*.

The four committees we have suggested thus far—boundary, census, community attitudes, and community organizations—although highly important to the first phase of the operation, will not be needed after the discussions of their reports have been completed in the general assembly. These four committees should therefore be regarded as temporary committees whose work will contribute substantially to paving the way for the work of other fact-finding committees which should continue throughout the first phase of the operation, and as we have indicated, will in some instances extend into the second operational phase. This brings us to the suggested continuing committees.

If the community is built around an incorporated municipality, such as a small town or city, another vital part of the internal structure to which we have referred will be the local government and its associated departments and agencies. Of necessity, this aspect of the community's makeup will occupy a central position in the operation, and without effective working relationships and understandings between the people and their local government, much of the potential for development will be lost. This function of community life suggests the need for a *Government Committee*.

There is an old adage which says, "When a community looks progressive it is progressive." Obviously, this is not necessarily true, but as we have noted, the physical appearance does have an important bearing on its desirability as a place in which to live. Moreover, it has become increasingly clear in recent times that if we are to develop the best possible conditions for human life, our communities are going to have to give a great deal more attention to the conservation and improvement of their physical environment than they have in the past. Essential fact-finding in connection with this aspect of the community's makeup suggests the need for an *Environmental Improvement Committee*.

No community can maintain itself, or even expect to survive, unless it has within itself, its surrounding area, or in other nearby communities, an economic base sufficient to support its population and provide the services and facilities people require for modern living. Certainly, this is fundamental to all of the parts and functions that comprise the community's physical and social structure, and must therefore be treated as an essential ingredient in the development effort. The type of economic development for which a community is best suited will, of course, vary from place to place. But if your community is suited to the creation or expansion of homegrown industries, or to the location of new industrial plants from outside, this should receive major attention. The fact-finding and action required for this purpose suggests the need for an *Industrial Development Committee*.

Another important aspect of the local economy comes under the heading of retail trade and services, which may include tourism. In many communities it may very well be that various retail or service enterprises offer the most promising opportunity for economic development —perhaps the only opportunity for such development. In any case this aspect of the economy will have a great deal to do with your community's desirability as a place in which to live, or in which to stop and stay a while, and will influence in many significant ways its civic vitality. Essential fact-finding and action in relation to this part of the community's life suggests the need for a *Retail Trade and Services Committee*.

Almost no aspect of the community's internal structure exerts a more profound influence on living conditions and the potential for development than its residential housing. Unless your community has no shortage of suitable housing within the economic reach of all its people, this category of community life and the fact-finding necessary to examine it suggests the need for a *Housing Committee*.

Another part of the community's makeup to which we have referred, and which will play a critical role in its development, is its school system. For the fact-finding and action that will be needed in this connection there should be an *Education Committee*. A somewhat separate but highly important part of the educational function concerns available library services, and suggests the need for a *Library Committee*.

Essential health services and practices, including sanitary facilities, comprise parts of the social and physical structure of all communities if they are to serve the life needs of their people. Some communities, particularly in rural areas, are not able to supply within themselves all these services. But somehow this vital factor must be dealt with, and therefore suggests the need for a *Health Committee*.

Another major function of the community's life structure which calls for attention in a comprehensive development effort, is recreation. This may also include what might be more accurately referred to as entertainment, or we might think simply in terms of adequate opportunities for constructive and satisfying ways of using leisure time. And we should also take into account all age groups and all recreational interests of all the people. This suggests the need for a *Recreation Committee*.

Another aspect of the community's makeup that could profitably receive attention is its local history. A good look at the events of the past from the point of view of how these events have contributed to making the community what it is today and what it may become tomorrow can provide valuable insights into the evolution of today's problems, and assist in important ways in the planning and development of a better future. This suggests the need for a *History Committee*.

Now, let's stop for a moment to consider once again the principles we have been following as a means of arriving at these possible fact-finding committees. We have taken a broad look at some of the internal factors and activities that go into the composition of all communities. By looking at the community in this comprehensive fashion, we have marked out various categories of the community's total makeup, and have designated a corresponding list of committees that we can use as instruments for analyzing and improving this internal makeup. We have approached the matter of deciding what fact-finding committees to establish, not from the standpoint of certain preconceived issues, projects, or reforms that would appeal only to certain special interest groups. Instead, we have considered the need to honestly and objectively examine the community in its totality, to look at its overall life conditions so that we can systematically diagnose its problems in all aspects of its social and physical makeup, pinpoint its resources or lack of resources, recognize more clearly its potentials, and thus make it possible for the citizenry as a whole to move itself into a position to proceed with whatever planning, action, projects, or services this self-examination may indicate. In this way we have made provision for a fact-finding machinery that is broad enough to reveal to all citizens any problem or need the community may have without resorting to tactics that lead inevitably to needless hostility. We have opened opportunities for participation by all local groups and interests, and we have provided an operational framework within which opposing views may be expressed without the wasteful consequences of destructive controversy and confrontation.

In summary, the fourteen possible fact-finding committees we have suggested are as follows: Boundary Committee, Census Committee, Community Attitudes Committee, Community Organizations Committee, Government Committee, Environmental Improvement Committee, Industrial Development Committee, Retail Trade and Services Committee, Housing Committee, Education Committee, Library Committee, Health Committee, Recreation Committee, and History Committee. Later in the guide a special section will be presented giving a suggested work outline for each fact-finding committee in this list. These sections will also indicate how the fact-finding committees can effectively relate themselves to whatever groups, agencies, organizations, or institutions may already exist either inside or outside your community whose cooperation and support will be essential to the success of the development effort.

This suggested list of fact-finding committees may, of course, be expanded or reduced if it is felt that certain alterations are needed to fit more precisely the local conditions and potentials in your particular community. But the basic approach we have used in arriving at the committees listed above should be carefully observed. If certain additional fact-finding committees are deemed advisable, the work outlines in the special sections that will be presented for the committees listed above should help indicate how work outlines may be prepared for these additional committees.

In looking at the fact-finding committees we have listed, it will be noted that there are certain interrelationships among all of them. This is as it should be. For inasmuch as the various component parts of the community's total makeup are themselves interrelated, so too are the fact-finding committees. This refers to the basic principle we have repeatedly emphasized—that community life is an organic whole, and that in an effective development effort we must at all times bear this in mind. Thus, it will not be uncommon to find two or more of the fact-finding committees bringing in similar recommendations for action, though from different points of view. Also, it will not be uncommon for various committees to draw on facts that have been revealed by other committees. For example, the census committee will supply information that will be used by virtually every committee. In any case, the work of all the fact-finding committees will be brought together in an integrated pattern of thought, planning, and action through the instrument of the general assembly.

From this comprehensive fact-finding machinery, information, problems, needs, and recommendations will be fed into the assembly meetings, there to be looked at, discussed, and analyzed by the citizenry as a whole. And the actions that are recommended will be approved, amended, or rejected by the citizenry as a whole. As this system of operations takes form, your community will acquire increased expertise in the art of decision-making and will develop on its own initiative a basis for action that will enable it to put to work the inherent precepts of democracy—the most potent force man has yet invented for the development of productive and humane communities.

In several sections in the guide we have referred to the fact that today many community problems can be solved only through an area approach in which all the communities in a given area pool their energies and resources and work together in a common effort. We have also pointed out that many community problems can be solved only on an individual community basis, and that for this reason development efforts are needed at both these levels.

Near the end of section 4 we indicated that the general assembly—once firmly established in each community in a given area—will provide an effective means through which to form workable partnerships among neighboring communities and enable them to move together toward phase two of the development effort—including operations at both area and local levels.

Now that we have described the second part of our phase-one organiza-

tional machinery—the fact-finding committees and indicated a rationale
for deciding what fact-finding committees to establish—we are in a
position to see still further how we can ultimately move toward this dual
approach, at the local level, and at the area level. And as we build and set
in motion our phase-one organizational machinery, we will find that in
many respects the operations that are essential at both these levels will
gradually blend together until in time they can, with high effectiveness,
function simultaneously.

But the place to begin is in each individual community of which the
area is comprised—and with phase one as the basis for the ultimate
building of phase two. Otherwise, we are not likely to build the solid
local foundation upon which successful area development must rest.
Without this local foundation, community development at the area level
may well become an artificial thing, supposedly an effort by the people,
but not really; or it may become little more than another payroll operation
in which the planning and decision making are primarily the work of a
paid staff—either of which is sterile at best, and neither of which will
develop the quality of community to which this development guide is
committed.

6

Procedures and Responsibilities
of the Fact-Finding Committees

WITH certain exceptions pertaining to the four temporary committees,
there are a number of procedures and responsibilities that apply to all the
fact-finding committees. The exceptions concerning the temporary
committees will be detailed in the work outlined for these committees in
sections 9 through 12. Briefly, these exceptions are as follows:

Boundary—By means of a short written report accompanied by a map, this committee presents recommended boundaries to the first public meeting which is described in section 13. This report can be handled without dividing the assembly into small discussion groups.

Census—Compiles basic statistical data for the use of most of the other committees. Gives a brief presentation of findings at the first public meeting, pointing up underlying community problems with which the development operation will deal as it goes along, but inasmuch as census data is not the kind of material that lends itself to public discussion, no recommendations or small group discussions will be needed.

Community Attitudes—Functions in the same manner indicated below for the continuing committees, except that when the discussions on the community attitudes report are completed the problems calling for action will be referred to appropriate continuing committees.

Community Organizations—Same as for the community attitudes committee.

After the four temporary committees have submitted their reports, their work will have been completed. All fact-finding committees, including the four mentioned above, must first do a careful job of research. This may require interviewing, record searching, discussions within the respective committees, and various surveys. The information collected must then be assembled, tabulated, and written into reports.

Except for boundary and census, all the fact-finding committees will produce reports that will be used as the basis for the small-group discussions in meetings of the general assembly. This carries the responsibility of formulating specific recommendations for action, and the committees should focus their fact-finding on seeking out, identifying, and describing definite problems with this responsibility constantly in mind.

The reports of these committees should begin with a brief introduction that gives a statement of purpose, explains how the fact-finding was done, and presents whatever other background information may be useful for the purpose of conveying a clear understanding of the subject under consideration. The main body of these reports should present the committees' findings, pinpoint the problems or issues these findings reveal, and present the recommendations for action in as definite a manner as possible.

These reports should be sufficiently candid and complete to carry a strong wollop and make them interesting. They may include choice quotations, tables, charts, graphs, drawings, or other illustrations that give added emphasis to various points, thereby flavoring them with all the vitality that can be put into them. Care must be exercised to prevent the reports from being "too hot to handle," but they should be organized in ways that will ensure vigorous, frank, informative, and constructive discussion in the general assembly and throughout the community. Therefore, they should be provocative. They should be sharp and penetrating. They should bear down hard on community needs and failings, and be put together in ways that will enable people to quickly digest the problems and recommendations for action they present.

They should be well salted with pointed questions that will kindle thought, suggest ideas, probe for fresh insight, and help the assembly come to grips with reality even though it may not be pleasant. In essence, these reports should be far more than mere documentations of fact; they should be tools for self-discovery that make it easy for people to openly and honestly express their opinions about their community and its needs, generate a definite mood for constructive action, and make the assembly meetings so interesting everyone will want to come back for more. Copies of each fact-finding report should be distributed to each person attending the assembly meeting for which it is scheduled.

In some cases a committee's subject will be too large and complex to be handled by the assembly in one evening's agenda, and for that reason more than one meeting will be required to cover all the problems and recommendations the committee has to present. In such cases, the committee may wish to write a comprehensive master report divided into a series of shorter reports, each of which can be covered by the assembly in one evening's meeting—all persons receiving copies of each report in the series as it is scheduled. Anyone wishing to obtain a copy of the master report should be able to do so, but in all probability most people will be satisfied with the series of short reports, thus avoiding the necessity of reproducing more than a limited number of copies of the full master report.

With the exception of the boundary and census reports for which small-group discussions will not be necessary, copies of all other fact-finding reports should be delivered to the discussion leaders and recorders, the general chairman, assistant general chairman, secretary, and treasurer two or three days in advance of the assembly meetings for which they are scheduled so these leaders can get themselves well prepared to perform their respective roles.

As was noted under item 5 in the typical assembly agenda outlined in section 4, each fact-finding committee will also have the responsibility of making an oral or visual presentation to the assembly before it breaks into small discussion groups. This presentation should highlight the salient points in the written report to be discussed that evening so that people will have the benefit of a quick overview of what the report contains, thus paving the way for a lively discussion period.

To accomplish this it is essential that this presentation not be just a series of dull readings from the report, but a performance that will give added meaning to the problems and recommendations being reported. This may be done in the form of a panel, using the format of an informative television talk show. Or it may be given in the form of a skit. It may be done by the use of a film or series of slides with appropriate commentary, or by whatever other techniques the committees may think of to make their presentations alive and provocative. These presentations should therefore be carefully planned in advance. Some of the committees may even wish to rehearse their presentation, or go through a "dry run" ahead of time. If so, fine. This presentation must set the stage for the small-group discussion period, and for that reason it has to be good.

Following this presentation, a short time should be allowed for comments or questions from the floor before the assembly breaks into the small discussion groups. To keep the meeting moving the total time allotted for the committee presentation, including reactions from the floor, should consume no more than fifteen or twenty minutes. However, at least one member of the reporting committee should sit in with each discussion group and be prepared to answer questions, or supply additional information if needed.

At the close of each assembly meeting the reporting committee, as was indicated in section 4, then becomes responsible for seeing to it that necessary follow-up arrangements are made to carry out whatever specific actions the assembly approves, and at later meetings may be called upon for progress reports to make sure these actions are not being ignored.

This follow-up responsibility does not mean that the fact-finding committees themselves will necessarily carry out every action project. In some instances they will. But as will be further pointed out in section 17, the actual carrying out of a given project will depend on its nature. Some action projects will be carried out by the municipal government, some by other official legal bodies. Some may be carried out by various service clubs. Some will require no more than just a few people, some perhaps only one person. Others may require hundreds of people or virtually the entire community. Some long-range projects may call for setting up an entirely new agency. But whatever the requirements of each action the assembly approves, it will be the responsibility of the reporting committee to see that appropriate follow-up is accomplished. This is one of the means by which the development effort will ultimately move from the first phase of operations into the more formal and permanent second phase.

In summary, the steps for completing the work of each fact-finding committee after its membership has been named are as follows:

1. The committee chairman in consultation with other members sets a date for the first committee meeting.

2. Each member of the committee gets prepared for this first meeting by reading the development guide, giving special attention to this section and to the special section on that committee which is presented later. Having done this reading, each member of the committee formulates in his or her own mind various means of conducting the committee's research, then attends the first meeting ready to help the committee get started with its work.

3. Adopt a plan of operations and distribute specific tasks with deadlines for completion. The committee's plan of operations should take into account the necessity of preparing and duplicating whatever survey questionnaires may be needed, the methods to be used in doing the fact-finding and compiling the results, the formulation of recommendations, the writing of the report, and the need to get it duplicated in time to have it ready for distribution at the assembly meeting for which it is scheduled. Also, with the exceptions noted above concerning the boundary and census committees, don't forget the advance copies for the discussion leaders, recorders, general chairman, assistant general chairman, secretary, and treasurer.

4. Make preparations for the highlight presentation which is to set the stage for the small-group discussions.

5. Except for the four temporary committees, each committee remains

intact after its report has been discussed in the general assembly to see that all recommendations for action which have been adopted are carried out, and stands ready to report back to the assembly from time to time on how this follow-up is progressing.

7

The Administrative Committees

WE turn now to the third part of our phase-one organizational machinery—the administrative committees. To help achieve the coordination required for maximum effectiveness we will need a small working group we may call the *Advisory Council*. Widespread representation is important in all aspects of the development effort, including the advisory council. But in this case it is equally important to obtain individuals who are firmly committed to seeing to it that the effort succeeds, and are willing to go to whatever lengths may be necessary toward that end.

Led by the general chairman, this group should meet whenever a situation arises that calls for special action to strengthen or improve the workings of the operation, and should be prepared to move quickly in any emergency. It should also function as a major instrument of review and evaluation aimed at continuously sharpening the total effort. It should act as a special planning body in the preparation of recommendations to the general assembly that may be too large for any one fact-finding committee alone, and be prepared to serve in a coordinating capacity in situations that involve two or more of the fact-finding committees. Also, the advisory council should make a special effort to help maintain cooperative relationships between the development effort and all organizations, institutions, or agencies—either inside or outside the community —whose services or assistance may be needed.

The general assembly may from time to time refer various matters to the advisory council for the formulation of plans for action to be reported back to the assembly for final decision. Any number of situations may arise that will require deliberation by this small working group. It, along with the general chairman and assistant general chairman, should serve as the central guiding and promotional element in the development operation. The advisory council should consist of all committee chairmen, the secretary, treasurer, general chairman and assistant general chairman, and any other persons in the community whose services will aid its effective functioning.

As was indicated in section 4, the work load of the secretary will be too heavy for one person to handle alone. For this reason there should be a *Secretarial Committee*, chaired by the secretary. This committee should supply the typing and duplicating services needed to produce the reports compiled by the fact-finding committees, plus any other typewritten material that may be needed. Private and public offices in the community, or in the area of which your community is a part, should be willing to make available the typewriters, duplicating machines, and office supplies that will be needed by this committee, and should also be willing to donate a reasonable amount of "company time" for clerical work. Other persons willing to volunteer for this important committee may wish to do their part of the work at home. But in keeping with the informal nature of phase one, the secretarial committee should operate on a strictly voluntary basis—not as a staff of workers to be paid by the development effort. During the second phase of operations, particularly at the area level, there may be a paid staff, but as we have repeatedly emphasized in regard to phase one, local voluntarism and a willingness on the part of the citizenry to help itself by evolving a comprehensive development effort strictly on its own are some of the essential keys to ultimate success.

The administrative committees may also include a *Publicity Committee*, to which there may be attached a group of what may be called *Block Captains*. This committee will have the important responsibility of devising and carrying out special means of advertising and promotion, and of making certain the entire community is kept fully informed of each aspect of the development effort as it goes along. The block captains, scattered throughout the community, will have the specific responsibility of encouraging through direct personal contacts and timely reminders of meeting dates, maximum community participation in the general assembly and in all other facets of the operation. Thus, in effect, the block captains will serve as recruiters whose job is to visit as often as necessary every home in their respective territories to get every citizen and family engaged in the development work. The work "block," as used here, is not necessarily intended to mean literally one block, as in a town or city. It could mean one block or several blocks. Or it could mean any geographical section within the community, such as a neighborhood in town or in the surrounding countryside in which it would be possible for one individual serving as block captain to contact in person, or as a neighbor by phone, all households in that section.

To be most effective the work of the publicity committee, along with its block captains, should not be done piecemeal. Each move or action should be planned as part of a systematic campaign carefully worked out in advance. Yet the campaign should be flexible enough to take advantage of any special opportunity that may arise.

Taking into account each aspect of the community effort, the publicity committee should work out the best way of making use of all available media through which advertising and promotion may be accomplished, and each member of the committee (including the block captains) should be responsible for specific tasks in the overall campaign. Among the various media that may be available for use are:

1. Newspapers;
2. Newsletters published by various community organizations;
3. Church bulletins;
4. School publications;
5. Radio and television stations;
6. Community bulletin boards;
7. Posters telling in eye-catching ways interesting information being discovered by the fact-finding committees;
8. Direct mailings;
9. Word-of-mouth.

In dealing with radio or television stations special items should be inserted in local newscasts, and special interviews and talk shows should be held. Word-of-mouth from person to person should be spread through street conversations, visits in people's homes, telephone calls reminding people of meetings and giving them ideas as to what the meetings will cover, speeches or talks before various community organizations, announcements by ministers in the churches, and any other means the publicity committee may devise.

A good publicity and informational campaign should tell what has already happened in the development effort, what is in the process of happening, and what is being planned. To merely remind people of a meeting without conveying any interesting information as to what may be expected is not enough. Extra copies of the secretary's reports may be distributed as a form of news report, or interesting highlights may be excerpted from these reports for that purpose. All information put out by the publicity committee should carry definite news value, human interest, and have reader or listening appeal. If this is done there will be no problem getting stories on the air or into print. Also, the publicity committee and block captains should not hesitate to offer to pick up people and take them to the meetings. These are just a few suggestions for purposes of publicity and promotion.

The development group may think of other administrative committees, but this completes the three basic parts of the organizational machinery for the first phase of the operation as was outlined in section 4—a general assembly, a series of fact-finding committees, and the administrative committees. We are now ready to discuss the steps that will need to be taken to put this machinery together and get it into operation.

8

How to Get Started

OBVIOUSLY, the development effort we have been talking about will not just suddenly appear out of thin air. Some specific group of civic leaders in your community is going to have to make the decision that such an effort is needed and worth working for. These leaders are then going to have to take it upon themselves to go out and persuade enough other leaders and residents to agree with that decision, then take the initiative to do the preliminary groundwork which is outlined in this section to pave the way for actually building the organizational machinery we have described.

This immediately raises an urgently important question. Who, or what organization, or what institution in your community should sponsor this initiating group? This is an extremely difficult question. It is difficult because there are certain facts of life that have to be faced. In almost all communities every existing organization or institution becomes the target of a wide variety of attitudes ranging from highly favorable to highly unfavorable. It is simply a normal characteristic of community life to make all individuals, organizations, and institutions subjects of gossip —frequently gossip that misrepresents the truth and therefore causes a great deal of misunderstanding. Almost all of them have their own sets of followers, friends, confidants—and perhaps, enemies. Many of them are looked upon by at least some people—or by each other—as being interested only in themselves. This may paint the picture a bit darker than it is in your community, but the fact is that in most communities this situation does prevail to a considerable extent. This, of course, is one of the many problems a constructive effort in community development should help correct. But in getting the effort started this fact of life must be taken into account, else the effort may never start.

Ideally, the development effort should be sponsored by nothing less than the community as a whole, thus avoiding the possible suspicion that a particular organization is trying to "put something over" for that organization's own benefit, or that there is to be no real opportunity for community-wide participation. This ideal type of sponsorship is a condition that can be achieved over a period of time, but not until after a considerable amount of groundwork has been accomplished.

Therefore, at the early outset when the civic leaders referred to above are first beginning to introduce the idea of starting the development effort and are engaged in the preliminary groundwork that will be required to get it organized, this initiating group will need to acquire a sponsorship that will necessarily be something less than the whole community, yet be as broadly based as possible. The creation of this initial sponsorship may be accomplished by getting a combination of existing organizations and institutions—both private and public—to enter into a local consortium, this consortium to serve as the sponsor of the initiating group. The sponsorship of this consortium will provide the local endorsement and the pool of voluntary workers that will enable the initiating group to get the community prepared to bring the first phase of the operation into being.

Examples of organizations and institutions that might be included in this sponsoring consortium are as follows: The local community college, if such an institution exists in or nearby your community, would be an excellent possibility; utilities and other business firms are also excellent possibilities; local banks and other financial institutions would be ideal for the sponsoring consortium; local newspapers, radio, and television stations should by all means be included. The nearly one thousand rural electric cooperative systems serving twenty-six hundred of the nations's thirty-one hundred counties are exceedingly valuable resources for community development.

Certainly, your town or city government should join the consortium that will sponsor and help recruit workers for the initiating group. Equally important would be the chamber of commerce, Jaycees, Lions, Rotary, Kiwanis, Civitan, women's clubs, and other service groups in the community. The PTA, the local public school, farm organizations, clergymen and other church leaders should join the sponsoring consortium. With a broad combination of such organizations and institutions, this sponsoring consortium will provide the initiating group of civic leaders with a solid base of support, and will make it much easier to project the effort as a program in which all local organizations and institutions are actively interested, actively involved, and actively supportive.

Each of these organizations will have a vital role in the preliminary groundwork that must be accomplished to generate the state of community readiness that will be needed. And beyond that, after the first operational phase is under way, there will be numerous instances in which one or more of these existing organizations will have to assume the major responsibility for various action projects approved in the general assembly. But in thinking of the important role of these organizations, we must not forget the ultimate goal: An effort by the community *as such* which will make it possible for all action projects to emerge and be carried out with widespread community understanding and support. During the period of preliminary groundwork which will lead up to the first phase of operations, this concept should be repeatedly pointed out.

Now let's take a special look at the initiating group. As we have said, this may be any group of civic leaders who are willing to dedicate themselves to getting the citizenry interested in organizing and carrying out a comprehensive development effort in which a substantial portion of the community's citizens, young and old, as nearly as possible *all* of them, may become active participants. This is the initiating group's basic mission.

To accomplish this mission the civic leaders who form this group should assume the role of an *ad hoc* steering committee, select one of themselves as chairman, take a mutual pledge to get the development effort started, then begin making plans and taking actions that will enable them to realize this pledge. The *ad hoc* steering committee itself need not be a particularly large group. A dozen or so should be enough, whatever number the group feels is sufficient. This committee should be open to anyone who wishes to attend its meetings and contribute to the success of its mission, but commitment, persuasive leadership, and staying power—not size—should be the major criteria. To whatever extent is practical and advantageous, this committee should represent a cross-section of the community, including both men and women and people from different segments of the population. But it is even more important that this initiating committee be a tight-knit group of leaders whose words and deeds carry weight in the community, and who have the personal ability to generate trust and enthusiasm among all elements of the citizenry.

All persons in the *ad hoc* steering committee should first read thoroughly and completely the development guide—not merely skim it once-over-lightly—but really study it from cover to cover, then discuss it among themselves so all of them have a thorough grasp of its contents and are prepared to explain to the community the organizational machinery through which the first phase of the development effort will operate. The second phase will be determined largely on the basis of problems and needed long-range actions identified during phase one.

In section 3 we discussed at length the advisability of avoiding any move toward formal or corporate organization, and of not seeking special project funds under state or federal aid programs until after the first phase of the operation is well under way. But suppose one or more special projects have already been set up under state or federal aid programs and a formal agency has been established before the *ad hoc* steering committee has begun its preliminary groundwork? If this is the case, then the steering committee will need to consider several immediately important questions. What effect, if any, might this formal agency have on the possibility of achieving the community-wide citizen participation which is vital for the development effort we have been talking about? What steps, if any, should be taken to prevent any possible stifling influence this agency might have on getting the effort started? Is there likely to be any unnecessary conflict between the comprehensive development operation the *ad hoc* steering committee is introducing, and the work of this formal agency? If this is a serious possibility, how might such conflict be avoided? Hopefully, any such prior existing agency will welcome the move toward starting the development effort, for once this effort is organized and set in motion, that agency's capacity for effective service will be greatly enhanced, and the community will discover how to make increased use of the resources it represents.

Ideally, the relationship between the community development operation and any state or federally supported agency that may already exist should be one of mutual cooperation. Therefore, unless there are compelling reasons to the contrary, any such existing agency should become a part of the *ad hoc* steering committee's sponsoring consortium, thus making it possible for this agency to help in every way it can with the preliminary groundwork that will be necessary to get the development effort started.

Another question the *ad hoc* steering committee should think about is how much will the first phase of the development effort cost, including the preliminary groundwork. In a general guide such as this, there is no way of giving a specific cost estimate. However, we can indicate certain items to help reach such an estimate. We will not include any items of cost for the second phase of the operation, for when the point of transition is reached between phase one and phase two, the development effort will be well established, and the question of cost will then be quite a different matter. At that point the community will be able to determine with much greater precision what further action is needed. It will be in a position to consider specifically what outside financial assistance may be appropriate to supplement its own resources, and what the community must do for itself to make the most effective use of such outside assistance. Also, at that point the community will in all likelihood be considering various new services, facilities, and improvements that can be achieved only on a long-range basis, some of which will undoubtedly involve planning and action at the area level in cooperation with other communities.

Copies of the development guide should be made available to as many people as possible who become engaged in the work. As has been pointed out, this is in essence a textbook for citizens on community development.

Therefore, the more people who read it, the more thoroughly the citizenry will understand the concept and the practical workings of the development effort and the more effective the operation will be. Many people will want to purchase their own individual copy. But an ample supply should also be made available at the local public library, or if your community does not have a public library, extra copies should be placed in a central location where they can be borrowed and returned. This, then, is one of the first items of cost—the acquisition of enough copies of the development guide.

The matter of a central location raises another possible item of cost —that is the desirability of establishing a suitable community development headquarters. This headquarters could be used for committee work sessions, and will give the operation a special identity. It could provide a home base for much of the development work, and could be the place in which to stock survey forms and other supplies and reference materials. Such a facility may be available in any of several possible locations—the chamber of commerce, the city or town hall, a community college, a civic center, a church, or in quarters provided by a private company. In line with the general thrust of voluntarism and the avoidance of a paid staff during the first phase of operations, this facility should, if at all possible, be made available without rent, but even if it is rent-free there may still be relatively minor costs—for example, a telephone, though free telephone service may be a logical donation by the telephone company.

During the period of preliminary groundwork the *ad hoc* steering committee will need to determine the place where the general assembly is to meet. As we have mentioned previously, this will probably be a public school building, but whatever building is used for this purpose, it too should be rent-free. However, extra help may be needed from time to time for additional work caused by the community development meetings—for example, janitorial services. Insofar as possible any such extra help should also be on a voluntary basis, but there may be certain relatively minor items of cost in this connection.

Probably the major item of cost will be the paper and miscellaneous office supplies needed to produce the survey forms and reports of the fact-finding committees, plus other typewritten or printed materials. This can vary greatly from one community to another, depending on how elaborate the committee reports become, and on the amount of printing and duplicating required. For example, certain printed materials will be essential to the industrial development committee in connection with the business of plant location.

During the preliminary groundwork, the *ad hoc* steering committee should draw up a written statement, to be duplicated and given wide circulation, explaining the highlights of the development operation. This statement, perhaps accompanied by flyers, will be of considerable value in helping the citizenry acquire an advance understanding of how the operation is to be put together, how it will work, and how it will provide a practical means for broad citizen participation in resolving local problems and improving the community. This informational material may be adapted from the development guide—including direct quotations—and from problems and situations the steering committee knows are of serious local concern. It should be brief enough to be read quickly, and organized and written in ways that will give it the strongest possible local appeal. This will be an item of cost.

Also, as will be more fully explained below, the four temporary fact-finding committees listed in section 5—boundary, census, community attitudes, and community organizations—should be activated during the period of preliminary groundwork so their reports will be ready for use in the early formative stages of the first phase of the operation. The survey forms and reports of these committees will therefore be another part of the cost to be taken into account by the *ad hoc* steering committee.

The other fact-finding committees which will continue throughout phase one, and in some cases carry into phase two, should not be organized until the first community-wide public meeting is held for the purpose of moving phase one into full operation, thus avoiding any more advance organizational structuring than is absolutely necessary to ensure a successful beginning. This first public meeting will be discussed in detail in section 13. Suffice to say for now, this meeting will be primarily organizational in character and will provide an opportunity for everyone in attendance to participate in the crucial process of moving from the period of preliminary groundwork into full activation of the first phase of operations.

Following this first public meeting, there will necessarily be a lapse of time before the continuing fact-finding committees will be able to get organized and supply the general assembly with their reports for discussion. This is why the four temporary fact-finding committees must get organized and prepare their reports in advance of this first public meeting;

otherwise there could be a delay of several weeks after the development effort is fully launched before it would be possible for the general assembly to begin its regular schedule of meetings. Such a delay would cause a serious loss of momentum, which could be extremely damaging.

The boundary committee, though highly important, will have less work than the other temporary committees, and its membership can therefore be drawn from the *ad hoc* steering committee itself. The steering committee should obtain additional volunteers in the community who are in a position to handle the work of the census committee. One of the member groups of the steering committee's sponsoring consortium should be asked, as a group, to serve as the community attitudes committee. A lively local service club would be ideal for this purpose, or if there is a nearby community college, this could be a class project with the instructor serving as the committee chairman. In order to prepare the community organizations report, information will be needed from all organizations in the community, and for that reason the steering committee should recruit persons from each existing organization to serve on this committee.

In addition to making it possible to activate the regular schedule of general assembly meetings immediately following the first public meeting, the work of these four temporary committees will contribute in significant ways to generating community-wide interest. For example, the community organizations committee will stimulate added interest among all membership organizations. The community attitudes committee will need to survey all households in the community, which will provide an ideal opportunity to explain the development idea in a direct personal way to a large percentage of the entire citizenry. The work of the boundary committee will help people begin thinking more comprehensively about their community as a whole, and the work of the census committee will reveal some of the underlying reasons why the development effort is needed.

As the date approaches for the first public meeting, the *ad hoc* steering committee and its sponsoring consortium should do whatever promotion is deemed necessary to ensure a large attendance. This will involve a major publicity campaign. Also, when the publicity committee is formed during the time the development organization is being completed, following this first public meeting, this committee will be engaged in promotional activities on a continuing basis. Thus, promotion is an item of cost to be considered. Now, to summarize where we are at this point in our move to get the development effort started.

The *ad hoc* steering committee has formed itself into a solid working unit. It has read and digested the development guide and has a clear understanding of the operation to which it has committed itself. It has prepared and duplicated the written statement referred to above, explaining the highlights of the operation, plus any other typewritten or printed matter it feels will be useful for explanatory and promotional purposes. It has on hand extra copies of the development guide. It has considered operational costs, arrived at an estimate of what these will probably add up to, and has devised plans for raising the necessary funds. It has recognized the need for a sponsoring consortium to be made up of existing organizations and institutions, and has formed definite ideas as to how to recruit and activate the four temporary fact-finding committees which will supply their reports during the early formative stages of phase one.

With these accomplishments, the *ad hoc* steering committee is now ready to begin its major push toward eliciting widespread public interest. Upon reaching this state of preparedness, the next move of the steering committee is to actually form its sponsoring consortium and make the development effort a major topic of conversation all over the community.

Although the *ad hoc* steering committee is not a formally appointed body, but simply a group of concerned civic leaders who have come together informally to promote the development idea and cause it to be put into practice, it is quite probable that most of those who make up this initiating group will be leaders or influential members in several, if not most, of the organizations and institutions that will form the sponsoring consortium, and will already have obtained substantial support for putting the consortium together. However, to make certain no group is overlooked, the steering committee should draw up a list of all existing organizations and institutions—both private and public—including the names of key leaders and members in each, divide the list among the steering committee members, and visit these persons individually.

Identify to them what and who the steering committee is. Explain that after exploring the idea of starting a community development operation along the lines suggested in the guide, this group has decided that such an effort will enable the community to do something of real significance for itself, but that this effort can succeed only if all organizations and individuals who care about the well-being of the community become active participants in organizing and carrying it out. Describe the organizational machinery that will make this participation possible—the general assembly, the fact-finding committees, and the administrative committees—and how this machinery will function. Point out the need for the four temporary fact-finding committees that must be formed during the period of preliminary groundwork, and describe what these committees will do. Explain the need for the sponsoring consortium, and ask each person called upon to help in its formation.

Point out the need discussed in section 3 for the community to set aside a definite period of six or seven months from its business-as-usual existence—preferably beginning in the fall—and the need for the general assembly to meet regularly during this special period of commitment —preferably no less than once a week. Raise the question for people to begin thinking about as to what would be the best night in the week to hold the assembly meetings, and the desirability of clearing that one night of all other activities for the duration of this special period so the community will be free that evening to devote full attention to the development effort by attending the assembly meetings.

Leave copies of the written statement explaining the highlights of the operation for each person called upon to read and distribute to others. Wherever it may be helpful, leave a copy of the development guide. Then go back for more conversation as many times as it takes to make sure a thorough understanding of the operation and solid support for getting it started have been established.

After talking personally to each person the steering committee has listed, plus any other people these persons feel should be visited, and having won their personal support and enthusiasm, the steering committee should then make arrangements to address the community's various membership organizations—its service clubs and public bodies such as the town or city council—to explain to these groups collectively the community development idea and the need for the sponsoring consortium.

Get as many institutions, official groups, business firms, and voluntary membership organizations as possible to agree to be listed as members of the sponsoring consortium, and see that this list is well publicized. Obtain written resolutions endorsing the development effort—the more the better—and see that these are made widely known.

And, again, don't forget to enlist through these groups the workers that will be needed for the temporary fact-finding committees so these committees can get started as soon as possible.

The *ad hoc* steering committee should facilitate as much intergroup communication within the consortium as possible, obtaining representatives from each group to serve on the community organizations committee. But it is not necessary for the sponsoring consortium to become a formal delegate body—which, in effect, would create another organization—or for the consortium as such to hold general meetings. Indeed, it is preferable that such formal action *not* be taken. To do that would run the risk of creating an impression in the community that participation in the development effort is to be limited to members of these existing organizations, thus making it more difficult to build the operation into an effort by the whole community. It *is* necessary, however, for all groups in the consortium to get out into the community and talk up the development idea, to help generate as it were a "community development bandwagon."

After the sponsoring consortium has been formed and its member groups are actively engaged in the promotion, after the *ad hoc* steering committee has recruited the boundary, census, community attitudes, and community organizations committees and they have completed their reports, after the development effort has become "the talk of the town"—meaning enough public enthusiasm has been created to ensure its success—the steering committee, in consultation with its sponsoring consortium, should set the date for the first community-wide public meeting. This meeting will provide all citizens in the community the opportunity to come together and move into the full organization of the first phase of the operation, decide which committee they would most like to be on, volunteer to be discussion leaders, recorders, or block captains, and elect the general chairman, assistant general chairman, secretary, and treasurer.

Hopefully, this election can be accomplished by a kind of informal consensus, rather than through hotly contested campaigns among rival groups which could lead to resentments or embarrassments that could set up unnecessary obstacles to the work. But even though such a consensus appears to have been reached the election should be finally determined by a vote; otherwise there could be feelings among some people that the whole thing was "railroaded," a situation that would be unhealthy to say the least.

Advance preparation for this election is one of the most important jobs of the *ad hoc* steering committee. Taking into account the duties and qualifications of the four elective positions, careful advance thought should be given to who would make an effective general chairman, assistant general chairman, secretary, and treasurer. The committee should consult with the groups in its sponsoring consortium and with other persons in the community and see to it that this matter is widely and thoughtfully discussed during the period of preliminary groundwork. By generating serious thought and discussion in the community in this respect, the election of these four leaders will be much more apt to be accomplished by a legitimate consensus and with wisdom and community acceptance.

No one should be nominated for any of these elective positions without first having given his or her prior consent. Therefore, it would be both productive and proper for the *ad hoc* steering committee, having thought this matter through and counseled with others in the community, to actually approach and sound out a few individuals who are highly regarded, would be well qualified for these elective posts, and obtain their personal agreement to serve if nominated and elected—not excluding the possibility of persons who are a part of the steering committee itself.

Almost nothing can be more damaging to the beginning of the development effort than to go into the first public meeting without having given careful advance thought to who would be ideal choices for these four elective positions. If a situation is allowed to occur in which several people are nominated on the spur of the moment, then get up and decline, seriously harmful confusion will almost inevitably result, and the process of getting started could be thrown into chaos. In this same vein, another extremely damaging situation would be for someone at the first public meeting to offer a nomination as a joke or to propose a person who is so controversial as to turn the meeting into a state of turmoil that would cause many people to have nothing further to do with the operation. It may be said that such things could never happen in your community, but such things can happen in almost any community, and if they do, the work required to repair the damage is not simple.

Also, if individuals are placed in positions of leadership for which they are not suited, who are either unwilling or unable to devote the required time and responsibility, or give the necessary attention, patience and persistence to accomplishing what is expected of them, the development

effort will be hurt. Indeed, it is virtually impossible to conduct a successful community development effort without effective local leaders who
are firmly committed to its success, and are able to work cooperatively
with all sectors of the population.

All this further points up the importance of the basic groundwork that
some group in the community must get accomplished before the first
public meeting is held. I have referred to this group as an "*ad hoc* steering
committee." But whatever this initiating group is called, a decision
must be made by some specific group of local civic leaders to perform this
essential preliminary work if the development effort is to be started and
carried out on a solid footing.

We will now move into the operations of the four temporary fact-
finding committees which will be a highly important part of this groundwork—boundary, census, community attitudes, and community
organizations—following which, we will discuss in detail the conduct of
the first public meeting.

9

The Boundary Committee

AS we have noted, your community covers a certain geographical
territory that can be plotted on a map, and inasmuch as the development
operation is to be community-wide in scope, a decision needs to be made
as to what is the actual extent of this territory. What area of ground does
your community occupy? How far does it extend—north, south, east,
west? Where in each direction does your community end and its neighboring communities begin? Just what are the boundaries of your community?

In a small town which is an incorporated municipality these boundaries
may be thought of in a legal sense as the official city limits. But in a
broader sense the community's boundaries may extend considerably
beyond these official limits. Because of proximity of location or established lines of communication and various mutual services, people who

live just outside these limits or varying distances away, while not being legal residents of the municipality—or town proper—may feel just as much a part of the community and be just as concerned about its development as anyone who lives inside these limits. This may be their post-office address. It may be the place where they do at least part of their shopping. Your town may be the place in which people outside the official city limits visit friends, join organizations, go for entertainment, attend church, check out library books, send their children to school. Some of them may work here, or operate businesses here.

And so in a broad social sense, the town proper is not really the entire community. Reaching out into what we might think of as zones of transition between neighboring communities, there are families, some of them on farms, who think of this as their home town. The people who live in these outlying parts of the community are of great importance to the town, just as those who live in town are of great importance to them, and if the development effort is to achieve maximum success it is essential that we take into account the whole community—not just that portion which is inside the official municipal limits—and that all residents of the whole community be included in the development operation.

Thus, it is necessary to determine the geographical boundaries of your community—or, let's say, "social boundaries"—so that steps can be taken to make certain the entire community becomes a part of the operation. This is of utmost importance because if the community is to develop the best possible life conditions for all its people and the greatest possible degree of solidarity as a citizenry, it is essential that those who live in town and those who live out of town learn to work together for the solution of their mutual problems and think about what is good for all sections of the community as a whole. If the people, as a unified social body, learn to face and deal cooperatively with their community problems, whether these problems are in town or out of town, and increase their sense of common loyalty and civic pride, they can build a stronger, more satisfying, more prosperous, and more attractive community life. Otherwise it is doubtful that the community can ever rise to its full potential for problem solving.

This makes the boundary committee very important, for it must provide the leadership in helping to decide exactly what is your *total community*. This determination is not always easy to make, for it often depends upon factors that are intangible and sometimes there is a certain amount of overlapping between neighboring communities, which makes the kind of boundaries we are talking about somewhat fuzzy. In some of the more remote parts of rural America, such as in the West, there are enormous gaps of virtually uninhabited stretches between communities, though regardless of how sparsely settled these stretches of land may be, there is some sense of community even in these remote areas.

In some areas, certain intangible factors make it rather easy to determine the boundary lines between communities. For example, in two small towns located seven miles apart, each of which conducted a successful community development effort, then joined forces with other neighboring communities in an area development operation, it was determined that the boundary between these two communities was a point along the road at which people ceased rooting for the football team in one town and began rooting for the team in the other town. This may be thought of as a kind of "loyalty line," and almost everywhere people feel more attached to one community than to any other.

Professional planners often lump all the communities in a given area together, and refer to them collectively as one—using such designations as "dispersed city," "metro-community," or a variety of other terms. But regardless of how many area-wide similarities there may be, or what common interests the individual communities within an area may have, these professional-planning designations are more artificial than real and have greater meaning on the planners' drawing boards than they do in the minds of the people. And what the people think and feel is of far more importance to effective local development—and ultimately to area development—than what any professional planner may decide in the isolation of a planning office.

Where two or more towns have contiguous city limits, it may be decided for purposes of community development to treat them as one and organize the operation as a single mutual effort—but, only if the people themselves decide this is the way it should be done. In unincorporated settlements strung out across the landscape, such as exist in parts of the rural South, as well as in other parts of the United States, the geographical extent of a given community may be decided on a sort of local district basis. If the community is a local neighborhood in a large city or metropolitan area, its boundaries will be along certain streets, in some instances along only one side of a street, and will be determined by patterns of activity and familiarity that create within the people who live there a certain "feeling," or informal and often unspoken understanding as to where their community ends and other communities begin. But whatever the geographical situation of your community may be, one of the first things that needs to be done in organizing for its development is to determine its boundaries in the broad social sense we have indicated so the whole community can become engaged in the effort.

In making this determination, however, one cautionary point that already has been inferred should be made explicit. Don't become overly expansive and assume the boundaries of your community extend over into another town whose residents regard themselves as a different community, unless the people who live there really want to join with your community in a partnership development operation. For to try to push them into such a relationship against their will, or to assume they are a part of your community when they don't agree with that assumption, is likely to produce more disharmony than harmony. The temptation to make this mistake is especially great where a development effort is being started in a community of, say, ten thousand population which is immediately adjacent to another community of, say, eight hundred.

In a situation such as this, the residents of the smaller place often feel a certain touch of jealousy, sometimes outright resentment, toward the larger place, and if such feelings exist, they will only be aggravated by the notion that people in the larger place think of the smaller place as simply an extension of their community. This is somewhat analogous to the feeling of being relegated to second-class status, and where this condition prevails, it is mere illusion to pretend there is only one community when in fact there are two. For this reason it is better to look upon the smaller place as what in actual fact it is—a neighboring community that happens to be located in the same area in which your community is located, and in the absence of an expressed desire to join in a common effort, it will be much more effective for each community to start its own development operation which in time will pave the way for legitimate partnership operations at the area level.

With these principles in mind, the members of the boundary committee should obtain whatever maps are available and through discussions among themselves decide tentatively the extent of the community—geographically. This tentative decision should then be checked by talking to various local residents, particularly in what seem to be the outermost reaches of the community and in sections or neighborhoods in which there may be reasons for honest doubt as to whether people feel they are a part of your community or of some other community—or perhaps a community unto themselves. Explain to each person called upon the nature of the development operation which is being started, that it is to be community-wide in scope, and describe the "whole community" concept as described in this section. Make clear that all residents whether located inside or outside a set of official city limits are welcome—indeed, urged—to become active participants in the operation.

Moving outward from the community's geographical center ask people what they think of as their hometown, or what community they generally feel they belong to. Ask questions about the community in which they usually do their shopping or in what town they usually conduct various business transactions, take part in organizational or church activities, or visit friends. If they live in the open countryside, what town do they use as their mailing address? Where do their children go to school? Is the school located in the same community they feel they live in? What would they say is about the last house or farm down the road that could be thought of as being located in the community to which they feel they belong? Where in each direction do people feel this community ends and another one begins?

Seek to reach as clear an understanding as possible the points in each direction at which people cease to feel a part of your community and feel more closely attached to another community, and note these outer perimeters. After analyzing the findings obtained from these inquiries and conversations the committee should settle on the community boundary lines it believes best describe the geographical limits of your community.

Once the committee has agreed on the boundaries it is to recommend, it should draw up a large-scale map of what it sees as the whole community, showing as much detail as possible—streets, roads, streams, railroad tracks, power lines, airport facilities, public and commercial buildings, parks, vacant lots and open spaces, even residential houses, showing both occupied and unoccupied dwellings, and insofar as is feasible the names of individual families. This map will be an extremely valuable tool in the overall development operation, and arrangements should be made to duplicate as many copies as will be needed after it has been publicly adopted or amended as an appropriate representation of the whole community.

In section 6, procedures and responsibilities were set forth that with certain exceptions apply to all fact-finding committees. That section should be carefully reviewed by the members of the boundary committee, but as will be noted, this particular committee was one to which several exceptions applied.

The boundary committee must complete its fact-finding and have its report and presentation ready for the first public meeting which will be held for the purpose of moving from the period of preliminary groundwork into phase one of the development operation. This meeting will be devoted primarily to getting the general assembly organized and will not break into small-group discussions.

Copies of the boundary committee's written report should be distributed to all persons as they arrive, and the committee should be prepared to display its map and give a brief oral presentation on the community boundaries being recommended for adoption. This presentation need not be as elaborate as that indicated in section 6 for other committees. It should state how and why the recommended boundaries were determined and allow opportunity for anyone who wishes to comment or offer suggestions to do so. But the allotted time for these purposes must be held to a minimum. The first public meeting will have considerable ground to cover and the total agenda should run no more than two hours—less if at all possible.

Once its presentation has been made and arrangements have been completed for duplicating enough copies of the community map as accepted or amended, the boundary committee will have finished its work and its members should move into other committees or positions of their choice.

10

The Census Committee

THE census committee has the responsibility of putting together a statistical report that will show what is happening to the community in terms of growth or decline and some of the underlying problems these facts reveal. This report, along with that of the boundary committee, should be ready for distribution to all persons in attendance at the first community-wide public meeting. A suggested research outline is as follows:

1. The total number of people and the total number of households. How many of them are in town, and how many are in that portion of the community which the boundary committee has determined extends beyond the official town limits?

2. How does the size of the population and the total number of households today compare with previous years? Is the community growing, declining, or remaining about the same?

3. What do these figures and population trends indicate about the community's current and future conditions? What problems, if any, do they reveal in regard to business and the local economy? Education? Health? Housing? Recreation? Churches? Other aspects of community life?

4. Does your community's population fluctuate from one season of the year to another? If so, to what extent? What problems, if any, does this cause?

5. Which sections of the community are undergoing the greatest population growth? Which sections are undergoing the greatest population loss? Which sections are remaining fairly stable? What are some of the reasons for this? Does this indicate any significant movement within the community? Does this pose any problems? If so, what problems?

6. How many families have left the community within the past ten years? How many individuals? Estimate how many will probably leave within the next few years. What are some of the reasons for this outmigration, what problems does it pose, and what does it indicate as to the community's future prospects?

7. What percentage of the community's graduating high school seniors in each of the past ten years have left the community permanently? What are the various reasons why they have left? What percentage of the community's young people who are now juniors and seniors in high school intend to leave the community permanently when they graduate? What are the various reasons these young people intend to leave? If lack of employment opportunity is given as one of the reasons, would those young people who intend to leave remain in the community even if suitable employment opportunities were available? If not, why?

8. What effect do these figures concerning the community's young

people have on the age levels of the population? Is this becoming a community of older people? What effect does this have on the starting of new families in the community? What does it indicate about the community's future? Does this pose any problems, and if so what are they?

9. What percentage of the community's population has been here less than five years? From six to ten years? From eleven to fifteen years? From sixteen to twenty years? More than twenty years? What does the length of residence reflect about the community? Does this pose any problems, and if so what are they?

10. How many people in the current population are less than one year old? One to five years old? Six to twelve years old? Thirteen to seventeen years old? Eighteen to twenty years old? Twenty-one to twenty-nine years old? Thirty to thirty-nine years old? Forty to forty-nine years old? Fifty to fifty-nine years old? Sixty to sixty-nine years old? Seventy and over?

11. Is the community becoming overbalanced toward any of these age groups?

12. What do these figures on age groups suggest in regard to the local economy? In regard to education and school planning? In regard to the need for health services? In regard to the need for recreation? In regard to other problems?

13. How many people in the population are male? How many are female? Does this suggest any community problems? If so, what problems?

14. How many marriages have there been in the community in each of the past ten years? How many divorces? Are the marriage and divorce rates rising or declining or remaining about the same? Do these figures indicate any community problems? If so, what problems?

15. What is the community's total labor force—that is, how many people are either self-employed, working for an employer, or would be working if they could find a job? What percentage of the labor force is male? What percentage is female? What percentage of the labor force is currently unemployed? How many unemployed persons in the labor force are male? How many are female? (Do not include in the labor force persons who are not gainfully employed and are not seeking work, such as retired persons, housewives who do not intend to get a job, or persons who are otherwise unavailable for employment).

16. What are the major occupations and occupational skills in the community's labor force?

17. What percentage of the labor force currently employed is working full time, year round? Part time? Seasonally? In what seasons of the year is the community's labor force most fully employed? In what seasons is it least employed?

18. How do the various economic activities—agriculture, industry, retail trade and services—rank in this community? Is there a healthy balance among these economic activities, or do all the community's "economic eggs" tend to be in one basket? What problems, if any, does this indicate?

19. What percentage of the community's labor force is unionized?

20. What races are represented in the community's population? What percentage of the population does each of these racial groups represent? Does this pose any community problems? If so, what problems?

21. Considering the population age twenty-five and over, what is the average number of school years completed? Does this suggest any need for adult education or vocational training?

22. What percentage of the eligible voters in the community (persons eighteen years of age and over) are registered to vote? What percentage are not registered to vote? What percentage of those who were eligible to vote in previous elections voted in each election over the past ten years? Is the voting rate increasing, decreasing, or staying about the same? On the basis of these past records what age groups are the most likely to vote? What age groups are the least likely to vote? What does this rate of voter registration and actual voter turnout say about the community's civic vitality?

23. To sum up, make a list of community needs and problems the committee has observed from these census figures.

Most of the data suggested above, plus other information the committee may decide to include in its report, can be obtained from existing records. Possible sources would include reports from the U.S. Bureau of the Census, the bureau of vital statistics of the state health department or any area agency engaged in comprehensive health planning, the county courthouse, the town or city hall, the state employment service, the public schools, banks, and utilities—electric, gas, water. Some of this information may have to be estimated. Some of it can be obtained by special surveys, such as questionnaires circulated among high school juniors and seniors.

All members of the census committee should review the procedures and responsibilities set forth in section 6 for all the fact-finding committees, noting the exceptions for this particular committee. The committee's written report may use charts, graphs, diagrams, tables, or whatever other devices will help make it clear and point out sharply the problems it reflects.

The oral presentation to be made as a supplement to the written report should make use of large drawings and charts, perhaps slides that can be projected on a screen, along with appropriate commentary so the presentation can be given in the least possible time, yet make a strong impact by pointing up in statistical form basic community problems.

As in the case of the boundary committee, the census committee's written report will not be discussed in small discussion groups. However, this report will point up in striking and specific ways some of the important reasons why the development effort is needed, thereby adding increased motivation for going ahead. The census report will also make factual information immediately available to the continuing committees for their use in developing plans and recommendations for action.

After the census committee has submitted its report and given its brief presentation at the opening public meeting, its work will have been completed. Its members, along with those of the boundary committee, should then move into one of the continuing committees or other positions of their choice.

11

The Community Attitudes Committee

WE have pointed out that human attitudes and life styles are among the most potent factors in determining the ability of a community to deal with its problems, and that very often these factors in themselves become some of the community's most serious problems. This has to do with the fact that every community has its own "character," its own manner of doing things that makes it different from all other communities—the ways people think and feel about it as a place in which to live, what they regard as its most pressing needs, what they consider important or unimportant, what they like and what they dislike. Just as emotions, thoughts, and attitudes influence the actions of an individual, the emotions, thoughts, and attitudes of the people collectively influence the actions of the community.

In a sense this whole complex of attributes is the sum total of all the varied attitudes, traits, and characteristics of all the people who live in the community and the many ways they interact and relate to each other. This makes the community's character a tricky thing to get at, hard to describe, even more difficult to comprehend. In many respects it is intangible and cannot be seen. Yet evidence of the community's character can be noted in the presence or absence of certain physical facilities and in their arrangement and state of repair. It is reflected in the appearance of streets and grounds, in the architecture of buildings, in the nature and vitality of the economy, in actions and patterns of behavior in various sectors of the population.

There is an intricate network of customs, habits, values, and ideals that grows up over generations, and as this network of traits evolves, it gradually shapes and conditions the community's inner character. This character includes the ways people respond to emergencies and to all sorts of situations and problems. It consists of the personal views people hold toward themselves and each other, the ways they look at their neighboring communities, their feelings about the area of which their neighboring communities and their own community are a part, and their differing reactions toward the many events and issues that occur in their state, nation, and in the world at large.

This character is not static. Just as the community and the people in it change, so too does the community's character. This change may be slow and go largely unnoticed as it is taking place. Or certain pressures and forces—both internal and external—may greatly accelerate the rate of change and bring on a sense of uneasiness and insecurity, sometimes outright fear, about what is happening.

But if the people are willing to examine the character of their community, if they have the courage to look realistically and objectively at the human attitudes that contribute to so great an extent to making it what it is, they can by their own effort largely control the direction of change and, to a substantial degree, make adjustments that will enable them to live with those changes they cannot control. It is this process of self-determination that lies at the heart of a truly democratic society, and when this process ceases to work or becomes weak as a result of civic apathy or a lack of concern for effective civic performance, then democracy begins to dry up.

As we have repeatedly emphasized, the prime purpose of community development is to increase the vitality of the local citizenry as a problem-solving unit of society, thereby continuously improving the community's capacity to see its needs and take action that will meet those needs by self-determined initiative. This is based on the belief that enlightened, active, self-reliant communities are essential to the growth of effective individual citizenship, to strengthening freedom and civic responsibility, to expanding equality of opportunity, and to ensuring the well-being of our nation.

Therefore, if your community has in it any attitudes or characteristics that tend to retard democratic initiative and thus prevent the citizenry from working together with enough underlying unity to openly identify and deal with its community problems, it is urgently important that these attitudes and characteristics be uncovered and brought to light so they can be looked at, examined, discussed, and seen for what they are. Only if this process is put to work can intelligent action be planned and carried out, or can needed alterations in thinking be achieved that will make it possible to revamp those attitudes and characteristics which create barriers to your community's social and economic advance.

We have indicated that an individual's personal sense of values has a major influence on that individual's mode of living and in turn will affect the character of his community. However, because each individual is largely a product of his environment—which to a considerable extent is the community in which he lives—his personal values will not only affect the community, the collective values of the community as a whole will greatly affect him. Thus, we are dealing with a two-way combination of influences in which all persons who comprise the total citizenry individually affect the character of their community, while at the same time the community profoundly affects them.

If, for example, the community is largely indifferent to its problems, a large portion of its people are likely to be of that character too, and by their civic inaction will contribute toward making their community still more indifferent. If there are groups whose values differ sharply with those of other groups, as there often are, or are in open conflict with each other, as often is the case, the chances are that until better communication of thought and feeling is created among these varied segments of the population they will not be able to develop enough respect and appreciation toward each other to function with the cooperative spirit the citizenry must have if it is to build a better community.

If human attitudes are such that various parts of the community tend to isolate themselves from each other, if there is an atmosphere of suspicion and jealousy, if conditions are such that many people are afraid to express openly what they honestly think, if the community is divided into factions that are continuously pitted against each other—if these and similar conditions are a part of the local character, then something needs to be done to bring about greater harmony before effective action can be initiated to resolve virtually any community problem.

It should also be recognized that the values and attitudes held by the community as a whole, or by certain groups within the community, are very often not what many citizens think they are. An individual is not always influenced by what other people actually think, but by what he *thinks* they think. This is to say that even though certain attitudes and opinions are not warranted on the basis of fact, it is a fact that such unwarranted attitudes and opinions exist. And the very existence of such attitudes or opinions, even though they are based on misinformation, will have just as much influence on the people who hold them as would be the case if they were based on truth. Misunderstandings of this kind are of great significance not only to individuals but to the community as a social body, for it is entirely possible that the problem-solving ability of a whole community can be seriously impaired merely because of mistaken notions or imagined ideas some people have about other people.

In a community that consists of a small town plus its immediately surrounding environs, as most rural American communities do, the attitudes between the people who live in the town proper and those who live in the outlying countryside will have an important bearing on the character of the community and its ability to get things done. Also of significance in this respect is the extent to which people feel a common loyalty to their community, the way they react to new ideas, their attitudes toward strangers and newcomers—all this will have a major bearing on the character of the community and the ability of the citizenry to diagnose its problems and muster successful action.

Another way of looking at the character of your community is to recognize that all communities have a certain life cycle. They are founded, they are settled, they may reach a certain level of maturity then, in many cases, deteriorate. A community may, however, by the actions of its people prolong indefinitely its period of maturity, for its state of maturity may have little bearing on its age.

Many communities, such as those which have become ghost towns, were founded suddenly, lived through a period of rapid expansion, then declined and disappeared almost as suddenly as they began. When the gold was mined out or the timber was cut away the place was finished. These communities never reached maturity; they never really grew up. Yet other communities now old in age are still relatively immature and stand at the threshold of bankruptcy. This applies even to some of our large and medium-size cities.

Other communities experience a gradual or even rapid growth, then at some point in time achieve a real quality of maturity. This maturity comes in varying degrees and as long as it is maintained at a fairly high level, the community remains an attractive place in which to live.

In a community that reaches and maintains a high quality of maturity, there is an air of self-confidence, a determined belief among the people that needed improvements can be achieved. There is a willingness on the part of the citizenry as a whole to work together, a seasoned ability to face local problems honestly and constructively without unnecessary conflict or unjustified ill will. It is this quality of maturity toward which a real effort in community development aspires. Indeed, it is the extent to which the communities of rural America are able to achieve this quality of maturity that will make the difference between success or failure in any nationwide move toward rural community development.

Your community necessarily fits into some stage of this life cycle. At just what stage it fits, and the direction it is going, are largely in the hands of you who live there. But this means that you, the people, must be realistic about where your community does fit into this life cycle and where it is headed. This does not mean harping on your community's shortcomings or disadvantages, or being critical just to find fault. It does mean looking objectively at your community as it actually is and discovering whether it has any aspects of character that are holding back its potential for improvement.

Now, let's take still another look at that word "maturity." In the case of an adult individual this word applies to one who is able and willing to stand on his own feet, examine facts, recognize his limitations, exercise self-discipline, and make decisions on courses of action that seem to be right even though they are not always pleasant. The mature person has learned to face life as it is, and by his own actions keeps to a minimum the situations in which he is unable to manage his own affairs. Most of the time he thinks in an objective, logical manner. He listens to advice from more experienced persons, and is not afraid to admit when he is wrong. He feels a sense of responsibility toward his family, his community, his country, and his fellow man. Probably few of us ever reach complete maturity in every respect, and the same applies to communities. But increasing maturity is a quality toward which every individual and every community may strive.

And so the relative maturity of your community will be largely determined by the willingness of your local citizenry to take a hard look at its internal character, face realistically its limitations and difficulties, recognize its needs, and work cooperatively toward meeting them.

Another point we should consider in this connection is that one of the fundamental institutions which determines the character and maturity of your community is the family. The families in your community are its primary social units. Anything that weakens them weakens your community. In short, the family, as an integral part of community life, is the basic form of human organization, and as such is the backbone of every community.

If the drift of young people away from the community becomes excessive and you begin to become a community of older people, if forces that cause family units to break down are allowed to go unchecked, if the qualities that hold individual families together are not continuously strengthened and maintained, the character of your community is in jeopardy and effective problem-solving in all fields of interest will grow increasingly difficult.

This does not mean that all of a community's youth must stay in the community for it to be strong. It does mean that when a community can no longer offer an attractive life to substantial numbers of its young people, and can no longer provide social and economic opportunities that contribute to building strong new families, the character of that community will be damaged and its civic vitality will decline.

The development of strong family units and the development of a healthy community life are closely interrelated, and unless the community's families are tied together by bonds of mutual concern and constructive activity, interfamily communications are likely to become so scattered as to reduce the positive effect of the community as a whole on individual family solidarity.

Relationships develop between families through marriage. Other relationships develop through business services that members of families perform for each other. Whether these business relationships contribute to local unity will depend upon how and with what attitude the services are rendered, and on whether the people involved find their dealings satisfactory. If, for example, a shopkeeper makes his customers "mad" or if some of his customers are habitually nasty to do business with, the relationships between these particular families are not likely to promote harmony and goodwill.

Other interfamily relationships that develop out of the flow of community life are in cooperative activities, such as working together in the community development effort. Others are in church, in meetings of social organizations. Some are formal, some are informal. Groups may get together to sing, to put on a play, to engage in sporting events, or to have a party. People visit each other. Friendships come into being. Clubs are organized. People stand around street corners to talk. These and countless other activities create interfamily relationships that go into the makeup of the community's character. And there are other relationships between families: Vice, crime, juvenile delinquency, drug use, promiscuous sex, and other illicit activities.

This complex pattern of community activities and interpersonal and interfamily relationships exerts a powerful influence on the individual character of both children and adults. If these relationships are direct, wholesome, and evolve out of mutual respect, people develop feelings of responsibility toward each other which create a community spirit that makes it easier to accomplish needed improvements, and the community grows up. It matures. It finds ways to develop an economy that enables its people to earn a satisfactory income. It becomes a place in which people want to live and work and raise their families. All these aspects of a community's character, plus many other aspects we could mention, bear on every facet of community development—social, economic, and cultural.

The community attitudes committee has the responsibility of doing the fact-finding and reporting that will provide the general assembly with

information needed to examine and discuss some of the important attitudes that shape the character of your community. This essential part of
the development effort may in some respects be a bit painful. But the
work of this committee and the community self-analysis it will make
possible will be an extremely interesting exercise. Through this opportunity for a very special kind of self-expression, unnecessary irritants that
have long festered under the surface and acted as hidden obstacles to
community progress will be uncovered. Problems and improvements of
most importance to the people themselves will be clearly identified, and
out of this airing of both positive and negative attributes will come an
increased incentive to get things done. To obtain the essential information for this analysis it will be necessary for the community attitudes
committee to conduct a community-wide survey of attitudes and opinions.

A suggested questionnaire which can be duplicated for this purpose is
set forth below. However, if the committee feels that certain questions
should be added or subtracted to tailor this questionnaire more specifically to conditions in your particular community, it should do so. It will
be noted that the questions in this suggested questionnaire are blunt and
candid. This is to help bring out blunt and candid answers, and the
committee should make every effort to obtain such answers. The more
frankly the questions are answered, the better. For unless the survey
reveals clearly and honestly how people *really* feel, as opposed to what
they might say in polite conversation, the survey will be of no value.

For this reason people should *not* sign their names to the questionnaires, and each person should fill out his or her questionnaire independently. Not even members of the same family should collaborate in
their answers, nor should they reveal their individual responses to each
other—at least, not until after the completed questionnaires have been
collected. The members of the community attitudes committee should
encourage all persons to write down *exactly* what they think individually,
no matter what, no matter how insulting or derogatory, with no punches
pulled, no thoughts withheld. This means the committee must devise a
system of distributing and collecting the questionnaires in a way that will
make it possible for all answers to be given anonymously with absolute
assurance that confidentality will be scrupulously preserved; otherwise
some people will not be willing to express how they actually feel.

One possible method of ensuring this confidentiality is to distribute the questionnaires along with envelopes in which they can be sealed when completed by the persons filling them out, then handed to members of the committee. Or the committee members could carry sealed boxes similar to secret ballot boxes into which the completed questionnaires could be dropped. There are many ways in which the necessary distribution and collection of questionnaires can be accomplished, but the main point to be emphasized is that the committee should devise whatever method it feels will obtain as nearly as possible a complete coverage of the local citizenry, and at the same time maintain the required secrecy as to who filled out each questionnaire. Whether the committee members wait, while people fill out the questionnaires, to pick them up or return later to pick them up is a matter for the committee to decide. But if a return trip is made, this should be done without delay; otherwise the chances of getting individual answers and community-wide coverage will be greatly reduced.

The importance of covering every household in the community, including those of the committee members themselves, cannot be overemphasized. Also, the questionnaires should be delivered and picked up at each household in person. Thus, this committee should be a fairly sizeable one. This is one of the reasons it was suggested in section 8 that one of the community's existing service clubs assume the responsibility of serving as this committee.

Enough questionnaires should be delivered to each house so that all adults who live there, including both husband and wife, may fill one out. This personal delivery and collection will provide an opportunity for the members of the committee to explain directly the purpose of the survey, stress the need for frank and complete answers and the importance of each person filling out the questionnaire individually without consulting anyone else in the household or letting anyone else see his or her answers. If the importance of each person answering the questionnaire without talking over with anyone else what he or she is putting down is sufficiently stressed, most people will do it this way, even though after the questionnaires are collected, many people will undoubtedly confide with each other as to how they answered certain questions. *But the important thing is that no one influence anyone else's answers at the time the questionnaire is being filled out.*

These house-to-house calls will also provide an opportunity for the members of this committee to explain the overall development effort that is being started, emphasize the need for all citizens to come out and actively participate, and distribute a copy of the written statement which has been prepared by the *ad hoc* steering committee outlining the highlights of the operation.

It would be of considerable value to conduct the community attitudes survey separately among the community's high-school-age young people. This would enable the committee to make two compilations of the survey results—one for the high-school-student population, the other for the adult population—thus bringing out any contrasts in opinion that may exist between the students and their elders.

If this is done, it is recommended that the committee find an appropriate way of consulting with various members of the student group to get their ideas as to how the questionnaires might best be distributed and collected among the students and ensure their serious attention. Perhaps the students might like to form a subcommittee among themselves to work with certain members of the community attitudes committee for this purpose. An arrangement such as this would increase the probability of obtaining fruitful results from the student group and help convey to the community's young people that they too are an important part of the development operation. In many, if not most communities, these advantages will be less likely to be achieved if the responsibility for distributing and collecting the questionnaires in the student population is simply left to the school administrators and teachers. Here is the suggested questionnaire.

COMMUNITY ATTITUDES SURVEY

(In duplicating the survey form be sure to leave enough space after each item for full information.)

Introduction: This survey is being taken in preparation for the community development program being started in our community. The purpose of this survey is to find out as closely as possible what we who live here think about our community and its problems. The overall results of the survey will be reported for discussion at a public meeting at which it is hoped everyone will be present so that we can all see and discuss what these results show about our community. Each questionnaire is confidential and nobody except *you* will know who filled it out. Each person in the community is therefore asked to fill out this questionnaire independently without telling how you are answering it, even to others in your own family. *Please do not sign your name.* Your cooperation in giving your *absolutely honest and frank opinions,* no matter how unflattering they may be to our community or to others who live here, will be extremely helpful in getting the community development program off to a good start and in providing information that will help make our community better.

1. What are some of the things you *like most* about our community?
   _____

2. What are some of the things you *dislike most* about our community?
   _____

3. What do you think are some of the most important problems or needs in our community today? _____
   _____

4. In your opinion are there any factions or groups of people in our community who do not get along with each other very well, or who generally disagree with each other on how and what things ought to be done? Yes ____ No ____
   If yes who are these groups, and what are the things they usually disagree about?

The Groups	Their Disagreements
_____	_____

5. If your answer to question 4 was yes, do you think this has anything to do with the ability of our community to get things done, or to carry out needed community projects? Yes ____ No ____ If yes, why? _____

6. In our community as a whole, including its outlying areas, what would you say is the general attitude between the people who live in town and those who live out of town? _____
   Are there any problems in this respect? Yes ____ No ____ If yes, what are some of these problems? _____

7. How well do you think our community gets along with its neighboring communities? _____
   _____

   Are there any problems in this respect? Yes ____ No ____ If yes, what are some of these problems? _____

8. Being absolutely honest with yourself, among the ten items listed below, which ones are the most important to *you personally*? Read through the list, then place (1) in front of the item you think of as the most important to you personally, (2) in front of the item you think of as the next most important, and so on up to (10) in front of the item you think of as the least important.
   _____ Getting an education
   _____ Going to church and being a religious person
   _____ Making a home and raising a family
   _____ The family you came from
   _____ Your length of residence in the community
   _____ Being a leader in the community
   _____ Financial success (the amount of money you make)
   _____ The material goods you own (car, clothes, house, TV, etc.)

_____ Your personal pleasure
_____ Your race or nationality

9. Among this same list of ten items, which ones, *in your private opinion,* would you say most of the other people in this community think are the most important? Number the same list of items below in the order of importance you feel most other people in the community look at them.

_____ Getting an education
_____ Going to church and being a religious person
_____ Making a home and raising a family
_____ The family they came from
_____ Their length of residence in the community
_____ Being a leader in the community
_____ Financial success (the amount of money they make)
_____ The material goods they own (car, clothes, house, TV, etc.)
_____ Their personal pleasure
_____ Their race or nationality

10. Being absolutely frank and blunt about it, how would you rate our community on each of the following points? Place an *X* in the column that you feel most nearly describes the community on each point.

	Excellent	Good	Fair	Poor	Terrible	No Opinion
(1) Friendliness and neighborliness						
(2) The ease with which newcomers are accepted and made to feel at home						
(3) The spirit of community progressiveness and civic action						
(4) Willingness to accept new ideas and ways of doing things						
(5) The extent of local unity						
(6) The degree of local community pride						
(7) The extent to which the majority of the people are truly interested in being informed and aware of local needs and problems.						
(8) The degree of willingness of most of the people to speak out honestly and openly in public on what they think about community problems without fear of what other people might think						

	Excellent	Good	Fair	Poor	Terrible	No Opinion
(9) The willingness of the people as a whole to get out and work long and hard to accomplish community projects						
(10) The ability of all groups to work together for the well being of the community without caring who gets the credit						
(11) Cooperation among the churches						
(12) Church attendance						
(13) The physical appearance and upkeep of church buildings and grounds						
(14) The extent to which there are active civic organizations willing and able to get things done for the overall good of the community						
(15) The extent to which there is cooperation and joint planning of community activities among the various civic organizations						
(16) The effectiveness of local government						
(17) The general level of citizen interest in local government affairs						
(18) The extent and quality of library services in the community						
(19) The extent to which library services are used by the people in this community						
(20) The physical appearance of most of the residential parts of the community (consider cleanliness, paint and upkeep of houses, landscaping, care of lawns, etc.)						
(21) The physical appearance and general upkeep of the business district						
(22) The physical appearance, upkeep, cleanliness, etc. of vacant lots						
(23) The physical appearance and upkeep of public buildings and grounds, parks, entrances to towns, etc.						

	Excellent	Good	Fair	Poor	Terrible	No Opinion
(24) The condition of grade school buildings and equipment						
(25) The quality of grade school educational programs						
(26) The condition of high school buildings and equipment						
(27) The quality of high school educational programs						
(28) Opportunities for adult education						
(29) Recreational opportunities for teen-agers						
(30) Recreational opportunities for adults						
(31) Prevention and control of crime and delinquency						
(32) The solidarity of family life						
(33) Availability of medical care						
(34) Availability of nursing care						
(35) Availability of hospital care						
(36) Availability of dental care						
(37) The local water supply						
(38) Sewage disposal facilities						
(39) Garbage collection						

After the questionnaires have been collected, the community attitudes committee then has the job of tabulating and compiling the results preparatory to writing its report for discussion in the general assembly.

For question 10 in which people were asked to rate the community on various items, the job of tabulation will be merely a matter of counting how many people marked each of the six possible ratings—excellent, good, fair, poor, terrible, or no opinion—for each item that was rated. Having completed this tally, the number of persons counted for each rating should then be converted to percentages of the total number of people who filled out the questionnaire as is commonly done in national opinion polls. These percentage figures can then be written in the appropriate rating column for each item on a blank questionnaire, which will provide a simple method of preparing this part of the committee's report. The use of percentage points, rather than absolute numbers, will give a sharper picture of the people's opinions, make the report much easier to interpret, and thus make for a more lively discussion in the general assembly. It would also be a good idea in this regard to total the percentage points for the first two possible ratings—excellent and good—then total the percentage points for the three possible ratings —fair, poor, and terrible—and include these figures in the committee's report. This will be helpful to the assembly's discussions because these totals will further bring out the major problem areas in which the discussion should be most concentrated. The individual ratings at this lower end of the scale—fair, poor, or terrible—will show the degree of seriousness with which people viewed the respective problems, but any item rated less than good by a significant percentage suggests the existence of a problem.

The tabulations for questions 1, 2, and 3 concerning people's likes, dislikes, and their opinions as to the community's most important problems, will be somewhat more difficult. However, by studying the responses to these three questions, it will be a fairly simple matter to devise a list of descriptive categories into which the answers to each of these three questions can be placed. Once these categories are determined, then the number of answers that fall into each category can be counted, and the absolute numbers can be converted into percentage points. The percentage figures in regard to these three questions will quite obviously not add up to a hundred because many people will have listed more than one like, dislike, or problem. However, the use of percentage figures here will again sharpen the report.

In addition to this, one further thing should be done in compiling the responses to the first three questions—particularly in the case of questions 2 and 3 which show what people dislike and what they consider to be community problems. A list of choice quotes should be taken from the questionnaires for inclusion in the committee's report as sample illustrations of what people actually said. These quotes, added to the statistical tabulations by problem categories, will further sharpen the report, give it greater vitality—in some instances a bit of humor—and show in vivid human terms just how strongly people feel about what they consider community needs and problems. This added touch will further stimulate the assembly discussions, thereby strengthening the motivation for constructive action. *One cautionary note, however: Some of these quotes may require a bit of judicious editing in order to omit direct references to specific individuals which could cause personal harm or embarrassment and for that reason be destructive rather than constructive.*

Questions 4 and 5 concerning the possible existence of opposing local factions and the effect this may have on the community's ability to accomplish needed improvements are companion questions, and the interrelationship between them should be clearly shown in compiling and reporting the responses. First, determine the percentage of returns giving a "yes" answer to question 4, and the percentage that gave a "no" answer. If the percentage of "yes" answers is insignificant or so far outweighed by the "no" answers as to make the "yes" answers virtually meaningless, it would appear that the community has no real problem in this respect, and the committee's report would reflect this without going into detail.

If the percentage of "yes" answers to question 4 is significant, the committee should compile an actual list of the groups that were mentioned in the questionnaire, along with the matters on which they were said to disagree, and put this data in the report just as bluntly as it was stated in the questionnaires—again, with the possibility of some editing the committee may deem appropriate to avoid unnecessarily increasing any hostilities that already exist. However, if the problem of local factions is significant, the answers to this effect should not be softened any more than the committee considers absolutely essential. Too much softening would not only be deceptive, but even worse, would cover up a basic problem that almost more than anything else can prevent community progress, and that can be resolved only by bringing it out for open and objective discussion within the framework of the overall development effort.

Following the percentage figures to question 4 and the listing of groups, along with what were said to be their disagreements, the committee should then tabulate the answers to question 5, giving particular attention to the "yes" answers and to the reasons stated as to why the existing factions and their disagreements influence the community's ability to carry out needed community projects—linking this information to that which was reported from question 4.

Taken together, the information from questions 4 and 5 should provide a bit of shock value that will stimulate the kind of discussion and self-examination which in itself will help reduce existing tensions and lead to greater understanding and unity.

Compilation of the answers to questions 6 and 7 can be handled in approximately the same manner as were the compilations for questions 2 and 3—computing the percentage of the returns that listed problems, then working out descriptive categories into which to place these problems, and extracting enough direct quotes from the questionnaires to give added life and emphasis to the committee's report.

Questions 8 and 9 are also companion questions, and provide an excellent means of bringing out significant attitudes that influence local civic performance. The list of ten items in question 8 should be tallied so that it can be rearranged in the committee's report in the order of importance the ten items were ranked, showing what percentage of the people filling out the questionnaire said the first item in this rearranged list was most important to them personally, the percentage that said the next item was most important to them personally, and so on, down to the item ranked as the least important to them personally. Then this same list of ten items in question 9 should be tallied so it can be arranged in the order of importance people felt others in the community regarded each item, and the percentages showing how people ranked each item in this list should be given as was done in the first listing. These two rearranged lists with the percentage ratings for each of the ten items on each list will point out clearly any differences between what people said were most important to them personally and what they felt other people in the community consider most important. These differences, if clearly stated in the committee's report, should make for highly interesting discussion in the general assembly, thus helping to further develop new insights and greater mutual understanding within the community.

After the results from each question have been compiled, the committee is ready to write its report. In all likelihood the discussion of this report will require at least two meetings of the general assembly. If this appears to be the case—which will be evident from the volume and nature of the information produced by the survey—the committee should prepare its report in two parts: The first part to be distributed at the first assembly meeting for which it is scheduled, with the second part being held for distribution at the next assembly meeting. This will have the advantage of maintaining a touch of suspense which will be an added inducement for more people to come out for the second meeting at which the discussion on community attitudes will be continued.

Also, in this connection, it is recommended that the committee not allow anyone to see any of the questionnaires while they are being tabulated and the report is being written, and that the report itself not be released to anyone in the community until the first meeting of the general assembly at which it is to be distributed for discussion. Until this time, the completed copies of the report should be locked up where no one will have any possibility of seeing them. As added precautions, members of the committee should not take copies of the report home with them, nor reveal even privately any of the survey results to anyone outside the committee. After the report is written in final form, the completed survey questionnaires and tabulation sheets should be destroyed.

People throughout the community will probably be speculating on what the survey found, and it is not unlikely that this will become a popular topic of local conversation. This speculation, coupled with the committee's secrecy about what the survey revealed, will help build interest and curiosity which can be satisfied only by coming to the meetings of the general assembly where everyone present will get a copy of the report.

The only exception to this withholding of information applies to the discussion leaders and recorders, and the general chairman, assistant general chairman, secretary, and treasurer. These people, as indicated in section 6, should receive their copies of the report two or three days before the first assembly meeting at which it is to be discussed. But they too should agree not to reveal its contents to anyone else prior to the meeting. For assistance in writing the report and completing other aspects of the committee's work, all members of the committee should carefully review section 6, "Procedures and Responsibilities of the Fact-Finding Committees."

From the standpoint of the community attitudes committee, the one exception to section 6 has to do with the matter of arranging appropriate follow-up action after the general assembly has completed its discussions of the committee's report. Inasmuch as this is a temporary committee whose report should be completed during the period of preliminary groundwork preparatory to beginning the first phase of the development operation, the problems and recommendations the report brings out, or that are brought out in the assembly discussions, should be referred by the general chairman to the various continuing committees for whatever follow-up may be in order, including, if necessary, the advisory council. Therefore, at the first public meeting, the members of the community attitudes committee, as in the case of the boundary and census committees, should sign up for other committees or positions of their choice —the one provision being that this committee must carry on with the responsibilities set forth in section 6, such as the oral or visual presentation, that need to be performed to see through the discussions of its report in the general assembly. The work of this committee will then be completed.

Adding to what was said in section 6 concerning the writing of committee reports, the report of the community attitudes committee should show what percentage of the adult and high-school-age population answered the survey questionnaires, and for purposes of clarity, include each question asked in the questionnaire. Also, a statement should be included in the introduction to the effect that all attitudes and opinions given in this report are those which were expressed by the citizenry as a whole during the community-wide survey, not merely by the committee itself. This report should thus be presented as a kind of mirror in which the community can look at itself as it has been described by its own people in response to the survey.

In regard to raising questions in the report to help generate discussion, as was mentioned in section 6, a few examples for the community attitudes committee are as follows: Do you agree or disagree with the attitudes and opinions expressed in this connection? Is this the way we really feel about ourselves and each other? Have we been as honest about this point as we should? Could this attitude be based on fancy or imagination, or is it actually based on reality? Does this give an accurate picture of this problem? Do the ratings on this point describe pretty well the situation as it is, or is it actually worse or better than the ratings show? What action can we take that would improve this situation? How might we go about solving this problem?

Questions along these lines phrased in ways the committee knows will have the most stimulating effect in your particular community, and inserted at strategic places through the report, will help get the discussions started and contribute toward keeping them moving in a lively manner.

12

The Community Organizations Committee

THE community's voluntary membership associations, such as service clubs and other private organizations, are important vehicles through which local residents form satisfying social ties, perform needed acts of public service, carry out many important improvement projects, and develop their capacity for civic leadership. All of these groups will be needed in the *ad hoc* steering committee's sponsoring consortium which we discussed in section 8. Collectively, they are a major part of the community's internal social structure, and no comprehensive development effort is likely to get very far without their active support and cooperation.

However, as we indicated in section 5, certain weaknesses may exist in this part of the internal social structure that can have an adverse effect on both the organizations themselves and the citizenry as a whole for purposes of community development.

For example, these organizations may overlap to such an extent in leadership, in membership, in purpose, and in function as to create a situation in which a relatively few people are nearly "meeting themselves to death" and are hardly able to find a free night in the week, while most local residents remain civically inactive and are content to let the relatively few go on wearing themselves out. In this situation healthy rivalries may be turned into inter-organizational envy, sometimes even outright hostility. As a consequence, an inordinate amount of the community's civic energy is often burned out for no useful purpose, and the end product of all the civic activity going on is much less than it could be.

This condition is well illustrated by the situation that existed in a town of less than two thousand people which had thirty-six civic organizations. Because some people belonged to more than one of them, there were actually more memberships in these organizations than there were people in the total adult population of the community. Yet nearly 70 percent of the town's adults didn't belong to any organization and never took part in any civic project. In these thirty-six organizations there were approximately two hundred leadership positions to be held, but these two hundred positions where held by thirty-five people, only fifteen of whom could be counted as active. One local resident was prompted to remark, "We've got too many irons in the fire, and no fire."

But while it may appear in such a situation that the community has been afflicted by a bad case of civic lumbago and that most citizens are dragging their feet, the difficulty does not always lie entirely with those who seemingly aren't interested. Often those who complain the loudest about being overworked in civic affairs are either consciously or unconsciously so eager to see themselves in the limelight that others who also have leadership ability are in effect frozen out. This situation may or may not exist in your community, but almost all communities have people with leadership ability whose services are never utilized.

Another weakness that often crops up in this part of the internal structure is that many of the community's membership organizations —even where memberships overlap—become so anxious to claim credit for themselves, while accusing other groups of refusing to cooperate, as to intensify the community's social fragmentation, each fragment walled off from the others, each more interested in its own identity and public recognition than in the community as a whole. There is, of course, nothing abnormal about people wanting to be recognized for their good works, and credit should be freely given when it is due. Also, every membership organization needs public recognition and approval if it is to maintain itself. But when credit and recognition become ends in themselves, and in the race for attention community-wide cooperation is seriously reduced, then real obstacles to community development begin to emerge.

Sometimes individuals of influence in their respective organizations become so conscious of their standing in "the club" they tend to think first as members of their organizations, and only incidentally as members of their community. When this happens, the community is divided still further into narrow interests between which there is little, if any, communication. This may lead to still another problem in which one group won't bother itself about any community project unless it concerns that group's particular interest, another is interested only in something else, and so on into a maze of disunity.

In communities where these conditions exist, it is not uncommon to discover that when a certain group attempts to initiate a community project which calls for cooperation from other groups, many people will oppose the project primarily because they don't like the group that started it or simply don't want to see that group get the credit. If these organizational ills are multiplied by the tens of thousands of communities in which they exist, then we begin to get a picture of some of the fundamental reasons why community development in America today can be extremely difficult.

In a community where the organizational aspect of the internal structure is healthy, people who belong to voluntary membership associations will think first of the well-being of their community as a whole and not be overly concerned with who gets the credit. They will recognize the distinct difference between a *club project* and a *community project*.

There are, then, at least two ways of looking at a voluntary membership association. One is to think of the organization itself as the center of importance, the other is to think of the organization as a resource to be used in cooperation with other resources for the development of the community. Probably the acid test of how valuable an organization is to its community is this: Are its members willing to subordinate recognition for their individual club to the larger need for community-wide cooperation in the difficult tasks of community problem-solving and overall development?

The community organizations committee has the responsibility of doing the fact-finding and reporting that will provide the general assembly with the information needed to examine and discuss any problems that may exist in this part of the internal structure of your community —again, not for the purpose of finding fault or fixing blame, but for the purpose of searching out possible needs, then openly and objectively talking about them in order to help strengthen this important aspect of community life.

As was pointed out in section 8, the *ad hoc* steering committee should draw members for the community organizations committee from all voluntary membership groups in the community, all of which we have said should be part of the steering committee's sponsoring consortium. This will mean the groups most directly concerned will themselves be fully engaged in this important part of the fact-finding, thus making the collection of the information needed for the committee's report a relatively simple matter.

Suggested questions are listed below to help guide the community organizations committee in gathering this information. Then following this list of questions, a special survey form will be suggested to further assist the fact-finding these questions indicate.

1. What are the private voluntary membership associations in your community? This should include a complete listing of all such organizations by name—meaning, all formally organized civic or service clubs, social clubs, fraternal organizations, patriotic organizations, professional organizations, community promotional organizations, farm organizations, juvenile organizations, and any other private membership organization in your community, with the exception of cooperatives and other types of corporate groups that are engaged in income-making business enterprises. Also, the survey should not include churches or organizations that function inside the churches.

Churches and inner-church groups are obviously a vital part of the community's internal organizational structure. However, from extensive experience and research, it has been found that it is extremely difficult to generate an effective discussion of the community's churches and church-related problems in open public meetings, such as those of the general assembly. People are simply reluctant to express themselves on this subject in this kind of a meeting. Therefore, if the community organizations committee wants to survey the community's churches, it is suggested that this be handled separately from the survey of other organizations, and that the results of the church survey be written up in a separate report for discussion—not in the general assembly—but in the various churches themselves. A separate list of questions and a questionnaire for this purpose will be suggested at the end of this section.

2. What is the total number of membership organizations in the community (not counting churches)? How many of them are adult organizations? How many of them are juvenile organizations?

3. What is the total number of memberships held in all the adult organizations combined? This refers to the total number of *memberships* held, not to the number of *people* who hold them. For example, one person belonging to six organizations would be counted as six memberships.

4. How does the community's total adult population compare with the total number of memberships held in all the adult organizations combined? Which is greater, the total adult population, or the total number of memberships? What percentage of the total adult population does the total number of memberships represent, or vice versa depending on which is greater?

5. How many adult individuals hold all these memberships indicated above? What percentage of the adult population do these individuals represent?

6. How many adults in the community do not belong to any of these organizations? What percentage of the community's total adult population do these people represent?

7. How many adults holding organizational memberships belong to: Only one organization? Two organizations? Three organizations? And so on up to the highest number of memberships held by one individual. Convert these numbers into percentages of the total number of memberships held in all organizations combined. Draw up a table showing the percentage of adults holding memberships in one organization, two organizations, three organizations, etc.

8. Of the total number of memberships held in all organizations, how many of these memberships can be counted as: Active? Somehat active? Inactive? What percentage of the total number of memberships held in all organizations does each of these three categories represent?

9. Considering all of the adult organizations collectively, what has been the average percentage of member attendance at general membership meetings over the course of the past year? Is this average percentage of member attendance increasing, decreasing, or remaining about the same? Prepare a table showing a numerical breakdown of the total number of organizations according to the percentage of member attendance at their regular membership meetings during the past year.

10. Considering all of the adult organizations collectively, how many offices and committee chairmanships are there to be filled in all of these organizations combined?

11. How many individuals hold this total number of offices and committee chairmanships?

12. Of the total number of persons holding all these offices and committee chairmanships, how many of these persons can be counted as: Active? Somewhat active? Inactive? (A person might hold office in two

organizations. If that person is active in one of them and inactive in the other, this would count as one active officeholder, and one inactive officeholder.)

13. Considering all of these offices and committee chairmanships collectively, what percentage of them are currently being handled on: An active basis? A somewhat active basis? An inactive basis?

14. From the above statistics, is there any evidence, and if so to what extent, that a relatively few people perform most of the leadership functions in the organizations in your community? Or, do the same few people usually do most of the work? If the answer to these questions seems to be yes, what are some of the reasons for this situation?

15. Draw up a calendar showing the dates, times, and days of the week or month the organizations listed above hold their regular membership meetings. How many of them meet weekly, monthly, quarterly, annually, or at other time intervals? How many of them meet on the same day? How many of them meet at the same time on the same day? Arrange the days of the week in the order of frequency of organizational meetings. Which days are the heaviest for meetings? Which days are the most free of meetings?

16. Are there any conflicts in the scheduling of organizational meetings? Does this present any problem from the standpoint of participation in the community development operation? If yes, what recommendation would the community organizations committee make for resolving this problem?

17. Classify the number of adult organizations in your community according to their stated purposes. How many have similar or closely related purposes? To what extent are those organizations that have similar or closely related purposes in the habit of setting up joint operations or projects in which all pool their energies to get certain jobs accomplished? Is there room for more inter-organizational cooperation in your community than that which now exists? If yes, what would the committee recommend in this regard?

18. Are there any membership organizations in your community that at times, or frequently come into conflict with each other—either openly or otherwise? If yes, what are some of the reasons for this conflict? Is there any good reason why it should continue? What would be the committee's recommendation in this respect?

19. Are there any particular segments of the adult population in your

community that are noticeably less active in organizational activities than other segments? If yes, what are the reasons for this? What would be the committee's recommendations in this respect?

20. Does all this information concerning the adult organizations in your community suggest any problems that have an adverse effect on the community's ability to work together to improve and further develop itself? If yes, list these problems. What would the committee recommend to remedy them?

21. To sum up: What would the committee consider to be strengths and weaknesses in your community as revealed by this study of voluntary membership associations? What recommendations would the committee make for any changes or improvements it feels are needed?

If the committee wishes, the same type of information indicated above in regard to the community's adult membership organizations may be gathered and compiled separately for the community's juvenile membership organizations.

FORM FOR USE IN
SURVEY OF COMMUNITY ORGANIZATIONS

(In duplicating this survey form be sure to leave enough space after each item for full information.)

Introduction: This survey is being taken in preparation for the community development program being started in our community. The purpose of this survey is to help determine the strengths and weaknesses in the organizational life of our community, the results of which will be reported at a public meeting at which it is hoped everyone will be present so we can all see and discuss what these results tell us about our community. One of these forms will be filled out for each membership organization in the community. However, the information obtained in this form will be treated as confidential and for statistical purposes only. Except for a listing of the organizations and drawing up an organizational meeting calendar, no names of any organizations or persons belonging to them will be revealed in reporting the results obtained from this survey. The information presented in the committee's report will give an overall picture of organizational life in our community as a whole, and will make no specific reference to any particular organization or person. After the necessary statistics have been compiled, the completed survey forms and tabulation sheets will be destroyed.

1. Name of organization _____

2. Purpose for which organized _____

3. Principal activities at present _____

4. Has the original purpose of this organization changed at any time since it was started? Yes ____ No ____ If yes, what changes in purpose have been made?

_____

5. Have there been any major changes in the type of activities of this organization since it was started? Yes ____ No ____ If yes, what changes have been made in its activities? _____

6. How many members are there in this organization at present? _____

7. Over the past year has the membership in this organization been: Increasing? ____ Decreasing? ____ Staying about the same? ____ What are some of the reasons for this? _____

8. Over the past year what has been the approximate average attendance at the regular membership meetings of this organization? _____

9. Type of membership in this organization: Male, female, or both? _____
   Approximate age group? _____
   Major occupational groups represented? _____
   Major interests represented? _____

10. What are the qualifications for membership, if any?

_____

11. Are there any restrictions as to membership? Yes ____ No ____ If yes, what are they? _____

12. What are the membership dues, if any? _____

13. Does this organization levy any special membership assessments from time to time? Yes ____ No ____ If yes, about how much do these assessments usually amount to? _____

14. Are there any groups of people in the community not included in the membership of this organization, but which the organization would like to have included? Yes ____ No ____ If yes, what are these groups? _____

_____

15. When are the meetings of this organization held?
    Dates (days of week or month) _____
    Time of day _____ Frequency _____

16. Where does this organization hold its meetings? _____

17. Does this organization ever engage in joint projects with other organizations? Yes ____ No ____ If yes, is this established practice, or does it happen only once in a while? _____

18. If this organization does engage in joint projects with other organizations, what are they?

Names of Other Organizations	Nature of Joint Projects

19. Are there any organizations in the community whose policies or aims are in conflict with those of this organization? Yes ____ No ____ If yes, how many

organizations are involved? _____ What is the nature of the conflict? ____

20. Are there any organizations in the community whose activities, other than regular membership meetings, conflict in scheduling with those of this organization? Yes ____ No ____
If yes, how many organizations are involved? _____ Why does this conflict in scheduling occur? _____
Does this present any problems? Yes ____ No ____ If yes, what are these problems? _____

21. What are the most outstanding projects or activities for community improvement accomplished by this organization within the past year?
If none, state none. _____

22. Being absolutely honest, how does this organization rate at the present time?
Active ____ Somewhat active ____ Inactive ____

23. Are all of the committees of this organization now functioning as well as they should? Yes ____ No ____ If no, about what percentage of them are not functioning as well as they should? _____
What are some of the reasons these committees don't function as well as they should _____

If some of the committees are functioning as well as they should, what are some of the reasons for this? _____
What are the major factors that make the difference between a poorly functioning committee and a well functioning committee? _____

24. Do newcomers quickly feel at home in this organization? Yes ____ No ____
Sometimes, but not always _____ Why? _____

25. Being absolutely honest, does this organization have any major problems within itself at the present time that prevent it from being as strong as it might be?
Yes ____ No ____ If yes, what are these problems? _____

26. Again, being absolutely honest, is there active participation in the projects and activities of this organization by all or most of the members, or do a fairly small percentage of the members usually do most of the work? _____

27. In order to make possible an actual count of the total number of memberships held in all organizations in the community, as compared with the number of individuals who hold these memberships, and as compared with the total population of the community, please supply on a separate sheet of paper, *which does not show the name of the organization,* a complete membership roster. Place the letter *A* in front of each member currently regarded as active, the letter *S* in front of each member currently regarded as somewhat active, and the letter *X* in front of each member currently regarded as inactive. The word "active" in this case means more than the mere payment of dues, but a person who attends meetings regularly, serves on committees if the organization has committees, and really works at making the organization strong. This roster of members, along with the membership rosters of all other organizations in the community will be used for statistical purposes only. No names of any organization's

members will be disclosed in the report of the community organizations committee, and when the committee has completed its count and statistical analysis concerning the organizational life of the community as a whole all membership rosters will be destroyed along with the completed survey forms and tabulation sheets.

28. On another sheet of paper *that does not give the name of the organization,* please list all existing offices and committee chairmanships, giving the names of the persons holding same. If any of these positions are currently vacant, indicate which ones are vacant. Using the same letter designations that were used in connection with the membership rosters—*A, S,* and *X*—indicate which persons holding these offices and committee chairmanships are currently regarded as active, somewhat active, or inactive. These lists will also be used for statistical purposes only, with no name of any individual or organization being identified in the community organization committee's report, and when the committee has completed its count and statistical analysis these lists will be destroyed along with the other materials mentioned above.

The importance of maintaining the confidentiality of the membership rosters and the lists of officers and committee chairmanships, along with other data from the survey, cannot be stated too strongly; otherwise some organizations may not be willing to reveal all the information the committee will need for this crucial part of the community's self-analysis. If the committee is made up of persons drawn from each of the various organizations being surveyed, as has been recommended, the survey form for each given organization should be completed by the committee's representative from that organization.

Without identifying which rosters they come from, the number of times a person's name appears on the various rosters can be tallied. This will make it possible to determine the total number of memberships held, the number of persons who hold them, the number of active, somewhat active, and inactive memberships, and various other statistics we have indicated. The same procedure can be used in obtaining the necessary counts and percentages pertaining to the officer and committee chairmanship lists, and similar procedures can be used in compiling the results for most of the other items included in the survey form. This will enable the community organizations committee to construct a realistic and detailed picture of this vital aspect of the community's internal social structure, pointing up clearly and objectively any problems or weaknesses that may exist without revealing anything that could be embarrassing to any specific individual or organization. For assistance in writing the report for discussion in the general assembly and completing other committee responsibilities, all members of the committee should carefully review section 6, "Procedures and Responsibilities of the Fact-Finding Committees."

As in the case of the community attitudes committee, the one exception to section 6 in regard to the community organizations committee has to do with the arrangement of appropriate follow-up action after the general assembly has completed its discussion of the committee's report. Inasmuch as this is one of the temporary committees whose report should be completed during the period of preliminary groundwork preparatory to beginning the first phase of the development operation, the problems and recommendations the report brings out, or that are brought out in the assembly discussions, should be referred by the general chairman to the advisory council for whatever follow-up may be in order.

Thus, as in the case of the other temporary committees, the members of the community organizations committee should sign up at the first public meeting for other committees or positions of their choice—the only provision being that this committee should carry on with the responsibilities set forth in section 6, such as the oral or visual presentation, that need to be performed to see through the discussion of its report in the general assembly. At that point the work of the community organizations committee will have been completed.

If the committee has enough definite material to make for a lively and constructive discussion at only one assembly meeting, then the committee should prepare its report for one evening's discussion. If there is enough discussable material for two interesting assembly meetings, fine. But don't push it to the point where the discussion is likely to deteriorate into ambiguity or become a rehash for lack of enough material that people can really take hold of and talk about in ways that give them a feeling of actually getting somewhere.

If the community organizations committee in consultation with the *ad hoc* steering committee and the community's clergymen decides it should do a church survey for discussion within the churches themselves, suggested questions for that purpose, followed by a church survey form, are set forth below.

1. What and how many churches are there in this community?

2. Considering all the churches together, what is the total church membership in this community?

3. What percentage of the community's total population does this aggregate church membership represent?

4. Over the past year what has been the total average attendance at the principal worship services of all churches combined?

5. Is this overall average attendance: Increasing? Decreasing? Remaining about the same? What are some of the reasons for this?

6. What percentage of the total church membership does this average attendance over the past year represent? What percentage of the community's total population does it represent?

7. Does the community, or any groups within the community, ever seek assistance from the churches for local improvement projects or for the solution of community problems? Is this assistance sought as often as it should be? How receptive are the churches to such requests? Why?

8. Do the churches seek to play an active role in local civic affairs on their own initiative—that is, whether asked to do so or not? If yes, how receptive is the community to this kind of church initiative? Why?

9. Is the influence of the churches on the life of this community: Growing? Declining? Remaining about the same? What are some of the reasons for this?

10. What are the major programs and activities inside the churches themselves? Do these programs and activities offer something of interest to all age groups? To what extent is the community aware of these programs and activities?

11. Do the churches in this community ever engage in joint projects or activities? Is there room for more interchurch cooperation? If yes, in what ways? How might this be accomplished?

12. Do the church properties add to the community's physical attractiveness or are these properties ill kept and run-down? If the answer to this question is on the negative side, what could be done to improve conditions?

13. Do the answers to these questions suggest any church or community problems? If yes, what problems? What ought to be done about them? By the churches? By the community?

CHURCH SURVEY FORM

(In duplicating this survey form be sure to leave enough space after each item for full information.)

Introduction: This survey is being taken in preparation for the community development program being started in our community. The purpose of this survey is to help determine the strengths and weaknesses in the life of our community with respect to its churches. The results of this survey will be written up in a special report which will be delivered to each local church. This report can be used as the basis for discussion and self-analysis by the various church congregations within their own individual churches or in joint meetings between two or more churches, if they wish. Also, if the churches wish, they may appoint spokesmen to present a synopsis of their discussions and conclusions at a meeting of the general assembly of the community development operation. One of these forms will be filled out for each church in the community. However, the information obtained will be used for statistical purposes only, and will be consolidated into an overall picture of church activity in our community as a whole, without reference to any particular church by name, except for a listing of the churches we have.

1. Name of church _____

2. Name of pastor _____

3. Current size of membership _____

4. Over the past year the average attendance at the principal worship services of this church has been approximately _____

5. This average attendance is: Increasing? ____ Decreasing? ____ Remaining about the same? ____ What are some of the reasons for this? _____
   _____

6. To what extent does this church receive requests for assistance in carrying out local improvement projects or for assistance in the solution of community problems: To a very great extent? ____ To some extent? ____ To only a minor extent? ____ Almost never? ____

7. Is the answer to item 6 above: About as it should be? ____ More than it should be? ____ Less than it should be? ____

8. Does this church welcome calls from local civic groups for assistance in carrying out community projects or for assistance in the solution of community problems? Yes ____ No ____ If yes, would it like to have more such calls? ____ Any special comments in this connection by the pastor? _____
   _____

9. Does this church ever seek to play an active role in local civic affairs whether it is asked to do so or not? Yes ____ No ____ If yes, how receptive is the community to this kind of church initiative? _____
   Why? _____

10. As nearly as can be estimated, the influence of this church on the life of the community is: Growing ____ Declining ____ Remaining about the same ____ What are some of the reasons for this? _____

11. List the major programs and activities that take place inside this church:
    _____
    Do these programs and activities offer something of interest to all age groups?
    _____
    To what extent does the community seem to be aware of these programs and activities? _____

12. Does this church ever engage in joint projects or activities with other churches in

the community? Yes ____ No ____ If yes, how often, in what projects or activities, and with what other churches? _____
_____

If no, why? _____
Is there room for more of this kind of interchurch cooperation? Yes ____ No ____
If yes, in what ways, and how might this be accomplished? _____
_____

If no, why? _____
13. What is the physical condition of this church property? Excellent ____ Good ____
Fair ____ Poor ____ Does it need repairs, paint, landscaping, or other physical improvements? _____
14. Do the responses to this survey form suggest any church or community problems? Yes ____ No ____ If yes, what problems, and what ought to be done about them? _____
By the church itself? _____
By the community? _____

13

The First Public Meeting

INASMUCH as the *ad hoc* steering committee does not represent any one organization, either private or public, but through its sponsoring consortium has the support and cooperation of virtually all organizations and institutions in the community, this initiating group should assume the responsibility for calling the first public meeting. Until the general chairman is elected, the chairman of the steering committee should preside, and until the secretary is elected another member of the steering committee should keep notes.

This first public meeting which, ideally, should be held sometime in the early fall, will be one of the most crucial moments in the whole process of initiating the development effort. For it is at this meeting that a call will be issued for a public declaration that the operation is now ready to be fully organized and carried out. This, then, is a meeting that has the potential of becoming an event of historic significance in your community.

Therefore, extreme care should be taken not to call this meeting prematurely—that is, not until there is solid evidence of community readiness to go ahead; that there is in fact a strong will and desire throughout the community to really take hold and get the effort moving. Until it is known with reasonable certainty that this state of readiness actually exists; that substantial segments of the community really mean business; that widespread determination to make the development effort successful is not just an illusion, this first public meeting *should not be called*.

It is equally important, however, that once it has been determined that these conditions for going ahead do exist, the date for this meeting should be announced forthwith so that this announcement will coincide with the "head of steam" or the community-wide enthusiasm that has been generated. *Thus, the matter of timing is of utmost importance*.

This also means that enough time must be allowed after the date is announced for a flow of publicity and advertising that will make certain every citizen in the community knows the meeting has been scheduled, the time and place it is to occur, that his or her presence is needed and wanted, and to ensure by every possible means—personal contacts, telephone calls, cars to pick up people who need rides, and any other appropriate action—a large attendance.

If, however, the attendance at this first public meeting should for any reason turn out to be smaller than expected, *do not be discouraged*. This has happened in other communities that have gone on to build some of the most successful development operations I have seen. A letdown such as this might be disappointing, but should only stiffen the determination to go forward. As we have indicated, the level of citizen participation essential to real community development does not always come easy, and the operation in your community will undoubtedly suffer a few temporary setbacks. But successful community development in today's America is simply too important and too urgent to allow any obstacle to stand in its way. Following is a checklist of some of the advance preparations that should be completed before this first public meeting is held.

1. The report of the boundary committee, including the community map.
2. The report of the census committee.
3. The report of the community attitudes committee.
4. The report of the community organizations committee.

5. Arrangements for the building in which the meeting is to be held, preferably the same building in which the general assembly will hold all subsequent meetings. As we have pointed out, this means a building in which there is a hall or auditorium large enough to accommodate the assembly when it is in general session, plus enough additional rooms or spaces that can be used when the assembly breaks into its small discussion groups which will become the practice when the operation moves into its regular schedule of assembly meetings.

6. Blackboards, chalk, ample seating, proper ventilation, extra pencils, pads of paper, arrangements to have the building unlocked and open, a podium for the presiding officer, a table and chairs at the front of the room, drinking glasses and a few pitchers of water, a public address system in working order, and anything else the *ad hoc* steering committe may think of that will contribute to the success of this first public meeting should be on hand and in place.

7. Enough copies of the development guide to supply all persons who wish to purchase their own copies, and additional copies for other persons who wish to borrow them. Several members of the steering committee should be designated to handle the sale of the guide, and to make records of borrowed copies. This may be done at the close of the meeting, and those who are to handle this job should be prepared with tables and supplies at the rear of the meeting hall.

8. Arrangements should have been made for a community development headquarters.

9. Cards numbered in series which can be used as a device for breaking the general assembly into small discussion groups once the regular schedule of assembly meetings begins should have been prepared, and one of the members of the steering committee should be ready to explain how this system will work. Or if some other device is to be used for this purpose someone should be prepared to explain that device. The procedure of breaking into small discussion groups will not be needed at the first public meeting, but the procedure should at least be explained so everyone will know that in this development operation there is to be full opportunity for all participants to express themselves.

10. Copies of a form called the Activity Preference Sheet should be prepared on which all persons present can fill in their names, addresses, telephone numbers, and signatures indicating their intention to take an active part in the development effort. This form should list each of the

continuing committees and the positions of discussion leader, recorder, and block captain, so all persons may indicate their order of preferences for those aspects of the development effort in which they would most like to serve. Ideally, everyone should serve in one of these capacities. However, anyone who wishes simply to attend the assembly meetings without serving in one of these capacities should feel free to do so. A sample copy of the Activity Preference Sheet is attached to the end of this section.

With these advance preparations in order, we are now in a position to discuss the major contents of this first public meeting. Because this meeting is essentially organizational in nature it will call for an agenda entirely unlike that which was outlined in secton 4 for a typical meeting of the general assembly. Basically, this initial public meeting has a twofold purpose.

First, to provide an opportunity for the *ad hoc* steering committee to review before as large a gathering of the citizenry as can be assembled the underlying meaning of community development, its philosophy and ultimate goal, the fundamental need for this kind of development in America, how it applies to your particular community, and the organizational machinery through which your community can put these concepts and procedures into practice.

Assuming the steering committee and its sponsoring consortium have done an effective job of introducing and promoting the development idea during the period of preliminary groundwork, a broad background of public understanding will already have been created concerning the aims and objectives of the operation and the wide range of benefits it will enable the community to achieve by simply putting to work in a very special way the basic tenets of American democracy. These concepts are not always easy to grasp, but the more thoroughly they are understood by all citizens in the community, the greater will be the likelihood of a successful development effort.

The second basic purpose of this initial public meeting has already been indicated: To provide as many citizens as can be brought together the opportunity to declare publicly their willingness to set aside a definite period of six or seven months in which to devote themselves to the intensive community effort the first phase of the operation will require. This declaration of commitment must be made—not only by the civic leaders who have taken the initiative to form the *ad hoc* steering committee, and those groups that comprise the sponsoring consortium—but by a public gathering of citizens speaking and acting for themselves as individual members of their community. Otherwise, the foundation of local self-determination that must be established by the community as a whole will not be complete.

Bearing in mind the importance of these two basic purposes, here is a suggested agenda for this first public meeting.

1. The steering committee chairman, serving as acting chairman of the meeting, calls the assembly to order.

2. An appropriate invocation concerning the importance of this special event is given by a local clergyman who has agreed in advance to perform this responsibility.

3. The acting chairman states briefly why this meeting is being convened, calls attention to the formation of the *ad hoc* steering committee, explains how, when, and why it got together, and gives an account of what it has done during the period of preliminary groundwork which has led up to this evening's meeting, pointing out the committee's use of the development guide. If anyone wishes to ask questions, fine. The object of this highlight review is to make sure all persons in attendance are brought up to date and have a clear understanding of what has been done thus far.

4. All persons who have worked on the steering committee are introduced and asked to stand and be acknowledged for the time and energy they have devoted to the preliminary groundwork the acting chairman has outlined, and the same is done for those who have worked on the four temporary committees—boundary, census, community attitudes, and community organizations.

5. A list of the member groups of the steering committee's sponsoring consortium is read and proper credits are given for the work they have done. The written resolutions issued by various organizations endorsing the development operation are read and acknowledged. If the full reading of these resolutions will require an inordinate amount of time, they may be summarized, but in any case they should be appropriately acknowledged and the gist of what they say should be stated.

6. One of the members of the *ad hoc* steering committee now gives what might be thought of as the keynote speech of the evening: A brief talk on the philosophy and purpose of community development. The person chosen to perform this responsibility should be a noncontroversial

figure, a good public speaker, and one who thoroughly comprehends the basic concepts set forth in the development guide. This speech should be inspirational in tone, create increased understanding of the community development idea, and generate further enthusiasm for putting it into practice. The central theme of this speech, as well as direct quotes, may be drawn from the guide itself, but based on the speaker's personal knowledge of conditions and concerns that apply specifically to your community, the speech should be couched in language that will give it the strongest possible local appeal.

7. Another person from the steering committee explains the two-phase strategy of operations which was set forth in section 3, and the concept of ultimately developing an area-wide effort in cooperation with other communities. Having clarified the distinction between phase one and phase two, and the rationale for proceeding in this manner, a brief reference is made to the three component parts of the organizational machinery for phase one—the general assembly, the fact-finding committees, and the administrative committees—leaving to other members of the steering committee the responsibility of outlining the details of each component.

8. A description is given of the general assembly, the core of the development organization which is to serve both as a public forum and a civic action body. It should be made clear how the assembly will operate, including the technique of breaking into small discussion groups as a means of making it possible for all citizens to be personally involved in the exploration of problems and the making of decisions. Emphasis should be given to the need for the assembly to meet on a regular schedule—preferably once a week during the first phase of operations —and to the importance of broad citizen participation in all assembly meetings. The leadership posts for the assembly that will call for election should be listed—the general chairman, the assistant general chairman, the secretary, and the treasurer—followed by a statement to the effect that before the meeting adjourns this election will be held.

9. Another member of the steering committee explains the functions of the fact-finding committees, describes how they will provide the general assembly with essential facts and recommendations for discussion, the rationale for deciding what fact-finding committees to establish, then presents a list of the committees, indicating that the four

temporary committees have already been at work, but that the continuing committees must now be organized.

10. A presentation is given on the administrative committees and the work they will perform.

11. The steering committee's estimate of the overall cost of the period of preliminary groundwork and of carrying out the first phase of the development effort is presented, along with the committee's thinking as to how the necessary funds can be raised.

12. The acting chairman opens the meeting for questions. Undoubtedly there will have been some questions and discussion as the meeting has gone along, but with the information which has now been presented, the assembly should be fully prepared to make comments, offer suggestions, and raise any questions needed for further clarification.

13. During the review and explanation it will have been pointed out that this development effort is to be an operation by and for the *whole community*, and that to help determine the geographical territory of the whole community, a boundary committee has done some advance exploration and drawn up a proposed community map. Referring to this aspect of the preliminary groundwork, the acting chairman now calls on the boundary committee chairman to present this map and report as briefly as possible on the boundaries the committee recommends. The assembly decides either to accept the committee's recommendations, or suggests amendments. On the basis of this decision, the acting chairman announces what is to be treated as the whole community geographically, makes it clear that for purposes of the development operation all persons living within this territory are to be regarded as members of the local citizenry, and are wanted and needed as active participants in the effort.

14. The acting chairman calls on the census committee for a brief summary presentation—the written census report having already been distributed as the people arrived for the meeting.

15. The acting chairman now calls for a motion that the first phase of the development effort be publicly declared to be in operation and ready to be fully organized. Assuming such a motion is forthcoming and is adopted, the acting chairman issues a statement to that effect.

16. The Activity Preference Sheet is then explained, and the importance of all persons filling one out is carefully emphasized. This form will provide a definite means by which people can record their personal intent

to take an active part in the effort, and choose for themselves which positions and committees they would most like to serve in.

17. Copies of the Activity Preference Sheet are now distributed, filled out by each person at the meeting, and collected for use in completing the development organization.

18. On behalf of the *ad hoc* steering committee and its sponsoring consortium, the acting chairman now introduces a definite proposal as to how often the general assembly is to meet—again, if at all possible, once every week for the duration of the first phase of operations—and the meeting reaches a decision on this proposal. The night of the week on which these meetings are to be held is determined, and the date and time for the next community-wide meeting which will begin the general assembly's regular schedule is set—preferably not more than one week later.

19. The acting chairman now refers to the community attitudes survey, in which virtually all citizens will have participated, and announces that the results of this survey will be the subject for discussion at the first regular meeting of the general assembly—the date and time of which have just been set.

20. The acting chairman briefly announces the location and opening of the community development headquarters.

21. Now comes the last major action to be taken at this first public meeting, an action that perhaps more than any other, can make or break the development effort. This is the election of the general chairman, the assistant general chairman, the secretary, and the treasurer.

In section 8 the importance of giving careful advance attention to this election, and the obstacles to a successful operation that can be created if this advance attention is neglected, were discussed in considerable detail. In the closing pages of that section it was suggested that because it is so important to place in these elective positions well-qualified persons whose commitment to the work can be absolutely depended upon, and who will have wide community acceptance, the *ad hoc* steering committee in consultation with its sponsoring consortium, and with people in general, should not only have given serious advance thought to who these leaders might be, but should have taken the responsibility of approaching and sounding out individuals believed to be especially well suited, for the purpose of obtaining their consent to serve if nominated and elected. It was further suggested that in the course of generating public interest in the development operation, the matter of choosing these four leaders should have been widely talked about through the community in preparation for this first public meeting.

If these steps have not been taken, and the people at this first public meeting find themselves in the tenuous position of engaging in an election to which no previous thought has been given, the outcome could be disastrous. But if this part of the preliminary groundwork has been given the attention it deserves, the persons present at this meeting should be fully prepared to choose individuals who will be ideal for these leadership posts—both from the standpoint of personal qualifications and from the standpoint of the broad public acceptance they will need to function effectively. Thus, the meeting should have no difficulty in reaching decisions that will ensure a wise election.

As one additional means of calling attention to the importance of this election, the acting chairman—before asking for nominations—should call on a member of the *ad hoc* steering committee to read from section 4 the duties and qualifications that should be taken into consideration in filling these elective positions.

22. Against this background of advance thought and discussion, the acting chairman now opens the meeting for nominations. If the acting chairman is placed in nomination—which could well be the case—this person should step down and ask another member of the steering committee to preside. After ample time for nominations and discussion the election process is completed. The elected leaders come forward and make whatever brief remarks they may wish concerning the challenge that lies ahead.

23. The newly elected general chairman now assumes the position of presiding officer, and calls on the person who has served as the acting chairman for last minute comments, which should include the following quick announcements:

—A reminder of the date and time of the next meeting, which will be the first session in the regular schedule of the general assembly.

—A reminder that the report of the community attitudes committee will be the principal subject of the evening, and that copies of the report will be distributed at that time to all persons in attendance so everyone can see and discuss what people throughout the community have said about themselves and each other, and about the community itself.

—That appointments of committees, discussion leaders, recorders, and block captains will be made on the basis of individual interests expressed in the Activity Preference Sheet, and will be announced at the first regular meeting of the general assembly—preferably one week later. These appointments should be made by the four elected leaders with the help of the *ad hoc* steering committee, and a time and place should be set to begin this work the following morning. If the community development headquarters is ready this could be the place.

—A reminder of the importance of reading the development guide, and that copies may be purchased or borrowed at the rear of the assembly room as people leave the meeting.

24. A local clergyman with whom prior arrangements have been made is called on by the general chairman to pronounce the benediction.

25. The general chairman issues a brief word of goodnight, and declares the meeting adjourned. *Total elapsed time, not more than two hours, less if possible*. The first phase of the community development operation is now under way.

ACTIVITY PREFERENCE SHEET

I (name) _____ agree that we should go forward with the community development effort, and intend to take an active part in its operation.

Address _____

_____ Telephone _____

The activities in which I would most like to serve are (place numbers in front of positions and committees showing order of preference):

Note: Inasmuch as the boundary, census, community attitudes, and community organizations committees which did their work in advance of this first public meeting will not be needed after their reports are presented to the general assembly, those who served on these four committees should also indicate their order of preference for the positions and committees listed below.

In the General Assembly:
_____ Discussion Leader
_____ Recorder

Fact-Finding Committees:
_____ Environmental Improvement Committee
_____ Government Committee
_____ Industrial Development Committee
_____ Retail Trade and Services Committee
_____ Housing Committee

____ Education Committee
____ Library Committee
____ Health Committee
____ Recreation Committee
____ History Committee

Administrative Committees:

____ Advisory Council
____ Secretarial Committee
____ Publicity Committee
____ Block Captain

Signature

14

Completing the Development Organization

THE first public meeting marks the end of the period of preliminary groundwork, but that does not mean the *ad hoc* steering committee should immediately go out of business. With the experience and cohesiveness it will have acquired in getting the development effort started, this initiating group will have become too valuable a resource to just suddenly do without. Those who have worked with this group will move into the various continuing committees and other essential parts of the organizational machinery for the first phase of the operation. Some of them will probably become committee chairmen. Others will move into other positions of leadership, and it may be that one or more of the four elective positions will have been filled by individuals who have worked with this initiating group. But while the organizational machinery for the first phase of the development effort is still being put together and becoming firmly established, the *ad hoc* steering committee should remain intact and be prepared to give an extra push wherever needed, offer advice and encouragement, or in the event of an unexpected crisis be ready to take whatever action may be necessary to see the operation through its early formative stage.

One of the most important roles of the *ad hoc* steering committee immediately following the first public meeting is to help the general chairman, assistant general chairman, secretary, and treasurer with the task of getting people placed in the fact-finding and administrative committees, appointing committee chairmen, and naming people to serve as discussion leaders, recorders, and block captains. This task will be too large for the four elected leaders to handle alone, and at this point in the operation the *ad hoc* steering committee is the group best prepared to help.

Insofar as possible, appointments to the various committees and positions should be made on the basis of the Activity Preference Sheets filled out by those who attended the first public meeting. However, because there will be other people in the community who also would like to serve in some of these capacities, though for one reason or another did not attend the first public meeting, the initial list of appointments need not be limited to those who were present at that meeting.

In making up this initial list of appointments, numerous problems may be encountered that will take considerable doing to resolve. For example, in the early stages of building the cooperation and esprit de corps that will make for a successful operation, certain combinations of people in the same committee may seriously disrupt the work of that committee. Or it may be that in filling out the Activity Preference Sheets some committees and positions will have received a high frequency of first preferences, others a low frequency, and some may not have been checked by anybody. These and other puzzling situations will call for considerable patience, a bit of compromise and shifting around, and some active recruiting in order to make sure all essential positions are filled by people who are suited to perform the functions of these positions, while also making certain that everyone who wants a specific job in the operation has one.

This sensitive task of matching people and positions will involve a great deal of personal contact so that decisions and agreements can be reached that will be satisfactory to all concerned, and that will contribute to a high level of morale in all facets of the development effort. Indeed, no one should be appointed to any committee or position which that person did not indicate as a first preference in the Activity Preference Sheet without being contacted and given an opportunity to accept.

This personal contact work will apply especially to the appointment of committee chairmen. Lists can be made of people who would be ideal for the various committee chairmanships, but no committee chairmanship can be made final until each prospect is approached individually, given a description of the duties and responsibilities of the committee concerned, and has agreed to serve in this capacity. Often when a person accepts appointment to a committee chairmanship only as a result of being pressured into it, that person does not make a very effective chairman. But this is another of those matters that will need to be carefully weighed, because this does not mean that in approaching one who is regarded as a particularly favorable candidate a certain amount of persuasion is necessarily out of order. Some people may need a little extra encouragement to overcome their inherent modesty. Others will probably say they are too busy. Yet the old adage, "If you want something done well find a busy person to do it," is a truism not to be entirely discounted.

Thus, the making and firming up of appointments to all necessary committees and positions will be a formidable and exacting task, requiring extensive thought, considerable tact and diplomacy, and a lot of running around to see and talk to people in person. As the operation expands and increasing numbers of citizens become engaged, they should take their places in various committees and positions they prefer. But to ensure a spirited and businesslike start, the initial list of appointments must be ready for public announcement by the general chairman at the first meeting in the regular schedule of the general assembly, thus making it clear that the filling out of the Activity Preference Sheet was not just an idle exercise.

This means that time is of the essence—particularly if the regular schedule of the general assembly is to begin the week following the first public meeting as we have recommended. This is one of the reasons why this important task of completing the phase-one organization should begin the very next morning following the first public meeting. Ideally, if the four elected leaders and the members of the *ad hoc* steering committee can make suitable arrangements to take at least this one day off from their normal business or employment or from their responsibilities at home, they should get together and begin their first work session no later than nine o'clock that morning. It would be a good idea to have coffee or soft drinks, and perhaps doughnuts, on hand. They should have lunch together, work through the afternoon, then if necessary come back for an evening session. By moving ahead in this prompt and determined way, the work will acquire a touch of excitement, word will soon get around the community that no time is being lost in getting the development effort off the ground, and within one day after the operation was publicly declared to be under way it will be possible to go far enough toward completing the organizational machinery to add substantially to the momentum, thus enabling the continuing committees to get started immediately. Here is a suggested procedure for this first day's appointment work session:

The secretary labels a large sheet of paper for each committee and position for which appointments are to be made, and posts the sheets on the walls around the room, or attaches them to an easel which makes it possible to flip them back and forth. The object is to have the appointment sheets arranged so everyone at the work session can see them. Then the members of the work session divide among themselves the Activity Preference Sheets, read aloud the names of all persons who filled them out, along with indications of first preference, and the secretary lists the name of each person on the appropriate sheet.

These listings will show at a glance which committees and positions have been given as first preference by enough people to get started, and which ones are short. When this sorting process is completed the secretary may draw a line at the bottom of each list as a means of distinguishing between those persons who designated a given committee or position as first preference, and other names that are added as prospects for recruitment.

Taking these lists one at a time, the work session then begins adding other names to the lists that are short until there are enough people on each list to get all committees and positions activated. These additional names may be obtained by again going through the Activity Preference Sheets to look for persons who indicated various committees or positions as a second or third preference. This is where some tentative shifting from one list to another may come in, but there is a limit as to how far this exercise can go, for as we have indicated, no attempt should be made to place a person in a position in which he or she would not be happy. Moreover, if the development operation is to grow into an effort by the whole community the work should include as large a portion of the total citizenry as possible. Thus, there is considerable advantage to be gained if as a general rule no one serves in more than one position at a time

—exceptions being the *ad hoc* steering committee and later the advisory council which ultimately will replace this committee, and the discussion leaders and recorders who will function only at meetings of the general assembly.

Therefore, in addition to looking for second or third preferences and making tentative transfers from one list to another, the members of the appointment work session should suggest other persons in the community who are felt to be well suited for certain committees or positions and add these names for possible recruitment.

In going through this process of adding names to the various lists, close attention should be given to the community map which was approved at the first public meeting. This will ensure community-wide coverage and help suggest names that might not otherwise occur to members of the appointment work session. Also, careful thought should be given to the duties and responsibilities of each committee and position as outlined in the guide, along with individual interests and talents of persons being listed. And one other important point: In adding names to the committee and position lists, don't forget the members of the *ad hoc* steering committee. The initial appointment lists should be completed in the order in which they will need to begin functioning as the development effort moves forward. Thus, the first two lists to be firmed up should be those for the discussion leaders and recorders who will be needed during the small-group discussion period at the first regular meeting of the general assembly one week hence, and who must have some advance time to study the report of the community attitudes committee, which will be the principal subject of that meeting. Also, to make sure they have a clear understanding of their responsibilities, the discussion leaders and recorders must be appointed soon enough to make it possible for them to get together at least once before this assembly meeting to talk over with the four elected leaders what they are going to do and how they are going to operate.

It cannot be emphasized too often that the success or failure of each assembly meeting will depend to a large extent upon how well the discussion leaders and recorders perform their respective functions. Therefore, if enough people have expressed one of these positions as first preference, and all of them are regarded as being well suited for these positions, the general chairman can simply notify them of their appointments, remind the chairman of the community attitudes committee to see that they get an advance copy of the committee's report for their private reading, and arrange the time and place to get together with them as a group before the first assembly meeting.

If, however, the list for either of these two positions is short the number of people needed, the members of the appointment work session will need to go through the process indicated above, adding others they feel would be well qualified and willing to serve as a discussion leader or recorder if asked—again, not excluding the possibility of some of those who have worked with the *ad hoc* steering committee. If one or more persons have marked one of these two positions as a first preference, but are regarded as not suited for this particular responsibility, this will be another of those puzzling situations for which the members of the work session will have to find an appropriate answer.

Once enough people have been added to these lists to provide the number of qualified discussion leaders and recorders needed to begin the regular assembly meetings, the general chairman should ask one or more members of the work session to immediately begin contacting them for the purpose of gaining their acceptance, while the other members of the work session move on to another list.

Another part of the development organization that needs to begin functioning early in the operation is the publicity committee. When a sufficient number of people have been listed to get this committee started, the members of the work session should decide who would make a top-notch publicity chairman and obtain the necessary consent. As a general rule it is advisable not to ask the editor of the local newspaper or the manager of the local radio or television station—assuming there are such facilities in your community—to chair this committee, unless of course, one of them would really like to do so. These people will be publicizing the development effort as it makes news whether they are members of the publicity committee or not, and further, will undoubtedly be willing to offer additional space for promotional purposes as a part of their normal public service responsibilities. Moreover, the work of this committee will involve informational and promotional activities other than those handled through the mass media.

Along with the publicity committee, attention should be given to firming up the list of block captains. To determine how many block captains will be needed, divide the community map into sections, each of which could be covered without too much difficulty by one person, then obtain one block captain for each section. If a title other than "block captain" is preferred for this position, fine. Should it turn out that this list is short the number of people needed, the task of recruiting additional block captains should be turned over to the publicity committee, for in practice the block captains will operate as a highly important extension of that committee.

However, no matter how quickly the organization of the publicity committee and block captains is started, it will probably require at least a week or so to build a publicity apparatus that will ensure effective coverage of the whole community. This, then, is another instance in which the *ad hoc* steering committee and its sponsoring consortium should be prepared to lend a strong helping hand. This assistance will be especially necessary in connection with the promotional campaign that should be mounted to ensure a large attendance at the first regular meeting of the general assembly.

The secretarial committee, which is to be chaired by the secretary, will also be needed early in the operation, and will provide one of the most vital services in the entire development effort. If the list of first preferences given for this committee is short, the recruitment of additional volunteers can be done on the basis of individuals who are willing to work at home or come in for special work sessions at the community development headquarters. But probably, as was pointed out earlier, the most efficient way of obtaining personnel for this committee will be to make suitable arrangements for the required clerical help with private firms or existing public agencies in the community that are willing to donate a bit of official time for this purpose. This could be any office that employs typists. It could be a group of churches or the chamber of commerce. It could be the school system, a community college, the local government, or any other tax-supported agency or institution. It could be a public or private utility. Arrangements with such organizations will probably be essential in any case because the secretarial committee will need not only workers who have clerical skills, such as typing, but will also need access to office equipment, such as typewriters and duplicating machines.

The paper, stencils, and other supplies needed by the secretarial committee and the publicity committee will immediately give rise to the matter of operating costs which was discussed in section 8. During the period of preliminary groundwork, the *ad hoc* steering committee in consultation with the member groups of its sponsoring consortium will have made plans for raising the funds necessary to cover these costs, and as was indicated in section 13, these plans should have been presented for consideration at the first public meeting on the evening before this

appointment work session. But even though the matter of financing has been largely resolved, it should be taken into account at this work session for the benefit of the treasurer who will have the responsibility of managing the operation's fiscal affairs, and making certain *before* expenses are incurred that adequate funds are available—or can be made available—to pay the bills.

When those parts of the organizational machinery covered thus far are completed, or definite steps have been taken to make certain they are well on the way to being completed, the first phase of the development effort should be in a position to move through its early formative stage without interruption. As was pointed out in section 11, it is likely that at least two meetings of the general assembly will be required to discuss the report of the community attitudes committee. Then at least one assembly meeting will be required to discuss the report of the community organizations committee. Thus, it will not be until at least the fourth meeting in the regular general assembly schedule that reports from the continuing fact-finding committees will need to begin coming in. However, this period of time can melt away quickly. Therefore, attention should now be focused on firming up and activating all of these continuing committees —environmental improvement, government, industrial development, retail trade and services, housing, education, library, health, recreation, and the history committee.

Giving careful thought to who could provide the essential leadership for each of these committees—again, not excluding persons who have worked with the *ad hoc* steering committee—the members of the work session should look closely at the responsibilities of these committees, settle on prospective committee chairmen, then move with utmost speed to gain the necessary acceptances so the general chairman can firm up their appointments.

Once prospective chairmen have been named for all of these continuing committees and personal contacts are being made to obtain their acceptances, the appointment work session should return to the task of building the committee membership lists which was started with the initial sorting of names according to individual choices expressed in the Activity Preference Sheets. Additional names for these continuing committees may be drawn from the discussion leaders and recorders, the four temporary committees, and from the *ad hoc* steering committee and the member groups of its sponsoring consortium. Also, as we have indicated, persons should be recruited from the community at large, and as more people begin coming out for meetings of the general assembly they should be asked to indicate committees of their choice, thus continuing to build the operation into an effort by the citizenry as a whole —including citizens who are not members of any existing organization or institution and who rarely if ever have previously taken part in civic affairs.

Obviously, all of the component parts of the organizational machinery for the first phase of the development effort cannot be firmed up in final form during this first day's appointment work session. However, insofar as possible, all of the discussion leaders, recorders, and committee chairmen should be named; a major start should be made toward obtaining the block captains; and over the next few days the bulk of the organizational machinery for phase one—including the initial membership lists for all committees—should be ready for announcement by the general chairman at the first regular assembly meeting. Certainly, all persons who attended the first public meeting prior to this assembly meeting and indicated a preference should be included in this announcement of appointments.

15

Special Notations on Meetings of the General Assembly

WITH phase one of the development effort now under way, we are in a position to indicate in further detail the planning that should be done for each meeting of the general assembly. In effect, then, this section is an extension of section 4.

Neither the general chairman nor the assistant general chairman should serve on any committee, except the advisory council which meets when called by the general chairman, thus leaving these persons free to perform their overall coordinating functions, plan the agenda for assembly meetings, and make certain that responsibilities for each aspect of the operation are clearly fixed and understood.

At the first regular assembly meeting at which the report of the community attitudes committee will be the principal subject of discussion, item 3 in the suggested agenda set forth in section 4—the secretary's oral report on the previous meeting—should in this case consist of a brief resume of the explanations given at the opening public meeting concerning the underlying goal of the development effort, the organizational machinery through which phase one of the effort is to operate, plus whatever decisions and actions were agreed upon. This, together with the distribution of the secretary's written report, will serve to reemphasize the basic meaning of community development as defined in section 2 and will be especially useful to those who did not attend the opening public meeting. The secretary should also bring everyone up to date on the work that has been accomplished to complete the development organization since that meeting was held, thus further showing that no time is being lost in getting the operation put together.

Item 4 in the agenda outlined in section 4 is the point at which the general chairman should announce the initial lists of appointments that have been made and accepted. If additional appointments are yet to be firmed up, this should also be announced, and all persons who did not attend the opening public meeting and have not yet been appointed to a position or committee should be urged to fill out an Activity Preference Sheet, to be turned in to the secretary, so their names can be added to the appointment lists of their choice. The general chairman then announces the subject of the evening, and calls on the community attitudes committee for its highlight presentation preparatory to the small-group discussion period.

As indicated by item 6 in the agenda outlined in section 4, the general assembly then breaks into the small discussion groups, each going into a prearranged location in the building with its discussion leader and recorder to begin the discussion of the community attitudes report. Thus, the procedure by which this division into discussion groups is to be accomplished must for the first time be activated and may require some additional explanation which will not be necessary at future meetings as the procedure becomes routine. Assuming the numbered-card procedure suggested in section 4 is to be used, the cards showing where each group is to meet should be arranged for distribution in series numbered from 1 up to whatever number of persons are to be in each discussion group. All persons receiving a card numbered 1 will form a group, those receiving a card numbered 2 will form another, and so on up to the total number of discussion groups. Inasmuch as it cannot be anticipated in advance exactly how many people will be attending a given assembly meeting, the general chairman may have to make some quick adjustments in the size and number of groups, but whether or not such adjustments are needed can be readily determined by the outcome of the card distribution. If, for example, one group is short enough persons to make an effective discussion, this group should be absorbed into other groups. Or, if there are more groups than there are discussion leaders and recorders, each group could be enlarged a bit for that particular meeting.

In regard to item 9 in the agenda outlined in section 4, it should be remembered that instead of charging the community attitudes committee—as well as the other temporary committees—with whatever follow-up action may be indicated, the responsibility for this follow-up should be distributed among the appropriate continuing committees, or in some instances referred to the advisory council. These notations on the agenda outlined in section 4, though focused chiefly on the first regular assembly meeting, should indicate procedures for planning and conducting all subsequent assembly meetings, recognizing that agenda variations will be required from time to time to meet special situations as they arise.

For example, a special situation that would call for variations in the agenda may arise when preparations are being made for a major community-wide action project which has been endorsed by the general assembly, but which requires the reporting committee to draw up a detailed action plan to be presented for discussion at the next assembly meeting. A situation such as this could alter not only the agenda, but also the scheduling of reports from other committees.

Also it should be noted that it is impossible to say how many general assembly meetings will be needed in every community to cover the problems and recommendations each fact-finding committee will be reporting. In some communities a given committee report may require only one assembly meeting; in others it may require several. Further, there will undoubtedly be instances in which recommendations for action rise out of discussions in the general assembly that were not included in a given committee's report. This may call for additional committee investigation and planning to be followed by a supplemental report, and this will influence the agenda.

If more general assembly meetings are needed for a given committee than have been scheduled for that committee, the question of how many more should be determined on the basis of the urgency of this particular subject matter in your community, on specific action projects being planned for the immediate future in that committee's field of interest, and on the amount of action that can be accomplished during the first phase of the development operation. Or the reverse situation could arise—that is, it may be found that more assembly meetings have been scheduled for a given fact-finding committee than are needed, which would call for adjustments in scheduling and agenda planning. Thus, the need for flexibility and possible changes in plans should be constantly borne in mind in order to keep the operation moving at a high level of interest and productivity.

While it is important that no committee report be covered so hurriedly as to leave people feeling they have not had time to come to grips with basic problems, it is also important that a certain subject not be covered in such exhaustive detail in the assembly meetings as to cause a falling off of interest. As a practical matter, it will simply not be possible for the general assembly to delve into every subject in as much depth as will be done by the fact-finding committees during their investigations and analyses. Still, the discussions in the assembly must be sufficient to enable all participants in the development effort to broaden their comprehension of problems in all aspects of community life, and to see clearly what actions are needed to bring about desired improvements.

The reports of the fact-finding committees, combined with the discussions in the assembly, should lead to a great deal of action. But this combination of fact-finding and discussion will also develop an increased recognition in the community as a whole that many desired improvements can be accomplished only on a long-range basis, in many cases requiring an area-wide effort in cooperation with other communities. This growing recognition is one of the important factors that will help build a firm foundation for the ultimate transition into phase two of the development operation.

The general chairman and assistant general chairman should keep in close touch with the chairmen of the various fact-finding committees to make certain all reports will be delivered to the secretary for typing and duplication far enough in advance to have them ready for distribution at the assembly meetings for which they are scheduled, and for distribution two or three days earlier to the four elective leaders and the discussion leaders and recorders.

From time to time, the general chairman and assistant general chairman should visit meetings of the various committees and be prepared to provide any special assistance they may need, especially when the committees are first getting organized. It would also be a good idea to check with the discussion leaders and recorders at least a day in advance of each assembly meeting to make sure they will be present and have received the committee report they will need to prepare themselves for the small-group discussion period.

Make it an established routine for the general chairman, assistant general chairman, secretary, treasurer, chairman of the reporting committee, and the discussion leaders and recorders to meet as a group at least a half hour before each assembly meeting to talk over the material to be taken up that evening and any procedures or agenda items that may call for last-minute review.

The general chairman and assistant general chairman, with the help of the discussion leaders and recorders, should make a personal check of all meeting rooms before each assembly meeting to be sure they are unlocked and that all equipment, chairs, tables, blackboards, chalk, erasers, heat, air conditioning, and whatever else will contribute to the success of the meeting are in readiness. During the small-group discussion period the general chairman, assistant general chairman, secretary, and treasurer should circulate from one group to another to make sure each group discussion is moving in a lively and productive manner, lending whatever assistance may be needed if one of the groups is confused or seems to be bogging down.

Other notations concerning meetings of the general assembly will be made in the following section which will deal specifically with the work of the discussion leaders and recorders, but the central point to be remembered is this: If the development effort is to realize its full potential for achievement *nothing should be left to chance or just taken for granted*. Good communities don't just happen. They are built by determined people.

16

The Discussion Leaders
and Recorders

EACH discussion leader and recorder should:

1. Read and become familiar with the development guide;

2. Obtain and study in advance of each assembly meeting a copy of the secretary's report on the previous meeting and a copy of the committee report which is to be the subject of the forthcoming meeting;

3. Meet with the general chairman, the assistant general chairman, the secretary, the treasurer, and the chairman of the reporting committee a half hour before each assembly meeting to go over the subject and procedures for that particular meeting and make sure all necessary details are in order;

4. Notify the general chairman far enough in advance to arrange for a substitute if circumstances are going to prevent a discussion leader or recorder from attending a certain assembly meeting.

In each group the discussion leader and recorder should operate as a team, their prime objective being to help develop and maintain a lively and productive discussion. The chief disadvantage will be that most members of the discussion group will not have had an opportunity to read the scheduled committee report in advance. This disadvantage, however, will be largely offset by the presentation that will have been given by the reporting committee immediately prior to the small-group discussion period, with all persons in the general assembly having a copy of the committee's written report to follow as this presentation is being given. Further, as was pointed out in section 6, each committee report should be written in a way that will lend itself to discussion, thus making it a useful tool in helping the discussion groups focus on specific problems and recommendations for action.

The members of each group should be seated around a table, or in a manner that enables them to face each other, not in rows that force them to look only at each other's backs. The seating arrangement should create a conversational setting, enable each discussant to talk directly to the group as a whole, and make it easy for all members of the group to hear and see what is going on. The expression on a person's face, various mannerisms and gestures, are frequently important parts of the process of communication. But none of these factors that help convey feelings and opinions can be seen on the back of a person's head.

Everything that can be done to make the members of the group physically and mentally comfortable should be done. Before starting the discussion, the leader should make sure that any member of the group who is not known to other members is introduced and help all members get personally acquainted on as informal a basis as possible. *Don't ask people to introduce themselves*. This is inclined to be an awkward procedure and for some individuals is downright embarrassing. The discussion leader should make sure everyone knows the recorder and should ask for their assistance in making it as easy as possible for the recorder to keep a good set of notes.

The leader should greet the group in the same manner that a considerate host or hostess would greet a group of people in one's own home. Try to create an immediately friendly attitude by helping everyone feel at ease, by making it clear that everyone's thoughts and ideas are both needed and wanted, and by making it evident that no one should hesitate to say whatever he or she feels like saying. While common courtesy and mutual respect should be observed, effective problem-solving cannot be achieved unless all members of the group feel free to speak their minds openly and candidly without fear of reprisal and without hesitating to express honest disagreement with a particular point of view.

As a practical matter, it must be recognized that in virtually all communities there are a host of reasons—business and otherwise—for some people not to feel entirely free to speak out in public on what they think about every matter. But it is the responsibility of the discussion leader and recorder to try by every means possible to remedy this, and as the reports from the fact-finding committees come in and the development effort moves along, considerable progress will be made toward overcoming this natural obstacle to effective communication.

Thus, the discussion leader should make it clear that everyone in the group is equally and mutually responsible for making the discussion productive—by listening carefully to what others have to say, by not dominating the conversation, by not allowing themselves to feel resentful if someone disagrees with them, by not going off on tangents that have nothing to do with the subject at hand, by speaking out on what they really think, by not making themselves disruptive by arguing just for the sake of argument, by holding to their opinions when convinced they are right —yet being willing to admit they can be wrong—by contributing to the development of constructive thinking that leads to positive action, and by sharing the responsibility of leadership.

And it should also be made clear that no problem can be solved by ducking it or being afraid to talk about it; that only as problems and recommendations are brought into the open, put on the table, looked at, examined, weighed, and analyzed in a spirit of honesty and good will can the development effort actually get anywhere. In emphasizing the point that everybody's ideas are wanted and needed, the discussion leader may further help pave the way toward productive conversation by mentioning in a good-natured manner that the more long-winded members of the group should not feel hurt if at times the leader cuts them off so other members may get in a word now and then.

At the opening of the small-group meeting, the discussion leader should briefly review the committee's report as the other members of the group follow their copies, pointing up the problems posed and the recommendations for action. All members of the group should be encouraged to ask questions or make comments as this review unfolds and to complete their discussion of each problem and recommendation as it is brought out in the committee's report, then move on to the next.

During the discussion the leader should do as little talking as possible, regarding it as his or her primary function to get the members of the group as a whole to do the talking. Some of the ways the leader may do this are to probe various questions, problems, and recommendations in the committee's report with additional questions that will help draw out the group's thinking and experiences concerning the points under consideration. Try to get each problem and recommendation explored from all relevant angles. Stimulate thought by offering brief suggestions at strategic moments, by asking for more follow-up on various points, by calling for clarification when necessary, by briefly challenging notions with which the leader may disagree, by summarizing from time to time where the discussion seems to be heading and asking if this is correct, by raising possibilities that will help develop further insight into a given problem, and by trying to alter individual prejudices through pointing out other ways of looking at a situation that will have the effect of helping create a broader understanding.

Try to create openings for the less talkative members of the group, perhaps addressing specific questions now and then to various people by name. Try to avoid allowing anyone to monopolize the conversation by asking what others think, by ignoring the monopolizer if necessary, and as a last resort, by referring to what was said at the beginning of the meeting about the leader's prerogative to cut people off; then politely but firmly suggest that it might be well to make a little more room for others to express what they think. This, however, is ticklish business, and should not be tried unless the leader has reason to believe it will be more helpful than harmful. After all, some people do have more knowledge and more useful ideas to contribute than others.

Don't let the group skim over important matters without due consideration and attention, or without making clear the meaning of what is being said. Likewise, don't let the group get unnecessarily stuck on unimportant details. If the conversation should at some point come to a sudden stop, the discussion leader shouldn't panic or launch into a lecture just to fill in words. The group may be thinking. Or it may be confused as to just how to deal with a complex problem. After a moment of waiting, the leader may get the conversation moving again by restating the problem, then asking a few provocative questions. If the discussion gets off the subject, don't let it wander too far. Get it back on the track by some such statement as, "Maybe we ought to take this up some other time and for now get back to the subject we are here to talk about." Then quickly follow with another provocative question.

Don't let the discussion drift into a one-to-one exchange of questions and answers between various individuals and the leader, or drift into a situation that is little more than an exclusive conversation between two or three persons. Instead, keep as much interaction going as possible among all members of the group, and don't fall into the habit of having people raise their hands for recognition by the leader before speaking. This, after all, is not a formal hearing before a public official in which *Robert's Rules of Order* are employed. Build the discussion into a real conversation among an informal group of people in which all persons contribute to the flow of conversation by simply speaking up when they have something to say, and by allowing others to do the same without undue interruption. Try to avoid merely listing and observing facts. Develop the discussion into an interpretation of the meanings and implications of facts.

If a certain member of the group sharply disagrees with the group as a whole, it is possible that this person has an insight into varied implications the other members have overlooked, or that this person comprehends the matter on which the disagreement is based more thoroughly than the others. But if the disagreement seems to be unreasonable, or if two or more persons get into a heated argument or personality clash in which emotion replaces reason, then the group may have a threatening situation on its hands. The discussion leader, working cooperatively with the group as a whole, may begin a line of probing aimed at stimulating supplemental questions that will help bring out all shades of thought in an attempt to reach an understanding of all sides of the argument, thereby achieving a cooling off of tempers.

If, however, the situation cannot be resolved by methods such as this, and reaches the point where it becomes a real menace to constructive decision-making, the discussion leader may find it necessary to take more drastic action, including in extreme circumstances, simply insisting that the argument stop and calling for a return to mature and reasonable behavior. Hopefully, no disagreement will deteriorate into such bitterness as to create a state of serious hostility—either openly or under the surface. But impasses of this kind can happen, and the discussion groups as vital parts of the development operation are too important to allow them to be wrecked by obstreperous or unreasonable behavior by a few individuals—regardless of the underlying causes for such behavior.

I am reminded of situations such as this that have arisen in some of the community development operations in which I have worked. In one instance, for example, an exchange of slanderous remarks among several members of a discussion group became so caustic that as a last resort I bluntly told them to shut up and calm down, that we could not afford this kind of childish behavior. It was a calculated risk, but it worked. After a second or two of stunned silence the entire group—including those who had caused the disruption—broke into applause. Almost as though I had waved a magic wand, the atmosphere cleared and the discussion returned to an amicable plane with no residue of hard feelings.

In another instance in which one person alone was acting out a particularly offensive mood that had the group so irritated it could hardly contain itself, I suddenly called for a halt and asked how much longer the group intended to tolerate this kind of obstruction. The group's response was immediate and definite, the offender apologized, and the discussion continued in a constructive manner. After the meeting I asked this individual out for coffee, and after a private talk that reached into the early morning hours I knew the background of his discontent. I listened attentively to what he told me about himself and his personal situation, asked a few questions, made a few understanding comments, and offered a few suggestions. Apparently this helped; at least he told me it did and repeatedly thanked me. Afterward he never missed a meeting of the general assembly, he participated productively in the discussions and became one of the most dependable workers in the development effort.

Fortunately, most people are reasonable. But when they aren't there is usually a combination of difficulties that can be rooted out and resolved if a genuine effort is made to do so when the opportunity arises. Further, in most cases in which a discussion group begins to deteriorate into a situation that is clearly damaging its ability to function effectively because of certain individuals' personal behavior, the discussion leader can usually rely on the group itself to take care of the situation by asking appropriate questions and placing the responsibility in the hands of the group as a whole.

People do hold differing points of view and different sets of values. And they will frequently engage in vigorous dissent. This is part of what free society is all about. But the discussion leader should inject a certain balancing influence and enough good will to maintain a healthy atmosphere of friendly relationships that will avoid the type of rancor and clashing of personalities that leads only to hostility and thus prevents constructive action. Mental barriers, either real or imaginary, often prevent human minds from meeting in a mature manner, and only when these barriers are broken down can effective discussion be achieved and real headway made toward community problem-solving. This is one of the basic reasons for dividing the general assembly into small discussion groups for a portion of the assembly meeting.

If the group disapproves of a recommendation for action that has been proposed in a committee report, the discussion leader should encourage the group to suggest possible amendments to which it can agree. Also, if the group thinks of a recommendation for action the committee did not include in its report, that recommendation should be put into words so it can be clearly entered in the recorder's notes for submission to the general assembly after the small-group discussion period has been completed.

As was stated at the beginning of this section, the discussion leader and recorder should work as a team. This means the discussion leader should help the recorder by calling for pauses whenever necessary to make sure the recorder has caught accurately and completely the salient points in the conversation. The recorder, in turn, should assist the discussion leader and the group as a whole by providing appropriate feedback from time to time that will contribute to the forward motion of the conversation. If the discussion becomes fuzzy at a certain point or there is a degree of uncertainty as to the precise meaning of what is being said, the recorder should not hesitate to break in and call for clarification.

By working together through the use of summaries whenever needed, through the use of strategic questions, and now and then restating specific points, the discussion leader and recorder should make it their business to help the group move toward definite conclusions and clear-cut decisions concerning specific problems and recommendations for action, avoiding by every legitimate means a discussion that is nothing more than fruitless or nonproductive talk which leads to a sense of frustration and leaves the group feeling its time has been wasted. If people can come away from each discussion period with a clear sense of accomplishment, a feeling that they have truly grappled with real problems, increased their knowledge of some of the obstacles to community improvement, and reached definite decisions on solid recommendations for action, the morale of the development operation will grow to ever-ascending heights and the community's capacity for self-determination and needed action will expand. If this does not happen, attendance will fall and the development effort will decline.

As the discussion goes along, the discussion leader should keep close watch of the time, recognizing that time in itself is a precious commodity and that every moment should be used as effectively as possible. About ten minutes before the period allotted for the small-group discussions is due to end, the leader should call attention to this fact and encourage the group to move toward a final wrap-up of conclusions. The last five minutes or so should be devoted to a final oral summary of the highlights of the recorder's notes to make sure they reflect accurately the group's thinking and decisions, indicating points of agreement and any dissenting positions that should be reported to the general assembly.

Referring again to the typical agenda outlined in section 4, the small-group discussion period is now completed and all persons reconvene in the general assembly. The recorders from the various groups seat themselves at a table at the front of the assembly meeting hall and, under the guidance of the general chairman, report to the assembly the gist of the conversation in their respective groups and the conclusions that were reached concerning the problems and recommendations for action in the committee report that has been the subject of the evening. If during the small-group discussions additional problems or recommendations for action relating to the committee report have been brought out, these should also be cited.

The recorders should make their reports brief, punchy, and to the point, avoiding unnecessary repetition, and keeping themselves aware of the limitation of time. If, for example, all or several of the discussion groups have reached the same conclusion on a given problem or recommendation, the recorders who follow the first one to report this conclusion should simply indicate that their groups agreed with that conclusion and have nothing further to add. Each recorder should report only information that differs from that which has already been reported or which is necessary to underscore or make a certain point more forceful, thus speeding up the reporting process and making it possible to move in a rapid and lively manner from one point to the next.

In leading this reporting session, the general chairman should avoid calling on the recorders in a set order, but instead, engage them in a discussion of each problem and recommendation for action that will result in the same kind of interaction among the group of recorders which the discussion leaders seek to achieve in their respective discussion groups. As a means of adding to this conversational tone, the general chairman should not hesitate to make comments of his or her own or ask questions for clarification of various points as the reporting session goes along.

For example, the general chairman may ask after one of the recorders has reported a given conclusion, "Do any of you have anything to add to this, or anything different, or do all the groups agree with this conclusion? Does any group disagree with this conclusion?" And whenever an appropriate opportunity arises, the general chairman should inject a little humor. This will provide a bit of light touch that will further enliven the reporting and help build the assembly meeting to a satisfying climax.

This discussion-type procedure will step up the pace of the reporting session and make it possible to bring out the conclusions reached on each problem and recommendation in a much more vigorous and interesting fashion than could be accomplished by having each recorder in turn give what could easily become just a round of dull and monotonous reading of notes.

At the conclusion of this reporting session the recorders—as indicated in section 4—hand their notes to the secretary for use in preparing the overall written report on that particular assembly meeting. The general chairman briefly summarizes the recommendations for action on which the groups have agreed, those on which there have been disagreement, and any amendments that have been suggested, then calls for any comments or questions anyone in the assembly may wish to add. If it is necessary to bring certain recommendations to a head or to confirm their adoption through a vote by the assembly as a whole, the general chairman should call for the appropriate motions and proceed with the voting.

As in the small discussion groups, each meeting of the general assembly should reach as firm and definite a set of decisions as possible, even if the decision on a certain recommendation is to hold off making a final decision until the appropriate fact-finding committee conducts further investigation and comes back at a later meeting with a supplemental report that either reaffirms the earlier recommendation or offers a modification.

As we have pointed out previously, all recommendations for action which the general assembly has approved are then referred by the general chairman to the appropriate fact-finding committee for necessary follow-up, or in some cases to the advisory council.

17

From Study to Action

AFTER the general assembly has completed its discussions of the reports of the community attitudes and community organizations committees, the community will begin to see itself in a new light. Social barriers that tend to prevent constructive action will begin coming down, and an increasing spirit of unity will begin to emerge. This will create a favorable climate for the fact-finding committees that will continue through the first phase of the development effort, and generate an increasing desire for action.

As the assembly meetings go forward, a considerable list of recommendations for action will accumulate. People will become increasingly aware of their community problems, and will begin getting restless. In addition to doing fact-finding, writing reports, attending committee and general assembly meetings, and analyzing and discussing problems, a mood will develop which says in effect, "Let's *do* something." This will be a healthy turn. But it will also be an extremely delicate point, for unless this urge is fulfilled it could have a dampening influence on the forward motion of the entire operation. This means the time for tangible action is *now*, and that from this point on, specific action projects must go hand in hand with the fact-finding and discussions if the development effort is to mature and the community is to achieve its full capacity for self-improvement.

From the list of recommendations that will have been approved when this point is reached, there will be the two major categories of action to consider that were mentioned in section 3: One, short range; the other, long range. As we have emphasized previously, and will continue to emphasize, some actions in these categories can be accomplished only on an area level in cooperation with other communities, while other actions can be accomplished only on a strictly local basis. Looking first at those projects in the short-range category that can be accomplished only on a strictly local basis, we have noted several possibilities:

1. Projects that have definite community support but require only one or two, or just a few individuals, to accomplish;

2. Projects that have definite community support but can be carried out only through an official institution, such as local government;

3. Projects that have definite community support but can best be handled by one or more existing private organizations, such as a local service club or chamber of commerce;

4. Projects that have definite community support and lend themselves to direct personal action by large numbers of people, in essence, the whole community—for example, a community-wide clean-up, paint-up, fix-up campaign.

All of these types of action are essential to successful community development. But in the early stages of the operation it is the fourth type—projects in which large numbers of citizens can work together in a direct personal way—that are most urgently needed if the civic muscle is to be built that will enable the community to rise to its full potential for problem-solving in all fields of interest. By carefully noting the frequency with which recommendations for such projects arise and watching for indications of readiness to act on these recommendations, patterns of interest in projects that would lend themselves to mass civic action will become apparent. The general chairman and all other leaders in the development effort should therefore put themselves on special alert and be prepared to issue a challenge for immediate action as soon as one or more projects of this kind appear likely to catch fire.

Bearing in mind the basic goal we discussed in section 2, it is not only important that the first action project be started relatively early in the development operation, the decision as to *what this first project should be* is equally important. Remembering that in keeping with this basic goal, no action is to be looked upon as an end in itself, but as one of the important steps in the development of an increasingly competent, problem-solving citizenry, here are some suggested criteria for selecting the first community-wide action project.

It should be something tangible, something physical, something people can do with their hands, something in which large numbers of people can become engaged personally and directly, and in which they can work together as fellow citizens. It should be a project that will result in improvements people can look at, photograph, point to with pride, and feel satisfied with themselves for what they have done. It should be a project that will have *deep personal meaning to your particular community*, something that will have emotional as well as intellectual appeal. It should be a project that will not be easy, but will not require major fund raising. It should be something that can be started on a specified date and completed quickly—within a few days or weeks—so the entire community can gain the immediate sense of achievement to which we referred early in section 3, be surprised with itself for what it has been able to do, and brag on the magnitude of civic cooperation this first community-wide action will have demonstrated. And above all, it should be something those in the community who are still skeptical of the development effort will be most apt to say cannot be done.

Virtually every community has some problem situation that might be called a "symbol of defeat," something that for years almost everybody has been saying ought to be done, and while blaming others for not doing it, feeling a little ashamed of themselves for their inaction—something the community clearly could do, would like to do, has half-heartedly tried to do, but has just never been able to develop enough cooperation and determined effort to actually accomplish. This is the ideal kind of first project to adopt for direct, mass civic action. Look for your community's "symbol of defeat."

By completing this kind of project as an integral part of the overall development effort, the community will have achieved far more than an isolated improvement. It will have forged a new vision of its civic potential, a new faith in itself, a belief that it can do things people had previously regarded as impossible. A new level of communication and interpersonal understanding will have been established. New friendships will have been formed and old ones deepened. Social barriers will have come further down. The community will have put itself through an acid test. It will have transformed a "symbol of defeat" into a "symbol of victory."

From this experience the surge for action will intensify. The committees will bear down. The assembly meetings will gain increasing importance. Everywhere in the community there will be new optimism, and all aspects of the operation will gain momentum. There are a number of ways of getting this first project initiated. Here are a few suggestions.

At the opportune moment when the mood to "do something" has become clearly evident, the general chairman may call a special meeting of the advisory council to discuss the need for such action and the importance of moving at once toward selecting the appropriate project. Reviewing the problems and recommendations for action that have been consistently raised in meetings of the assembly up to this point, and noting the emerging patterns of interest, the advisory council should be able to select one or more possible projects that fit the criteria we have indicated. These possibilities can then be set forth in the form of a concrete proposal for immediate action at the next general assembly meeting.

Thus, instead of one of the fact-finding committees providing a report for discussion, this meeting of the assembly is devoted to an action proposal from the advisory council, thereby giving this particular meeting a special tone of urgency. The council's proposal should be presented in a manner that will challenge and stimulate the small-group discussions, and before this meeting is adjourned, the assembly should have reached a definite conclusion as to what the first community-wide action is to be and when it is to begin.

If several possible projects are to be included in the advisory council's proposal, the council should indicate in its presentation to the assembly the order in which it thinks these possibilities best fit the criteria set forth above. The initial task of drawing up these possibilities can be most easily accomplished by a small working group, and the advisory council—which includes all committee chairmen—is a logical group to supply this essential leadership. But to ensure maximum participation in the ultimate decision so the project can be launched and carried out as a genuine community-wide effort, it is also essential that final approval come from the general assembly as a whole.

Another way of getting this project initiated is for the general chairman, sensing a state of readiness for this kind of action at one of the regular assembly meetings, to seize the opportunity to propose the idea for such a first action project as a special challenge, immediately following the recorders' reporting session, perhaps naming two or three possibilities that have been talked about in this and previous meetings. If this challenge meets with obvious acceptance, the general chairman should announce that a special session of the advisory council is being called immediately to come up with specific recommendations for this project to be presented for discussion at the next assembly meeting. Or this challenge may come from one or more of the discussion groups, or from the chairman of that evening's reporting committee.

But whatever means are used for getting this first major action launched, the important point is that after the development effort is under way and the urge for such action has caught on, then is the time to move with utmost dispatch toward putting together a detailed work plan —including such items as: A definite time and date the action is to begin and a target date for its completion; how it is to be organized to engage insofar as possible the total citizenry; who is to be responsible for what; and what kinds and sources of all materials, tools, and equipment will be needed to carry it out. One word of caution: Don't be overzealous and get stampeded into a project that would not be constructive.

Immediately after this first major community action has been completed, numerous other short-range projects should follow as the process of fact-finding, discussion, and community self-examination continues. Through the various continuing committees and other groups in the community—both public and private—several short-range action projects may be going on simultaneously while decisions are being reached and further detailed planning is going ahead for actions of a more long-range nature. Meanwhile, as we have indicated earlier, a system of evaluation and progress reporting should be adopted so that no decision to act is left dangling or simply forgotten, and to make certain that if various methods or procedures are found not to be working, remedial steps may be taken.

Thus, the first phase of the development effort moves from study to a first community-wide action project, followed by continued study, action, and evaluation carefully interwoven into a comprehensive flow of self-initiated civic performance. We now turn to the work outlines of the continuing fact-finding committees.

18

The Environmental Improvement Committee

ENVIRONMENTAL improvement has become a matter of national and international concern requiring public and private expenditures of a magnitude so vast as to be virtually inconceivable. But conserving our natural resources, and at the same time, finding the proper balance between protecting the environment and developing and maintaining a productive economy must go hand in hand. And as in all other aspects of community development, a great deal of constructive action for these dual purposes can be initiated without waiting for massive outside financial aid. This does not mean no outside aid will be needed. It does mean that to a significant extent environmental problems can be appropriately resolved only by the direct action of people individually and as communities, and there is no better place to begin than here—in the community where you live, and in the area of which it is a part.

The fact-finding and recommendations for action needed for informed discussion in the assembly concerning this important part of the development effort will be the responsibility of the environmental improvement committee. As in the case of the other fact-finding committees, all members of this committee should prepare for their work by carefully reviewing section 6, "Procedures and Repsonsibilities of the Fact-Finding Committees." The secretary's reports on meetings of the general assembly should be examined for problems that may call for further research by this committee, and the committee should confer with other committees concerning matters of common interest.

Probably the best and most logical way for the environmental improvement committee to begin is to first make a detailed examination of the community's physical appearance. Nothing makes a traveler more determined to keep moving toward another stopping place than a shabby-looking town. People are inclined to be drawn to communities where buildings are neat, painted, and in good repair; where there are attractive parks, well-cared-for lawns, trees, landscaping, and interesting places in which to eat and stay overnight. We have many communities like this in rural America, but we also have thousands of towns and small cities dotted across the country that are dingy and ill kept, and in which there seems to be little effort or desire by the people to improve the unsightly image.

Certainly the physical appearance of your community will have an important bearing on its social and economic development, on the overall quality of life, and on the attitudes and general morale of the people. If the community's very appearance is a reminder of deterioration and neglect, new families and new industry will hesitate to move in, property values will decline, retail trade will dwindle, and the population will tend to shrink even faster than it would otherwise. It is possible to live next to an unsightly junkyard over a period of time and become almost unaware of its presence. Many communities don't seem to realize the importance of maintaining an attractive physical appearance, or that the lack of such an appearance not only reflects an absence of local pride and a low level of civic enterprise but may actually have an adverse psychological effect on the community's ability to deal with any problem.

In section 17, "From Study to Action," we referred to the importance of initiating, fairly early in the development operation, physical action projects which lend themselves to direct participation by large numbers of people, and criteria were suggested for selecting such projects. The findings and recommendations of the environmental improvement committee are likely to offer particularly good opportunities for this kind of community-wide action. During the course of this committee's fact-finding, and in preparing its presentation and report for discussion in the general assembly, special attention should be given to section 17 with an eye toward identifying opportunities that would be ideal for these kinds of community-wide physical action projects.

A suggested outline for examining the community's physical appearance is as follows: Using the map prepared by the boundary committee, walk or drive through all streets and roads in the community making an actual count of all existing buildings and collecting on-site information on the items set forth below. (For each item make separate tabulations for inside and outside the city limits.)

Residential Buildings and Grounds

1. What is the total number of residential houses or structures in the community?

2. How many of these residential houses or structures appear to be in satisfactory condition? (Neat, clean, painted, well maintained, and in good repair.)

3. How many appear to need improvements? Paint? Repairs or fixing up? Seem to be structurally sound, but are badly run-down? How many appear to be so dilapidated as not to be worth fixing up, aren't fit to live in, and should be torn down?

4. How many of these residential houses or structures appear to have satisfactory yards? (Neat, clean, uncluttered, well-kept grass, trees, shrubbery, and general landscaping.)

5. How many yards are not in satisfactory condition? (Front, back, and sides.) Dirty, cluttered with trash or junk, or downright filthy? Aren't in that bad a condition, but still need cleaning up? How many yards need: Mowing? Weeds cut? Grass planted? Trees planted? Shrubs planted? Landscape maintenance? Trash hauled away?

6. Of the total number of residential houses or structures in need of improvement or in need of lawn care as indicated under items 3, 4, and 5

above, how many of them are: Owner occupied? Renter occupied? Vacant?

Barns and Sheds

1. What is the total number of barns and sheds in the community?

2. How many of these barns and sheds have a satisfactory physical appearance? (Neat, clean, painted, well maintained, and in good repair.)

3. How many of them seem to be structurally sound, but need to have their physical appearance improved? Paint? Repairs or fixing up? Landscaping?

4. Of the total number of barns and sheds in the community, how many of them appear to be so dilapidated they should be torn down?

Outdoor Privies

1. What is the total number of outdoor privies in the community?

2. How many of these outdoor privies are still being used? How many of those still in use are in satisfactory condition? (Neat, clean, painted, properly maintained from a sanitary point of view, and in good repair.) How many of those still in use are *not* in satisfactory condition? How many of them need: Paint? Repairs and fixing up? Landscaping? Sanitary maintenance? Are located in a way that could cause water pollution? Are so dilapidated they should be torn down and replaced?

3. How many of these privies could be replaced by a sanitary sewer system? How? At what cost? How could the cost be paid?

4. How many outdoor privies are there in the community that are no longer being used and should be destroyed?

5. Draw up recommendations for action to correct all unsatisfactory conditions.

Commercial Buildings and Grounds—
Retail, Wholesale, Storage, Industrial

1. What is the total number of commercial buildings in the community?

2. List by name those that are occupied, and indicate number. Note which of those occupied are in satisfactory condition. (Neat, clean, painted, well maintained, and in good repair.) Note which of those occupied need to have their physical appearance improved: Paint? Repairs or fixing up? Are so bad they ought to be torn down? Note condition

of grounds: Improvements needed that as a practical matter could be accomplished, considering cost and other factors.

3. List by name those that are vacant, and indicate number. Note the same conditions for vacant buildings as indicated above for occupied buildings. Note which of these vacant buildings could be used in their present condition: Purpose for which each could be used, either commercial or noncommercial. Note which of these vacant buildings could be used if repaired, renovated, or remodeled: Purpose for which each could be used, either commercial or noncommercial. Economic feasibility of needed repairs, renovation, or remodeling.

Public Buildings and Grounds

Collect the same information concerning all public buildings and grounds in the community, listing them by name, as outlined above in regard to residential and commercial buildings and grounds.

Religious Buildings and Grounds

This applies primarily to church buildings, and calls for the same information indicated above concerning residential, commercial, and public buildings and grounds. If the community organizations committee did the church survey outlined in the closing pages of section 12, this information may be obtained from that committee's church report.

Summary of Information Concerning
All Buildings and Grounds
in the Community

1. Adding them all together, how many buildings of all types are there in your community?

2. Of this total number, how many of them have a satisfactory physical appearance, how many have an unsatisfactory physical appearance, and what percentage of the total does each of these two categories represent? Consider both the buildings themselves, and their grounds or yards.

3. What specific action projects would the committee recommend to improve the physical appearance of all unsightly buildings in the community, or if deemed appropriate, get them torn down and the debris eliminated?

Streets and Roads

1. How many unsightly streets and roads are there in the community?

2. List them by name, indicating what stretches of each are unsightly, and describe the unsightly conditions.

3. Does the community have a sufficient number of attractive waste receptacles at strategic locations? Are they emptied often enough, and waste properly removed? What actions are recommended to correct any unsatisfactory situations?

4. Are there any streets or roads that need repairing? If yes, give names, exact location, the number of blocks or distance in each case, and describe what repairs are needed. Costs? Possible sources of funds?

5. Are there any streets or roads that need paving? If yes, give names, exact location, number of blocks or distance in each case, and kinds of paving that would be satisfactory. Costs? Possible sources of funds?

6. Are there enough streetlights in the community? If not, number of lights needed, and where. Kinds of posts and lights that would be most attractive? Costs? Possible sources of funds?

Sidewalks

1. How many unsightly sidewalks are there in the community?

2. List them according to the name and side of streets, indicating what stretches are unsightly, and describe the unsightly conditions.

3. Are there any sidewalks that need repairing? If yes, give exact locations, indicating number of blocks or distance in each case, and what repairs are needed. Costs? Possible sources of funds?

4. Is any new sidewalk construction needed? If yes, give locations, describe reasons for need, and footage or distance involved in each case. Costs? Possible sources of funds?

5. Indicate on a map all stretches of streets, roads, and sidewalks where improvements are needed, showing in each case the kinds of improvements needed, along with recommendations as to how these improvements could be accomplished.

Alleys

1. Are there any dirty, cluttered, or otherwise unsightly alleys in the community? If yes, make a list of these alleys describing the particular stretches that are unsatisfactory, and the conditions that call for im-

provement. What actions are recommended to eliminate any unsatisfactory alley conditions? By whom? Possibility for voluntary community project?

Vacant Lots

1. Are there any unsightly vacant lots in the community? If yes, give number, list locations, and describe unsightly conditions. What actions are recommended to eliminate these conditions? By whom? Possibility for voluntary community project?

Public Parks

1. Are there any public parks in the community? If yes, indicate whether neat, clean, and properly maintained. If not neat, clean, or properly maintained, describe existing conditions that ought to be improved, and draw up recommendations for community action.

Cemetery

1. How many cemeteries are there in the community?

2. Do any of them need to be cleaned up and better maintained? If yes, describe community action recommended to accomplish the needed improvements.

General Eyesores and Other
Miscellaneous Undesirable Conditions

1. Are there any trash piles or unauthorized dumping places in the community? If yes, give number and locations. What community action is recommended to get these cleaned up?

2. If trash, junk, rubbish, garbage, or other forms of litter are being indiscriminately dumped or thrown out at unauthorized places either inside or outside the city limits, what actions and educational campaigns would the committee recommend to stop these practices?

3. In addition to unauthorized dumping spots, are there any unsanitary places in the community such as stagnant water holes, cesspools, and the like that might be called mosquito breeders or other dirty health hazards? If yes, give number and locations of such places. Describe condition of each. Tell why they are allowed to exist. What community action is recommended to get rid of them?

4. Are there any rats or other vermin in the community? If yes, give locations and reasons. What community action is recommended to get rid of them?

5. Are there any automobile junkyards marring the community's appearance? If yes, give number and locations. Describe practical action that should be taken to remedy this situation.

6. How many public rest rooms are there in the community? How many are clean and sanitary? How many are dirty or unsanitary? Action recommended for any needed improvements.

7. Make photographs of selected eyesores throughout the community that can be projected on a large screen when the committee makes its presentation to the general assembly, printed in the newspaper, and displayed in other places in the community to attract public attention. These photographs should include such items as dilapidated buildings, dirty streets, unkept parks and cemeteries, unauthorized dumping places and trash heaps, unsightly vacant lots, unattractive entrances to town, and any other scenes that will help sharpen citizen awareness of any clutter or ugliness that is damaging the community's physical appearance.

Having examined each item listed above, plus any other items that ought to be considered in your locality, the committee should draw up a comprehensive plan of action for putting the community's overall physical appearance in top-notch condition—and keeping it that way. This plan should include:

1. Specific action projects and campaigns;

2. The order in which these projects should be initiated, with suggested strategies, beginning dates, and proposed deadlines for completion—giving special attention to the suggestions set forth in section 17 for mass community action;

3. A detailed work outline for each project showing how it can be started and carried out;

4. Who and how many people each project will require;

5. Materials, tools, and equipment that will be needed and sources from which they can be obtained;

6. Estimated costs and means of financing each project;

7. How these projects relate to each other and how each fits into the total plan.

This points up again the need for coordination between the continuing fact-finding committees and the role of the general chairman and advisory council for this purpose.

We have indicated that specific action by the community as a whole to clean up conditions that detract from its physical appearance will not only be a major step toward eliminating pollution but will also strengthen the community's ability to initiate other and more difficult projects. The fact-finding suggested below may indicate what some of these other projects might be.

1. Are facilities available to your community for the effective disposal of solid wastes—facilities such as well-managed and properly located sanitary landfills? If facilities of this kind are available, are they sufficient to handle the volume of solid wastes currently being produced in the community? What are the expectations for the foreseeable future? If such facilities are not available, or lack the necessary capacity for present and predictable future needs—including new industrial development—what corrective planning and action would the committee recommend? What technical and financial resources are available for this purpose? Municipal? County? State? Federal? Private? Would it be technically and economically feasible to use these solid wastes as raw materials for the production of fuels or other forms of energy? If yes, what actions would this require, and from what sources might these actions come?

2. What services are available to the community for garbage and trash collection? Are these services being handled in a clean and sanitary manner? Are they being provided on a regular and sufficiently frequent basis? If such services are lacking, or are in any respects inadequate, what corrective actions should be taken?

3. Does the community have a sewage treatment and disposal system? If yes, does it meet state and federal standards? Is it adequate for present and anticipated future needs? If no such system exists, or if the existing system is in any respects inadequate, what corrective planning and action would the committee recommend? What technical and financial resources are available for this purpose? Municipal? County? State? Federal? Private?

4. What about the community's water supply? Is the capacity sufficient to meet present and foreseeable future needs? What is the source, and is it secure and properly protected? Does it meet state and federal standards? Is there a sufficient watershed, and is it properly protected against erosion? Are water distribution lines up-to-date and properly

maintained? Are any individual family wells in current use for drinking purposes, and if so are they tested for purity at sufficiently frequent intervals? Describe any problems that exist concerning the community's water supply and distribution system, and what action the committee would recommend to resolve these problems. What technical and financial resources are available for this purpose? Municipal? County? State? Federal? Private?

5. Are there any polluted streams, lakes, or ponds in your community or area? If yes, describe the prevailing conditions and the causes for the pollution. What actions will be required to eliminate this pollution? What technical and financial resources are available for this purpose? Municipal? County? State? Federal? Private?

6. If there are swimming pools or other waters for swimming purposes in your community or area, do they pose any sanitary problems? If yes, what are these problems, and what action should be taken to correct them?

7. Is your community or area subject to any form of air pollution? If yes, how seriously? What are the causes? What practical remedies are possible? What technical and financial resources are available for this purpose? Municipal? County? State? Federal? Private?

8. Are there any problems in your community or area concerning the conservation of natural resources, such as land, forests, fish and wild life? If yes, what are these problems, and what practical actions can be taken to help resolve them? How can the needs for conservation and the needs for sound economic development be properly balanced and harmonized? What technical and financial resources are available for these purposes?

9. Does your community or area have any service available for the collection of glass and paper products for shipment to recycling plants? If yes, to what extent is this service being used? If no, is there any practical means of establishing such a service in your community or area, or that could be made available to your community or area?

As was indicated earlier in this section, much of today's environmental pollution can be resolved only by national and international action. Much must also be done at regional and state levels. But even a problem as vast as this comes back in the final analysis to people—and to the communities and areas in which they live.

19

The Government Committee

UNDER the impact of current social change increasingly heavier burdens are being placed on our institutions of local government. Never have these institutions been expected to provide more public services, nor have they been subjected to more criticism for rising costs. And there are other pressures. As it has become increasingly clear that the federal government cannot cure all the ills of today's communities and areas, there has been a steadily growing trend to use county, municipal, and other institutions of local government as funnels for nationally-manufactured policies aimed at attacking these ills.

Local government has always been an important political element in American life. But the expanding role it is now being expected to play in both private and public affairs is placing it in a position of even greater importance. New and increasing tensions are thus being created within local government itself, and with public discontent and a host of conflicting demands contributing to these tensions—often tearing the community itself apart—it is becoming ever more urgent for the electorate to know in factual detail what is going on and why. The difficulties now confronting our institutions of local government seem at times to create an almost impossible situation. This is one of the realities of modern life that must be handled and patiently worked out in any effective effort in community development.

Every American has the right to voice his opinions concerning the actions of his governmental institutions, but in exercising that right he also has the responsibility to be constructive, to try to see all sides of the issues, to understand the difficulties with which public officials are continuously confronted, and to register and vote. These are minimum requirements for good citizenship. For unless there is a bridge of mutual cooperation between the citizenry and its institutions of local government, democracy cannot function, and the development of vibrant communities within the framework of modern times will become increasingly difficult.

Yet in communities throughout the nation, both rural and urban, substantial percentages of the people old enough to vote don't bother to register, and many who do aren't sufficiently interested to actually get out and vote. Millions don't know the name of their congressman, are unable to name the U.S. senators from their state, and don't know the name of their governor. Vast numbers of people don't even know the names of all their elected local officials. This widespread ignorance not only adds to the difficulty of creating the relationships between government and people that are needed for sound community development, it also raises the question of how many citizens who do register and vote actually know what they are voting for.

These conditions may or may not prevail in your community, but if they do prevail to any significant extent this is a problem your development effort should help resolve. For if we Americans ever lose control of our governmental institutions, it will be nobody's fault but our own. We, the people, can have the kind of government we want and can afford only if we choose to exercise the necessary civic responsibility and understanding. If we are either unable or unwilling to do this at the local level, we will not be able to do it at any level. Thus, an alert, reasoning citizenry possessing enough factual information to exert a constructive influence on its institutions of local government is one of the most important ingredients in community development.

The fact-finding and recommendations required for informed discussions in the general assembly concerning this essential part of the development effort will be the responsibility of the government committee. To help get itself organized and obtain an overview of its work, the committee's members should carefully review section 6, "Procedures and Responsibilities of the Fact-Finding Committees." They should also look for problems that call for further research by the government committee in the reports of other committees and in the secretary's reports on meetings of the general assembly.

Turning now to the fact-finding, let's first look at municipal government. As creatures of the state, incorporated municipalities are authorized by state law to exercise a broad range of powers and functions which may be established by the municipal governing body through the enactment of local ordinances, or through measures approved by the voters in local referendums. A municipality may or may not choose to exercise all the powers and functions granted by the state, but neither can it take any legal actions that are not authorized by the state. Therefore, whatever official functions your municipal government performs depend upon the expressed will of the people and their elected municipal officials within the limits imposed by state enabling legislation.

Municipal government may be organized in any one of several ways. In the mayor-council form the distribution of power between the mayor and council varies from one locality to another. The office of mayor may have major executive powers, with the council serving as a legislative body. Or the office of mayor may be relatively weak in relation to the council. A variation on this is aldermanic government in which the mayor is elected at large, while each member of the board of aldermen or city council is elected from one of a number of wards depending on the size of the municipal population and provisions of state law. In some states there are provisions for a village form of government in which a village president and trustees are elected. There is also the commission form of municipal government in which a mayor and four commissioners are elected at large, the four commissioners serving as heads of the various municipal departments and the mayor serving in an overall coordinating capacity.

Another form of municipal government is the council-manager plan under which the people elect the mayor and councilmen who in turn appoint a professional city manager. The council, chaired by the mayor, functions as the policy-making body, and the city manager is given the responsibility of administering the council's policies and seeing that all municipal departments or units function accordingly. In this form of government it is essential that the mayor and councilmen confine themselves to legislative and policy matters and not interfere with the manager's administrative responsibilities. Otherwise undue confusion will ensue and the manager will be unable to do the job for which he is hired. The city manager, however, serves at the pleasure of the mayor and council and can be replaced by this elected body. Thus, if the manager is not performing properly the council may take steps to correct the stituation. Or if the people become dissatisfied with the manager they can convey their feelings to the mayor and council, and if they get no action and still aren't satisfied they can express their discontent in the next municipal election.

There are also townships, boroughs, and other forms of local government. But regardless of these variations, local government occupies a central position in your community and shapes in many important ways its social and economic condition. Each form of municipal government has its advocates, and what works well in some communities may not work well in others. So whatever form is most capable of providing essential services at the lowest possible cost in your particular community, along with due consideration of state law and the realities of politics, is in all probability the form best suited to your local situation.

The government committee should begin its report with a written description of your form of municipal government and compare its advantages and disadvantages with other forms possible under the laws of your state. Further suggestions for fact-finding concerning municipal government are as follows:

1. List the names and titles of all current elected officials and their terms of office. Also list the appointed heads of all municipal departments or agencies.

2. Draw up an organizational chart showing in visual form the structure of your municipal government, including all offices, departments, or agencies, and their relationships to each other. This should be accompanied by a written statement making clear the meaning of the chart and explaining how the municipal government operates overall. Does this organizational structure and the total governmental operation it represents pose any problems? If so, what are these problems and what are the causes behind them? What actions would the committee recommend to help resolve these problems?

3. Taking each office, department, or agency separately, prepare a written description setting forth:

(a) Its duties and responsibilities.

(b) Its current annual cost. Over the past several years has this cost been increasing, decreasing, or remaining about the same?

(c) The committee's analysis as to how efficiently the responsibilities of this office, department, or agency are being performed. Explain the reasons for the committee's conclusions.

(d) On the basis of this analysis, does the committee find the present annual cost of this office, department, or agency to be too much, about what it should be, or not enough for effective performance? Why?

(e) Is the staff for this particular unit too large, too small, or about right? Why?

(f) Does this unit overlap or duplicate in any way any other unit within the municipal governmental structure? If so, does this result in any conflict or waste? Or are there good reasons for this overlapping?

4. What is the total current municipal budget? Over the past several years has this overall budget been increasing, decreasing, or remaining about the same?

5. List all sources of municipal income, showing what percentage of the total is derived from each source.

6. Prepare a percentage breakdown showing how and for what purposes this municipal income is spent.

7. How does municipal income and expenditures compare with the total current municipal budget? Is the overall budget balanced? Is the total income less than total expenditures, or is there an income surplus? If income is less than expenditures, what are the causes of the deficit, and what does the committee think should be done to bring the budget into balance? If there is an income surplus, what are the reasons for this and what is being done with the surplus funds? What are the committee's conclusions in this respect, and why?

8. Does the municipal government operate any federally supported programs or activities? If so, what are they? Describe the purpose and function of each, and indicate the extent of federal funding. What is the committee's assessment as to the performance of these programs or activities?

9. In order to prevent sections of the internal municipal law from becoming obsolete or mired in a tangle of confusion, it is extremely important that all local ordinances be clearly and readily available to municipal authorities and to the citizenry. By keeping this legal information properly organized and up-to-date, municipal officials will be able to see with less diffficulty the current status of the ordinances under which they must operate, determine more easily and efficiently their powers and responsibilities, know whether or not they are in compliance with the laws of the state, and better understand what legal changes or adjustments may be made to meet current local needs. Further, all members of the citizenry will be able to learn more precisely what they can and cannot do according to law. How long has it been since your municipal ordinances were codified and revamped? Is there a need to bring them up-to-date and organize them in a more orderly reference form than they are in at the present time? If there is such a need, what action and expense would be required to remedy this situation?

10. Draw up a complete listing of all powers and functions available to your municipal government under state law, indicating which of these powers and functions are now being exercised, and which ones are not.

11. Does the committee think any of these powers and functions which are not now being exercised should be exercised? If so, which of these powers and functions does the committee think ought to be added? Explain the reasons for the committee's conclusions, and spell out what actions and procedures would have to be invoked to take advantage of these additional powers.

12. Are there any state authorized powers and functions now being exercised by the municipal government the committee thinks ought to be discontinued? If so, which ones? Explain the reasons for the committee's conclusions, and spell out what actions and procedures would have to be invoked to carry out these conclusions.

13. Make a listing of all existing municipal buildings. Are these buildings suitable for their current use? Do any of them need repairs or redecoration? Should any of them be replaced? If any of these buildings are unsuitable, in need of repairs or redecoration, or should be replaced, what would be the approximate cost of the needed improvements? This information may be obtained from the environmental improvement committee, or representatives from both committees may team up and do this part of the fact-finding together. Could any needed improvements revealed by this research be accomplished on a voluntary basis as a community action project such as we discussed in section 17, "From Study to Action"?

NOTE: In a midwestern community of about four thousand population, which was engaged in a comprehensive development effort, the people decided their city hall was so filthy and run-down that something had to be done. With donated building materials, a large voluntary work force of local tradesmen and businessmen moved in and renovated the three-story brick structure from top to bottom. A special committee of women came each day with free coffee, doughnuts, and box lunches. When the construction work was completed, more than three hundred men and women spent a weekend painting the interior of the entire structure —including the city jail, which they painted pink. The total job was accomplished in about two months with a cash outlay of less than two thousand dollars, all of which was raised through private contributions. What had been an old obsolete building, though structurally sound, was turned into an attractive new city headquarters with a long-needed teen-age recreation center. But of even more importance, the community gained an enormous sense of achievement, people from all segments of the citizenry learned to work together, renewed their civic vigor, and acquired a feeling of local pride that added fresh momentum to all aspects of their development effort.

14. To what extent do people in your community attend meetings of your city council or its equivalent? Do citizens attend these meetings only for protest purposes, or do they ever attend out of sheer desire to learn what is going on and lend their support and advice? To what extent are people made to feel welcome at these meetings? Does your community have any established mechanism through which the local citizenry can gain a better understanding of the workings of municipal government, and a better appreciation of the problems your municipal officials have to face in their efforts to provide essential services? How about the community development effort for this purpose?

15. Are there any other questions in regard to municipal government the committee feels should be looked into?

16. From the fact-finding indicated by the items and questions outlined above, has the committee identified any problems that call for attention, or any improvements it thinks ought to be made in municipal government operations? If yes, prepare a complete listing of these problems and operations, showing specifically what actions the committee recommends.

17. What is the thinking of your municipal officials in regard to these conclusions and recommendations for action? To what extent and in what ways do these officials agree or disagree with the committee?

Another institution of local government—the county government or its equivalent—is also a creature of the state. Technically, counties are legal subdivisions of the state, their boundaries and powers being prescribed by state law, and their primary legal purpose being to serve as local administrative units of state government. Counties were created for this purpose when distances and poor transportation made it much easier for certain governmental functions to be administered from the county seat than from the state capital.

Today many students of local government are of the opinion that there ought to be some consolidation of counties as a means of reducing costs and creating a broader tax base from which to raise funds for the public services counties provide. However, in the course of time, individual counties have acquired strong sentiments of local independence, and even though they are branches of state government, it does not seem politically realistic to expect any large number of county mergers in the near future unless the advocates of consolidation are able to mount sufficient political strength.

The influence of county government in state politics varies from a position of considerable influence in the southern and western states to relatively little influence in the New England states where local political power is more likely to be concentrated in legal subdivisions known as towns. The organizational structure of county government, along with its operations and services, also varies from region to region. But in most states, county government is an extremely important part of the local political scene and of major significance to community development.

The government committee should therefore conduct the same kind of fact-finding concerning county government which is suggested above in regard to municipal government. If other communities in your county, or all of them, are also engaged in community development efforts of their own as this guide recommends, the fact-finding and conclusions and recommendations for action concerning county government should be carried out as a county-wide cooperative venture with representatives from all these community development operations participating. This inter-community cooperation will be an important step toward the building of an area development effort, and the ultimate transition from phase one to phase two which we discussed in section 3, "Strategy."

As in the case of municipal government, a written statement should be prepared describing the existing form of county government. The names, titles, and terms of office of all elected county officials should be listed, along with all appointed heads of county departments or agencies. And an organizational chart should be drawn up showing in visual form the structure of county government, together with a written explanation making clear the meaning of the chart and how the county government operates overall.

Then, taking each county office, department, or agency separately, prepare a written statement covering the same items and questions outlined above under point 3 (a through f) in connection with municipal government. Also the equivalent of points 4 though 17 in the above outline should be applied in the fact-finding covering county government—including specific conclusions and recommendations for action.

The same kind of fact-finding should also be conducted in regard to all other local governmental institutions—township government, special district governments, such as park districts, road districts, cemetery districts, and any others that pertain to your community, with the exception of school districts which will be covered by the education committee. Included in the fact-finding report there should also be a written explanation of the various ways in which these local governments relate to each other.

Another important subject for the government committee to look into is local taxes. On this subject the committee should obtain:

1. The current assessed valuation: Of your municipality. Of your county. Of other tax-supported units.

2. Present local tax rates: Real estate property tax. Personal property tax. Other local taxes. Prepare a statistical breakdown showing where and for what purposes this tax revenue is currently being spent.

3. Over the past several years have these tax rates been: Increasing? Decreasing? Remaining about the same? What recommendations does the committee have concerning these local tax rates?

4. Bonded debt limits of local governmental units.

5. Bonded indebtedness currently outstanding and dates of maturity: Revenue bonds. General obligation bonds.

6. Over the past several years has the passage of local bond issues become easier or more difficult, or has there been no significant change in this respect? Cite statistics showing the actual record. Explain reasons for this record. What, if any, recommendations would the committee offer in light of this record?

As regards local voting patterns the committee's fact-finding should cover the following information:

1. The total voting-age population: In your municipality. In your county.

2. The percentage of the voting-age population currently registered to vote: In your municipality. In your county.

3. The percentage of the voting-age population that voted in the last general election: In your municipality. In your county.

4. How does this compare with previous general elections?

5. The percentage of the voting-age population in your municipality that voted in the last election for municipal officials. How does this

compare with previous elections for municipal officials? Give reasons for any significant changes.

6. The percentage of the voting-age population that voted in the last election for county officials, township officials, and other local officials: In your municipality. In the county as a whole. How do these figures compare with previous elections for the same offices?

7. How does your municipality compare from the standpoint of voter turnout with the county as a whole? With other municipalities in your county? With your state? With the nation?

8. How are candidates for public office in your various local governments placed in nomination?

9. Draw up a calendar of election dates for your local public offices, along with information concerning qualifications for voting, and when, how, and where local residents must register.

10. Do these statistics on voter registration and turnout suggest any community problems? If yes, how would the government committee characterize these problems, and what recommendations would it make? How do these conclusions compare with the conclusions set forth in this regard in the report of the census committee? If there are any major differences in the conclusions of the census committee and those of the government committee in this respect, what are the reasons for these differences?

In section 5 we pointed out that in most communities the man-made portion of the physical structure has grown up largely by chance and assumed whatever pattern circumstances happened to dictate. In recent years, however, more and more people have recognized the need for city or town planning in order to avoid the hodgepodge growth of the past, which has become one of the underlying causes of the physical deterioration confronting so many communities today and is becoming increasingly expensive to correct.

This recognition has also been extended to the concept of county planning, and in many areas a planning agency may cover several counties. Planning has also been extended to the state level, and there are regional planning agencies which cross state lines. As a function of government, planning has thus become a means of creating new laws to guide the present and future growth of communities and the areas in which they are located in ways that can help bring about the best possible conditions for modern living and sound economic and social development.

An official planning agency may help the community or area it serves determine which tracts of land are best suited for residential, commercial, industrial, agricultural, recreational, and other desired purposes. Land-use planning such as this should make it possible to establish a rational basis for dividing the total land available into generalized functional areas that harmonize instead of conflicting with each other, thus helping to avoid unwanted clutter which may lead to ugliness and objectionable living conditions. Within this broad planning framework, more detailed planning can be undertaken in the form of zoning, subdivision regulations, and building codes, which may protect both public and private interests by making for greater convenience, enhancing aesthetic values, and increasing and maintaining economic values. Official planning can help the community or area improve its network of streets and roads in order to make for better transportation and ease the flow of traffic. It can assist in determining the best-possible locations for public buildings, parks, and other community facilities, or help protect and improve those which already exist, and it can introduce greater efficiency into the task of budgeting for both short-range and long-range public improvements.

This kind of planning will require the establishment of an official planning agency by your municipality or county in accordance with the powers and functions granted by the state. Whether a function of municipal or county government, or both, the planning agency or agencies will be headed by a group of policy-making individuals—commonly called a planning commission which is usually appointed by the elected municipal or county governing body. The planning commission employs a professional staff which makes recommendations to the commission, and the commission in turn reports to the elected governing body that created it, which may in turn pass local laws or ordinances adopting various phases of the plans that have been recommended.

As a practical matter, however, this legal procedure is likely to be of minimum value from the standpoint of actually achieving desired planning objectives unless voluntary citizens groups in the community, or area concerned, exercise a genuine interest in the planning that is being done and are able to participate in the planning decisions. This means that for maximum success, city, county, or area planning must be deeply rooted in an active partnership between the people, their elected and appointed officials, and the professional planners they are paying. The creation and maintenance of such a partnership is an integral part of the community effort to which this development guide is committed.

If city, county, or area planning is done in this way—in partnership with the people—the plans will in the final analysis be the people's plans, not their hired planners' plans. If the planning is not done in this way, conflict, perhaps even bitterness, is likely to result, and the ensuing controversy may prevent or delay for years the benefits that official planning in accordance with formal legal procedures can bring. Moreover, city, county, or area planning is not static. Planning decisions must be periodically reviewed in light of changing conditions, revised, kept up-to-date, and subject to reasonable exceptions.

But if the citizenry is split into warring factions by planning that is done *for* the people instead of *with* the people, if decisions are simply handed down by arbitrary authority without giving the people a legitimate voice, the potential benefits of planning will at best be seriously retarded, at worst frozen into an impossible impasse. Instead of furthering the development of the community, this may contribute to its continuing deterioration.

Therefore, by supplying for discussion in the general assembly the essential facts about whatever official planning agencies may already exist at municipal, county, or area levels, or about the need for such agencies if they do not already exist, the government committee can help make the development effort a powerful vehicle through which to build the constructive citizen participation and democratic decision-making which—along with competent professional assistance—successful city, county, or area planning requires.

If your municipality is now being served by a city- or town-planning agency the government committee should therefore make detailed inquiries into how it is organized, how it operates, what it has done since it was established, what plans it is projecting for the immediate and long-range future, its annual cost and sources of funding, and what provisions have been made for citizen participation in its decisions. The same inquiries should be made into any existing county or area or regional planning agencies whose actions bear on your community. If your municipality is not being served by an official planning agency, the government committee may wish to consider the advisability of recommending that steps be taken to establish such an agency.

The committee may also see the need for a county- or area-planning agency. If this conclusion is reached it would be another move toward building an area-wide effort to bring about needed improvements that no one community in your area could accomplish alone, and again, would help pave the way toward the transition from the first phase of your development operation to the second and more formal phase which we discussed in section 3.

20

The Industrial Development Committee

VAST numbers of communities in today's small-town America are faced with the grim prospect of economic stagnation and ultimate decline —unless they can develop new opportunities to earn a living. In most rural areas any significant expansion of such opportunities will in the long run require an effort by the area as a whole in which all communities in the area work together, each acknowledging that what helps one of them helps all of them. Later in this section we will deal specifically with this matter of area-wide cooperation. First, however, we will focus on your community individually.

We may begin by thinking of three possibilities for industrial development: Bringing in outside companies that are looking for new plant locations; expanding industrial establishments already operating in your community; and starting "homegrown" industries based on promising new ideas or opportunities that show real potential but have yet to be developed.

Let's begin by looking at the possibility of attracting new industry from outside. Each year many companies reach the decision that it would be to their advantage to move an existing plant operation or establish a new branch plant, and in recent years there has been a significant trend toward locating in small communities that are able to meet the requirements of particular plant operations.

This industrial mobility and expansion, coupled with the need for economic renewal in communities throughout the nation, have made community industrial development one of the most competitive businesses in America. Thousands of industrial development organizations have been established at local, area, and regional levels; private industrial development consulting firms have opened; virtually all state governments have set up tax-supported industrial promotional agencies; and every new plant being contemplated is wanted by numerous communities.

This means that getting outside companies to choose your community for new plant locations is fraught with limitations, for inasmuch as the number of communities wanting a new plant greatly exceeds the number of plants likely to become available, there simply aren't going to be enough plants to go around. Some communities are going to get several new plants, others aren't going to get any, and unless your community is prepared to meet the competition it is likely to be one of those left out.

Attracting new industry from the outside thus becomes a matter of looking realistically at your community's assets and liabilities, trying to see it as outsiders would see it, determining what industrial activities it is suited for and that would be in keeping with local desires, then selling it to the appropriate companies. The act of selling your community is in many respects not much different than selling anything else, except that in this particular case the product you will be attempting to sell—your community, a human social organism—is an exceedingly complicated product which has to be as good a product as the citizenry can make it, and that means a lot of things.

Therefore, the development of a sound and expanding economy through plant locations by outside companies is dependent not only upon the economic resources your community currently has available—or, as a practical matter, could build or create—to meet the physical requirements of certain plant operations, it is also dependent upon many other factors, both tangible and intangible, including every aspect of community life. Thus, while the industrial development committee will play a special role in the task of plant location and economic expansion, the success of this task will depend to a large extent on the work of every other committee—and, in the final analysis, upon the effectiveness of the overall community effort which which this guide is concerned.

We have said your community must be prepared to meet the competition. "Prepared." In community industrial development that word cannot be overemphasized, for unless your community is willing to do all that is necessary to really get prepared, and until it actually is prepared, no amount of searching for industrial prospects, no amount of selling, or no amount of anything else is likely to be of any value. So, what are the crucial steps that must be taken to get your community prepared?

Let's consider some of the characteristics of modern industry and what reputable industrial management is likely to look for in choosing a new plant location. Obviously, the location of some industrial operations, such as mining, are dictated by the presence of certain natural resources or other technical factors that may have no bearing on the nature of the community, or on whether a community even exists at the point of location. But for manufacturers that have a choice of many locations, the nature and quality of the communities under consideration will be seriously scrutinized before final decisions are made.

All manufacturers must continuously improve their service and output if they are to remain in business, meaning that numerous physical requirements for a profitable operation must be met—an efficient plant facility, adequate transportation, competitive freight rates, an adequate supply of energy, a sufficient water supply of the essential quality, feasible access to raw materials, proximity to markets, and other such requirements that this section will specify. The compilation of this kind of data, so that the economic resources your community has to offer can be accurately presented, is one of the crucial steps in getting prepared to deal in a businesslike way with industrial management.

But let's assume that a given company has looked at a number of communities and has found that several of them have all the physical requirements for the plant operation being planned. By what criteria does the company then make its final choice?

Modern industry is not only interested in making money, it is also interested in being a good corporate citizen. This may have a certain ring of altruism, but in light of current social change, these two interests are virtually inseparable. Progressive management is becoming less and less willing to place itself in the position of contributing to blight, pollution, substandard housing, inadequate municipal facilities, ill public health, social disorder, community conflict, or in contributing to any other conditions that make for irresponsible citizenship and a poor environment in which to live. Modern industrialists simply want no part of that kind of a community. Today's industry wants up-to-date plants, and it wants up-to-date communities in which to locate them.

To a steadily increasing extent, corporate management is willing to apply its knowledge, imagination, and leadership to help improve the communities it chooses for new plant operations, for this responsibility is being recognized as a social and economic necessity if our system of free enterprise is to survive. But modern industry is also looking for communities in which the citizenry shares this concern, is willing to face up to its problems, and take practical steps based on fact—not blind emotion or hysteria—to resolve those problems. These are the communities most likely to provide a favorable climate for business and a desirable home for modern industry.

Industry, to put it bluntly, is looking for communities that will make it glad it came, communities in which there are progressive attitudes toward solid growth and an informed appreciation of the problems of business. It wants communities in which there is honest and efficient government willing to help, not hinder, industrial development. It wants communities in which there is an enlightened electorate, industrious people who believe in a day's work for a day's pay, and who are as much interested in seeing their industrial operations succeed as is management itself. Industry wants communities in which salaries, wages, and fringe benefits are fair and equitable to both employees and employers. It wants communities in which there are satisfactory banking and retail establishments. It wants educational, cultural, recreational, health, and other community facilities that make for desirable living conditions. It wants communities in which workers can enjoy life—communities which the families a new plant may bring in will regard as desirable places to live and raise their children.

All these factors, both physical and social—including a justified sense of local civic pride—will be closely taken into account by companies that would make desirable new additions to your community. The creation and continuous improvement of all these factors are a major part of getting prepared to meet the competition for industry.

Having discussed this critical matter of preparedness, we are now in a position to deal specifically with the fact-finding reports for which the industrial development committee will be responsible in starting this important part of the overall community effort. Basically, two major types of reports will be needed.

1. An *economic resources report* showing as accurately as possible what the community has to offer that will help industrial management make at least a tentative determination as to whether your community can meet the requirements of certain plant operations. This report, along with related materials which will be indicated below, is addressed to industry.

2. An *industrial problems report* concerning local needs and short-comings that influence your community's state of industrial pre-paredness, with specific recommendations for corrective action. This report is addressed to the general assembly.

In gathering the information for the economic resources report it is suggested that the committee divide itself into a number of task forces, each responsible for one or more of the categories in the economic resources outline which follows. These task forces can obtain much of the information they will need from other fact-finding committees in the development operation—boundary, census, community organizations, environmental improvement, government, retail trade and services, housing, education, library, health, recreation, history. The following suggested outline, designed to help compile your community's economic resources, may also suggest a table of contents the industrial development committee will need in organizing this particular report.

1. List and appropriately identify the persons who prepared the report.
2. Introduction.
   A. The purpose of the report, briefly indicating the kind of information it contains, and how this information was obtained.
   B. A brief explanation of the comprehensive community development operation of which the industrial development committee is a part, how this operation is engaging the citizenry as a whole, and what this means in terms of community-wide cooperation and the hopes and aspirations of the people.
   C. A brief sketch of the community's history with emphasis on its economy, and a description of local living conditions.

3. Location.
   A. A brief written statement telling where in your state your community is located, giving the name of your county, and describing the distance and direction of your community from major cities and points of interest. Describe briefly the nature of the area in which your community is situated, and give an approximation of the population within a five-hundred-mile radius.
   B. A series of maps that can be photographed and reduced in size to fit into the report. These should include: An outline map of the section of the United States where your community is situated, showing its location in relation to large and medium-size cities, indicated by concentric circles at intervals of fifty miles up to a five-hundred-mile radius around your community. A map of the community itself. Road maps, county and state. Plat maps covering the community and as much of the surrounding area as may seem useful.
   C. A series of photographs, including: An aerial photograph of the community and its environs. Photographs of community facilities, such as the downtown section, a selection of public buildings, schools, churches, residential areas, parks, and other features that will convey a pictorial image of your town and its surrounding area to be reproduced in the printed report.
4. Population and labor force: The number of persons employed and unemployed. A breakdown by age, sex, and race. Major occupational skills and industrial groupings. Average number of school years completed by persons age twenty-five and over. These figures should be given for the community itself, the county, and to whatever extent deemed appropriate, the immediately surrounding counties.
5. Labor relations, including: A listing of all unions covering workers in your community and surrounding area. Portion of the labor force unionized, and the portion not unionized. A history of labor-management relations for the past ten years, showing any work stoppages and the nature of settlements.
6. A listing of all manufacturing and wholesale operations in your community and surrounding area, including: Names of establishments. Ownerships. Types of businesses. Length of

time in the community. Reasons for locating in the community. The number of employees. A written statement from the management of each existing company on its view of your community and surrounding area as a locality in which to conduct its plant operation.

7. A listing of all retail establishments by trade groupings, including: Newspapers, radio and television stations, motels and hotels, and other eating and entertainment facilities.

8. Prevailing wage and salary rates and fringe benefits by industry and trade groupings.

9. A listing of all professional services.

10. Transportation, including: Railroads and railroad maps. Highways and mileage to principal cities. Trucking companies serving the community, giving addresses, telephone numbers, and names of owners or managers. Bus lines, giving addresses, telephone numbers, and names of presidents or managers. Airports and airline service, with map showing proximity to community.Rental car services, giving addresses, telephone numbers, and names of managers. Water transportation and water transport companies, giving addresses, telephone numbers, and names of managers. Freight rates.

11. Utilities.

   A. Electric power, including: Name, address, and telephone number of utility and president or manager. Map of service lines, rate schedules. Capacity. Average seasonal loads. Peak loads. Available surplus.

   B. Natural gas, including: Name, address, and telephone number of utility and president or manager. Map of service lines. Rate schedules. Capacity. Average seasonal demand. Peak demand. Available surplus.

   C. Other fuels, including: A description of each. Costs. Quality and quantity available. Names, addresses, and telephone numbers of companies and presidents or managers.

   D. Water, including: Name, address, and telephone number of utility and president or manager. Source of supply and capacity. Map of water lines. Rate schedules. Average daily consumption. Available surplus. Chemical analysis and total hardness. Temperature range. Finished water, with data on hydrogen-ion concentration, residual chlorine, and other chemical properties.

E. Telephone service, including: Name, address, and telephone number of utility and president or manager. Services available. Rate schedules.

F. Sewage disposal, including: Name, address, and telephone number of utility and president or manager. Detailed description of system, map, charges, treatment process, usage, capacity and potential, plans for expansion if needed.

12. Plant sites. (NOTE: A plant site is not merely an open piece of land, but a property at least partially developed with essential roads and utilities so the site can be fully developed within minimum time limits to meet specific plant operational requirements.) The following information should be given for each site: Detailed description of location and boundaries. Acreage, contour of land, and drainage. Load-bearing capacity of soil. Ownership. Railroads and spur lines serving the site, or possible arrangement for spurs if needed. Highways and roads serving the site. Power available to the site, electric, natural gas, other. Water lines serving the site, size of mains, pressure and capacity. Sewer lines, size and capacity. Zoning. Taxes. Fire insurance classification. Employee transportation. Maps, topographic, aerial, and black-and-white glossy photographs. Acreage adjoining this site now available that would be suitable for possible future expansion.

13. Available industrial buildings, including: A complete description of each. Availability for occupancy. Service facilities. Fire insurance classification. Floor plans. Photographs. Ownership. Land area, and other information as indicated above for plant sites.

14. Contractors, including: Building contractors, giving names, addresses, and telephone numbers of companies and presidents or managers. Other types of contractors, with the same information as that given for building contractors. Job capabilities.

15. Capital resources, including: Banks, and available assets. Building and loan associations, and available assets. Credit unions, and available assets. Other sources of financing, including indi-

viduals, community industrial fund, and state and federal sources.

16. Government, including: Form of government, municipal, county, other local government. Services available from each. Zoning, building codes, and other regulations concerning construction and industrial plant operations. Taxes, including: Municipal. County. State. Other local taxes.

17. Geography, including: Climate. Topography. Natural resources. Nonfuel minerals. Fuel minerals, coal, oil, gas, others. Stone deposits. Clay deposits. Forests and forest products. Describe location, quality, quantity, type, and availability of each natural resource.

18. Agriculture, including: Soil types. Types and sizes of farms. Farm products. Potential other farm products. Farm labor. Greenhouses.

19. Community facilities.

    A. Education, including: Public school system. Community college. University. Opportunities for adult education and manpower or vocational training. Availability of job aptitude testing. A brief description of each educational institution, giving enrollments, research capabilities, and public services offered.

    B. Churches and names of pastors.

    C. Directory of community organizations.

    D. Public library services.

    E. Health facilities, including: Hospitals, clinics, nursing homes, others.

    F. Parks and other recreational facilities not elsewhere listed.

    G. Special tourist attractions not elsewhere listed.

This completes the general outline for the economic resources report. A supplemental outline is set forth below which the committee may use to obtain the information called for under category 6 in the economic resources outline concerning manufacturing and wholesale establishments already existing in your community and area. It may also be useful in determining potential opportunities for expanding current operations or starting new industrial operations. This supplemental outline is in essence an *industrial inventory*. In taking this inventory, the following questionnaire—with whatever alterations may be needed to fit your local or area situation—should be duplicated and filled out for each existing industrial operation.

QUESTIONNAIRE FOR INDUSTRIAL INVENTORY

(In duplicating this questionnaire form be sure to leave enough space for complete answers for each question. Also, bear in mind that much of the information called for in this questionnaire is confidential in nature and must be treated and tabulated accordingly.)

Name of firm _____

Address of local plant _____

Home office of company _____

Is this plant located inside or outside the city limits? _____

Name and title of the official completing questionnaire _____

1. How long has this plant been in its present location? _____

2. What are the major reasons this plant was located here? _____

3. Have you found this location to be satisfactory? Yes ____ No ____ In some ways yes, in other ways no ____

4. What are the principal reasons for your answer to question 3 above? _____
_____

5. If you had it to do over again, would you still choose this location? Yes ____ No ____ Why? _____

6. How old is your present building? _____

7. Do you own or lease this building? Own ____ Lease ____

8. How many square feet of floor space do you use? _____

9. Does the floor space you use include the whole building, or just part of the building? _____

10. If the space you are using includes just part of the building, how many square feet of floor space is there in the remaining part of the building? _____
Is this additional floor space now being used, and if so, by what firm and for what purpose? _____
Is this additional space currently available for occupancy? _____
If this additional space is currently available for occupancy, what kind of business would you recommend as a suitable occupant? _____

11. Do you need more floor space than you are now using? Yes ____ No ____ If yes, how much? _____

12. Could your present building be economically expanded? _____

13. Do you have any plans for expanding your present operation within the next few years? ____ If yes, about how much expansion do you plan, and about how soon? _____

14. Is your present building one-story or multistory? _____
    Which do you prefer? _____

15. What are the present products or services of your operation in their order of importance? _____

16. Could you profitably increase the production of any of these products or services? _____ If yes, which ones? _____
    Could this increased production be accomplished in the space you now occupy, or would you need more space? _____
    Would this increased production require an additional building? _____
    If yes, how large would this building need to be, and under what conditions would such a building be feasible for acquisition? _____
    Would this require you to move your entire operation to another building, or would it mean using two buildings? _____

17. Is there enough land adjoining your present location for any expansion you have in mind, or would you need another site? _____

18. What products or services in addition to your present ones could you produce in this community or area? _____
    What would be required to make this possible? _____

19. Do any unused waste products result from your present operation? Yes ____
    No ____ If yes, what are they? _____
    Could these unused waste products be used commercially? Yes ____ No ____ If yes, what requirements would have to be met for this purpose? _____

20. What raw materials do you use? _____

21. Where do these raw materials come from? _____

22. How are these raw materials transported to your plant? _____

23. About what volume of these raw materials do you use annually? _____
    _____
    About how much do they cost? _____

24. If any or all of these raw materials are obtained from outside this area, would it be economically feasible to obtain any or all of them from inside this area? Yes ____
    No ____ If yes, would this be desirable from the standpoint of other business considerations? Yes ____ No ____ If the answers to both of these questions are yes, what would have to be done to make local acquisition of these materials possible? _____

25. What parts and supplies other than raw materials do you use? _____

26. What quantity of each of these parts and supplies do you use annually? ____
    _____
    At about what cost? _____

27. How are these parts and supplies transported to your plant? _____

28. Where do each of these parts and supplies come from?

     Part or Supply   Place from which it comes

_____   _____

29. If some or all of these parts and supplies come from outside this area, would it be economically possible for them to be produced within this area? Yes ___ No ___ If yes, which ones and to what extent? _____

30. Would you buy any or all of these parts and supplies from sources inside this area if they could be obtained under the right conditions? Yes ___ No ___ If yes, what conditions would have to be met? _____

31. What are your present major market areas? _____

32. Are there any feasible possibilities for new industrial operations inside this community or area that could provide an additional market for your operation? Yes ___ No ___ If yes, what would be required to make such new operations practical? _____

33. How many people do you employ at the present time? Men ___ Women ___ Total _____

34. What is the breakdown of your work force by occupations, skilled, semi-skilled, and unskilled? _____

35. Are there seasonal variations in the size of your work force? Yes ___ No ___ If yes, what is the maximum and minimum size of your work force by seasons? _____

    Are there any practical ways your season of maximum employment could be extended? Yes ___ No ___ If yes, does this provide an opportunity for one or more new commercial operations within the area that would supplement or complement your operation? _____

36. What is the average hourly wage of your employees by occupational group? _____

37. About how much (in round figures) is your annual payroll? _____

38. Would you recommend this community or area to other companies for other plant operations? Yes ___ No ___ If yes, why? _____ If no, why? _____

39. If your answer to question 38 above was no, could any corrective actions be taken that would reverse your answer? Yes ___ No ___ If yes, what actions would you recommend? _____

40. What types of new industrial plant operations would you suggest as most suitable for location in this community or area? _____ Please summarize reasons _____

With the information obtained from the economic resources outline and industrial inventory, plus any other information the industrial development committee may deem appropriate, a small subcommittee should be appointed to write the economic resources report. In writing this report, care should be exercised not to reveal any information gained from the industrial inventory that companies supplying this information might not want included. This can be handled by consolidating the industrial inventory data in a manner that shows whatever opportunities may exist for new industrial activity without naming specific companies except to list those that have current plant operations in your community or area. Further, the writing committee should check its draft material with appropriate management executives before the report is printed. Close working relationships between the industrial development committee and existing management in your community or area are of utmost importance and should be carefully cultivated—bearing in mind appropriate limitations. Information not included in the economic resources report can be kept on file for use in helping to determine how certain new industrial operations may be located or started in your community or area.

Inasmuch as the basic purpose of this report is to show outsiders what your community has to offer industry, it should also be kept in mind that this report is in essence a selling tool. Therefore, this report should put your community's best foot forward, but make no claims that cannot be verified. The economic resources report should be neatly arranged, carefully indexed, easy to read, and put together in a manner that makes it possible to insert new pages as needed to keep it up-to-date. Ideally, it should be printed and bound in an attractive notebook cover that gives it a professional and businesslike appearance.

The number of copies needed will depend upon how much circulation the report is to be given, but this is not a document to be mailed out indiscriminately. Wholesale mailings of this report to recipients from whom there has been no prior indication of interest would be wasteful. A few copies should be on file in your state industrial development department, in the industrial development sections of all utilities and transportation companies serving your area, and in the offices of all other agencies interested in your area who are in a position to receive inquiries from manufacturers looking for new plant locations—for example, an area chamber of commerce or similar type of organization. Certainly, copies should be placed in your local chamber, also in your local banks and other appropriate business firms, plus any public offices such as your municipal government, that may be queried by a potential industrial prospect. Beyond this, the economic resources report should be distributed only to companies from which an indication of possible interest has been received.

The industrial development committee should also prepare a brief brochure that provides a quick glimpse of the community and highlights some of the major points of local interest, care being taken not to oversell or distort prevailing conditions. This brochure may contain a few well-selected photographs, and if cost permits, should be printed in color. One item this brochure definitely should include is a succinct description of the overall community development effort, thus showing the context in which the industrial development portion of this effort is being conducted. This will convey the important message that here is a community whose people, organizations, and official public bodies are fully committed to *all* aspects of local improvement, and who are demonstrating that commitment by seriously working together to build the best possible place in which to live and work and make a home. An extra supply of large-scale maps of your community and area should be on hand for use in dealing with industrial prospects who may come in for personal inspection tours.

We now turn to the industrial problems report to be addressed to the general assembly. In preparing this report, the industrial development committee should carefully review section 6, "Procedures and Responsibilities of the Fact-Finding Committees." This report will be quite different from the economic resources report in that instead of cataloging what your community has to offer industry, this report will focus on local conditions that could cause companies seeking new plant locations *not to choose your community*.

Material for the industrial problems report may come from other committee reports and from the secretary's reports on previous assembly meetings that have brought out negative factors on which corrective action has yet to be taken, or has been started but not completed. Additional material may come from the industrial development committee's own fact-finding. In gathering the material for the industrial problems report, the committee should ask itself in all candor such questions as: What major defects does your community have that make it ill prepared to meet the competition for industry, or that could make it unacceptable for purposes of a new plant location?

Defects such as these may be revealed by the fact-finding that goes into preparing the economic resources report, and in making the industrial inventory. In what categories called for in this research is your community lacking? Or in what respects does your community not really measure up? For example, does your community have adequately developed plant sites readily available on attractive terms? Does it have any existing vacant buildings suitable for modern industrial operations? If yes, are these buildings readily available on attractive terms? Does your community have adequate water and sewage systems with sufficient surplus capacity to accommodate new industry, and how much and what kind of new industry? If not, would it be feasible to create such surplus capacity, and to what extent and under what conditions? Do you have adequate fire and police protection? What about your fire insurance rates?

Have any industrial operations moved out of your community in recent years, and if so, why? Have any industries considered moving into your community in recent years, then decided not to, and if so, why? If either or both of these events have occurred, have they been due to dissatisfactions with your community that could be corrected? If there are any industrialists that currently have plants in your community, what do they say about the desirability of operating there? Don't be irritated if they state some truths that may be less than flattering. If such truths exist they must be faced and constructively considered. Why did these industrialists choose your community as a location? Do they have any suggestions for actions they think would make your community more attractive to industry?

If your community has a local chamber of commerce do the chamber and the industrial development committee work together as closely as they should? What about the local government, the banks, utilities, and other business firms in this respect? Are all such organizations fully supportive of the overall community development effort? If not, why? What corrective action may this suggest?

Suppose an industrial scout came to look over your community, and without identifying himself asked questions about the community to people at random—filling station attendants, barbers, waitresses, bartenders, shopkeepers, and the like—what kinds of comments would he be likely to hear? In what ways, if any, is your community lacking from the standpoint of desirable living conditions? What about available housing? Health services and facilities? Are there sufficient recreational, cultural, and entertainment opportunities either in the community itself or at reasonable distances within the area?

Take a look at some of the fact-finding reports that have to do with intangible community attributes—for example, the report from the community attitudes committee. Do these reports reveal any unfavorable or negative traits that have yet to be changed? Also, look at the positive actions that have been taken as a result of the discussions of these reports, and consider the improvement projects that have been mounted since the overall development effort began. What do these factors say about the state of your community's preparedness for industry?

In making this critical examination, the committee will find many positive features for purposes of industrial development. It is also likely to find some disadvantages. Indeed, it will probably find some disadvantages that as a practical matter simply cannot be changed or eliminated, and which therefore place definite limitations on the types of industries for which your community is suited. But it is far better to recognize these limitations than to waste time and energy chasing the impossible.

However, by thoughtfully examining the community's problems and limitations from the standpoint of potential industrial development, it is possible to discover certain changes or adjustments that could be made to correct or get around some of these deficiencies and limitations, thus enabling the community to increase its state of industrial preparedness. This is why it is so important to submit for discussion in the general assembly the industrial problems report, organized and presented as indicated in section 6.

This will make it possible for the assembly as a whole to wrestle with the needs that confront the community concerning industry. Thus, whatever decisions are made, whatever solutions are determined to be appropriate, whatever actions are taken for the purpose of industrial development will become a product of the total community effort, not merely of a small inner circle—meaning, that these decisions, solutions, and actions will have the public understanding and acceptance they will need to be fully carried out. And this will further the basic goal of community development we discussed in section 2. The citizenry will thus feel a stake in the success of these actions, and the state of community preparedness for industry will steadily increase.

One practical means of overcoming certain limitations for purposes of plant location is to join forces with other communities in your area so that industrial development will become a cooperative enterprise at both local and area levels free of the kind of fruitless competition between individual towns that in so many areas has become a major deterrent to industrial development. Hopefully, as we have repeatedly recommended, each community in your area will engage in an overall development effort of its own, thus making improvements that can only be made locally, while all communities in the area work together to make improvements that can be made only through an area effort—one of which may be the business of obtaining new industry.

A decision to work cooperatively with your neighboring communities on an area-wide basis for the purpose of attracting new industry would make it possible to give practical and objective consideration to exactly where in the area, or what particular communities in the area, would be most advantageous for the development of new plant sites and locations. The area—which may be your county or two or more counties—must be determined through consultation by representatives from the individual local communities. But whatever the area is determined to be, new industry whether located in your community or in a neighboring one will strengthen the economy of the entire area, increase the number of jobs, produce expanding business opportunities, and result in a growing tax base to support essential public services and facilities. As we have pointed out earlier, this may be for many communities the only practical means of developing and maintaining a sound economy.

In section 3, we recommended that phase one of the community effort not be started by setting up a formal incorporated agency. We further recommended that special loan or grant funds from state or federal agencies be avoided until the effort becomes firmly established through local initiative. We made these recommendations because nationwide experience has repeatedly demonstrated that by building a solid base of local action through an informal structure such as the general assembly and its varied committees before formal development tools are introduced, the community will increase significantly its ability to make effective use of these development tools.

By the time the industrial development committee has conducted the research for the economic resources report and is preparing its industrial problems report for discussion in the general assembly, phase one of the effort should have become a strong civic enterprise, and a series of specific community improvement projects to which we referred in section 17, "From Study to Action," should have been completed or at least well under way.

Assuming the operation has reached this state of maturity, it may now be appropriate to consider the formation of a formal industrial development corporation legally empowered to deal in industrial real estate and to transact whatever other business may be necessary for the purpose of attracting industry. This could include such actions as the acquiring of land and the development of plant sites or industrial parks, the acquisition of existing vacant buildings, the construction of industrial buildings to meet specific plant specifications, the sale or leasing of such properties, advertising and promotion, and trips to meet with corporate executives or industrial realtors who are in a position to help find industrial prospects.

The development corporation may be set up as an official industrial commission as a part of municipal or county government authorized to receive and make use of local tax funds, in some states issue revenue bonds for industrial facilities to be paid off by the new plant operations using the facilities. Or the community's industrial development organization may be a private nonprofit corporation or foundation supported by voluntary subscriptions or the sale of shares. This organization should be set up in a way that makes it eligible to generate funds for the specific purpose of industrial development. Decisions as to the legal form of this organization will depend on prevailing laws and ordinances applicable in your particular locale, and upon the expressed wishes of the people. Also, decisions must be made as to whether this corporate entity should be organized on a strictly local basis serving only your community, or set up on a county or area basis with appropriate representation from all communities concerned.

The industrial development committee should explore the organizational possibilities best suited to your community, then settle on *one* entity to deal with industrial prospects and sources of possible prospects. Cooperation among all relevant groups is essential, but more than one group dealing with industry independently of each other would be disastrous. The committee's conclusions in this regard should be included in its report to the general assembly.

If your community already has an industrial development corporation, the committee's report to the general assembly should include a description of this organization, its activities, problems, needs, and the like, so the citizenry may obtain a thorough understanding of its activities, realistically assess its practical value, and determine what action may be needed to strengthen its work.

As a further step toward getting prepared for industrial development, two important selling teams should be formed: A traveling team, and a home team. The members of these teams may be interchangeable so it will not be necessary for the same persons to be available every time the teams are needed. However, for purposes of continuity and coordination, someone—perhaps the chairman of the industrial development committee or of the development corporation—should chair the group from which these two sales teams are drawn.

The traveling team, consisting of two or three well-qualified persons, has the responsibility of taking trips from time to time to make known in person what the community has to offer industry and establish close working relationships between the community and strategic outside sources that are in a position to help find industrial prospects.

One of the most important sources for this purpose will be your state industrial development agency. This agency is charged with the task of attracting new industry to your state and trying to prevent industrial movement out of the state. And it is anxious to succeed in this task. It is probably the principal center in the state to which companies considering a new plant location write for information and send specifications for new plants they are planning to locate. This agency is therefore especially interested in communities and areas that are well prepared to meet these specifications and to deal in an effective and businesslike manner with its industrial prospects. It is virtually impossible for this agency to help a community or area for which this agency does not have detailed information, and obviously this agency is not inclined to refer an industrial prospect to a community it feels is likely to bungle the matter—or "blow the deal." Thus, it is essential to see to it that this state agency is made fully aware of what your community or area has to offer, that you are indeed prepared, and organized to conduct business with industrial prospects in an effective manner. This is one of the jobs for the traveling team.

Also, personal contacts should be made with all other public offices, both state and federal, that may receive inquiries from companies looking for new plant locations. Other important sources with which these personal contacts should be made are the principal offices of utilities and railroads that serve your area, your state chamber of commerce, and any other organizations that solicit new plant locations and receive inquiries in this regard. Organizations of this kind will cooperate closely with you *once they are convinced your community and area are prepared to meet the competition and are really engaged in constructive action*.

The traveling team should make advance appointments to visit the appropriate officials in these public and private offices, become well acquainted, and make sure they are kept supplied with up-to-date copies of your economic resources report, brochure, maps, plant site reports, and any other material they may request. They should also be kept informed as to your comprehensive community development work. These visits should be discreetly followed up by correspondence, telephone, and additional visits to maintain relationships and keep them current. *But don't "bug" them*! Whenever possible it would be a good idea to get these officials to visit your community, to see for themselves what you have to offer, and become further aware of your comprehensive development effort.

The traveling team will also have the responsibility of visiting executives in the home offices of specific industrial prospects. The prime selling task on such trips will be to get the prospects to visit your community or area so negotiations can be carried on in your home territory, *and until the prospect gives written authorization no public announcement should be made of the fact that the contact has been made or that negotiations are in process*. Failure to maintain strict secrecy in this respect until the company itself is ready for a public announcement is one of the best ways to lose a good industrial prospect. It is also a good way to raise the hopes of the community for a possible letdown that could be damaging to local confidence, thereby causing a loss of community support.

The home team is responsible for acting as host and guide for any industrial prospect or executive who comes in to visit and inspect your community or area. Each member of the home team, as is true of each member of the traveling team, should become an expert on one or more categories of the economic resources report and be fully prepared to answer whatever questions the prospect may ask. One person should act as the chief spokesman for the team, referring questions as necessary to other members of the team. If a question is asked to which no one on the team knows the correct answer, the response should be exactly that —followed by assurance that the desired information will be obtained by a certain time and reported. In this way the representatives of an industrial prospect or development agency can hold a businesslike meeting with the home selling team and in a minimum of time obtain the information they wish, then be taken on a personal tour to inspect whatever is of interest to them. If entertainment is in order, such as an evening dinner party, this should be arranged in a manner that will convey a warm and friendly feeling to the outside visitors.

It is not necessary to accept an industry that the community would not wish to have or to make concessions that would be detrimental to the community's interest. However, it should be remembered that in the competitive business of industrial development the community is usually the seller, the industry the buyer, and until an industrial prospect is really sold, the selling team should keep on selling without asking questions about the prospect's private affairs that might have the effect of scaring it away.

To avoid becoming involved with a company that would not be good for the community, such as one which is not credit-worthy, or that would bring in a plant the community would find more harmful than helpful, each prospect should be discreetly investigated. One bad experience can sour the whole community and become a serious obstacle to future industrial development. Insofar as possible, the investigation of a potential prospect should be completed prior to meeting with the company's representatives and without the company's knowledge. This is another instance in which the various development agencies mentioned above, such as your state industrial development office, can be helpful. But it is not always possible to make this investigation in advance, and it is in these cases that the community's sales teams must be especially careful not to make any moves or ask any questions that would risk the loss of what could be an excellent opportunity before the prospect is thoroughly sold.

For example, I am reminded of a community that was visited by representatives of an industrial prospect, and immediately following the introductions a local businessman said, "Before we get started the first thing I'd like to see is your financial statement." That killed the negotiations. After about an hour of disjointed talk the prospect's representatives politely excused themselves and left. They were never heard from by this community again, but a few months later located their new plant starting with more than two hundred employees—in a different state.

You can always decide not to make a final agreement for the actual location of a given plant—after you have done the selling job. Further, if you are dealing with a reliable company it will respect your desire to know what your community is getting into, if expressed at the appropriate time. For the success of a plant operation depends to a large extent on establishing relationships between the company and the community that are mutually satisfactory.

The question of what concessions may be warranted in attracting new industry must be determined on the merits of each individual case and the extent of economic benefit the community or area may realize over a reasonable period of time. No community should "give away Main Street." A stable industrial operation is not likely to be achieved unless the company is willing to make a sufficient investment of its own. However, it should also be noted that many good companies are interested in some form of local or area participation as an indication of community faith and continued interest in the success of the industrial operation.

There are many ways of prospecting for industry, several of which we have already mentioned. Advertising, searching for news items in financial and business journals that suggest possible leads, conversations with sales representatives that call on local retailers, sending out judicious letters of inquiry are other possible ways. But to emphasize the point one more time, it is first essential to get prepared. Once this is accomplished and news of that fact, along with news concerning the total community effort, gets around, many possibilities will begin to appear—particularly if this overall effort and state of preparedness are extended into all the communities in your area and accepted as matters of basic concern by the area as a whole.

Now, let's go back to the second route to industrial development mentioned at the beginning of this section—the expansion of industries already located in your area—especially small enterprises with definite growth potential. Many communities and areas make the mistake of devoting enormous amounts of time and expense trying to lure industries from outside, while ignoring the industries they already have. These existing industrial operations may have any number of problems which constructive and timely action by the community could help solve. The industrial development committee should therefore make a special point of finding out about such problems and of learning what actions the community could take that would be helpful. This in itself may result in a significant increase in job opportunities. The industrial inventory is an important instrument for this purpose. Careful analysis of the information obtained through this inventory may suggest a number of sound possibilities for industrial expansion from within, while at the same time helping to determine what kinds of additional industrial operations are well suited for your area, thus suggesting possible ideas and leads that would otherwise be overlooked.

A third route to industrial development mentioned at the beginning of this section is "homegrown" industries that could be started locally on the basis of promising new ideas. This too is closely related to the industrial inventory, but in addition to this information, there may be people in your community or area who are not now in business but have some good ideas, who with a bit of assistance in the form of financing and technical advice could become successful local entrepreneurs. Many of the nation's largest industries started from a one-man operation in a homemade shop, and many communities have found this form of industrial development highly beneficial.

For this purpose it is suggested that what might be called a "home industry council" be established. This could be a part of the industrial development committee or the industrial development corporation or commission. It could be set up as a branch of the chamber of commerce, or as a special entity under whatever sponsorship seems most appropriate in your particular locale. This committee or council should consist of people who are skilled in the varied aspects of business, who know the hazards of starting a new business enterprise and are willing to volunteer a bit of time. Additional counsel may be called in as needed from a community college or state university or from interested state or federal agencies. The functions of this special committee would be to assist persons who have ideas that appear to be economically sound, help these persons get started, then stand by with free guidance as needed to get them successully established.

New industrial potential may also be discovered through new uses of existing natural resources in your area, and all possibilities in this regard should be carefully investigated. Community industrial development in today's economy has become a challenge of great magnitude. But with determination, effective organization and action, and a realistic assessment of the potentialities and limitations of your community and area, it is a challenge that can be met.

21

The Retail Trade and
Services Committee

NO community in today's small-town America can hope to satisfy all the demands of its people for consumer goods and services. Even taking into account those towns which have remained fairly stable or attained a fair amount of growth, it is inevitable that a large percentage of local shopping dollars are going to be spent outside the home community, often in cities at considerable distances away. If, however, within the limits of practical economics a respectable portion of this money can be recaptured and put into local circulation by inducing people to do more shopping at home this would be an important stimulant to your community's economy. In fact, a successful effort to increase the volume of retail trade and services in your town can be regarded as the equivalent of a new industrial payroll.

This is not an easy task. For in the face of modern mass production, sophisticated merchandising practices in metropolitan areas, high-speed transportation, and interstate highways, the small-town merchant is severely handicapped by outside competition. The growing number of empty store buildings in thousands of once-thriving towns attests to this trend. Indeed, the time has come when the local merchant who fails to exercise every legitimate means to please his customers is not likely to be able to stay in business. Or, he will manage to exist only as something of a hanger-on. The problem is not only that of meeting the competition of lower prices and wider choices available in urban shopping centers, it is also a matter of having to compete with the growing desire for travel, for entertainment, or for just an overnight outing.

Then too there are often internal factors that weaken the position of small community merchants, such as complaints and countercomplaints concerning local business practices. This kind of wrangling sometimes becomes so rife as to actually drive shopping dollars away, thus increasing even more the difficulty of meeting outside competition.

All these competitive factors, both external and internal, are powerful obstacles for your local merchants to overcome. They influence the sale of virtually every retail item or service, and they influence deeply your community's economy. The vitality of your community therefore rests in no small part on the ability of your local merchants to maintain profitable enterprises and make themselves a vital force in civic affairs.

This calls for a great deal of cooperation among the business people themselves to develop the best and most attractive trading center they can. But it also calls for a degree of cooperation within the citizenry at large that will cause all local residents to look upon the community's business district as theirs, recognizing that its success is essential not only to the well-being of those who are in business but to the well-being of the entire community. This gets back to the intangible ingredients of human behavior we discussed under the heading of community attitudes. It means neighborliness. It means a common bond of good will, a network of friendly personal relationships between customers and those who serve them. It means a pervading spirit of community loyalty, local solidarity, and civic consciousness. It means all those qualities that enable people to know, enjoy, appreciate, and feel responsible for each other. These are extremely important assets for building your community's economy, and they apply to retail trade and services just as they do to industrial development.

Within the framework of these qualities of human feeling and mutual concern, the community as a whole—customers and merchants alike —can look objectively and realistically at itself with an eye toward discovering what practical actions can be taken to maintain and perhaps increase its volume of retail trade.

Research and the formation of recommendations for this purpose will be the job of the retail trade and services committee. All members of the committee should carefully review section 6, "Procedures and Responsibilities of the Fact-Finding Committees," the report of the community attitudes committee, and the secretary's reports on meetings of the general assembly—then map out plans to accomplish the work this section suggests.

One of the most effective instruments of fact-finding concerning retail trade and services is a consumer buying habits survey. This is used by virtually every major merchandising organization to determine the likes and dislikes of its potential customers, get as clear a picture as possible of their shopping habits, learn what they are buying, where they are buying, and why. If from this information the merchandiser finds that his store layout, his stock, service, prices, advertising, merchandising practices, or the very appearance of his place of business are causing him to lose sales to his competition, he quickly makes whatever changes he can to improve his position in the market. Most merchants in small communities cannot afford the cost of this kind of research, but as a part of your community development effort it can be done on a voluntary basis at very little cost.

In this case the object of the consumer buying habits survey is not to measure the competitive positions of your local businesses against each other, but to determine how well all of your community's businesses collectively are meeting the competition from other localities. Thus, it is a means of devising actions to improve the competitive position of your community as a trading center.

A survey form for this purpose is outlined below. The committee can make whatever alterations to this form it deems necessary to best fit your specific local situation. The members of the committee may themselves serve as the survey team, or other persons in the community may be recruited for this purpose. However, it is suggested that those who make up the survey team *not* include anyone who is in business, which the committee itself undoubtedly will. A survey team consisting entirely of consumers will reduce the possibility of evasive answers and increase the likelihood of learning what the citizenry as a whole really thinks about your community as a place in which to shop or not to shop. Suggested possibilities for the survey team would be a group of articulate housewives, or a high school class supervised by its teacher, or a class of community college students if there is such a college in or nearby your community. If the survey team consists of students with their teacher serving as the team chairman, it would be a good idea to select a class engaged in a subject for which the conduct of the consumer buying habits survey would provide a practical learning experience—for example, home economics or business administration. This would accomplish the primary purpose of the survey, and as a by-product add to the students' education.

The survey can be done on a sampling basis, or if feasible cover virtually all households in the community. The more extensive the coverage the better. Using the map prepared by the boundary committee, divide the community into districts and make sure each district is thoroughly surveyed. Arrange for the persons who are to form the survey team to assemble at a central location—ideally, the community development headquarters—on the morning the survey is scheduled to start, and organize themselves into crews, one crew for each district. After receiving final instructions and street assignments, the crews then move out into their respective districts with the survey questionnaires. If the sampling method is used, a questionnaire can be taken to every other house or every third house along each side of every street and road in the community. In any event, it is highly desirable to try to complete the actual field work in one day, at least by the second day. By completing the field work quickly, the survey will be more likely to reflect immediate attitudes or first thoughts—which will provide a more reliable index of actual shopping habits.

Also, it is essential for the members of the survey team *not to reveal* who answered which questionnaire. This means, as was the case in the community attitudes survey, that a system must be devised which assures each respondent that his or her answers are given anonymously, and that this anonymity will be scrupulously preserved. With this assurance, all respondents should be urged to answer the questionnaires with complete candor, expressing what they like or dislike about shopping locally and why and to what extent they shop elsewhere. If the questionnaires can be filled out by personal interviews without causing the respondents to doubt the anonymity of their answers, this would be much the best method from the standpoint of completeness. If this is not possible, then the questionnaires will have to be handed to the respondents to fill out themselves. The members of the survey team should explain to each respondent the purpose of the survey and its importance, stress the fact that no names will be identified, and make sure the respondent understands the questions. If it is necessary to leave the questionnaires to be filled out by the respondents themselves, arrangements should be made to pick them up later that same day or at the very latest the following day. As we suggested in connection with the community attitudes survey, two possible ways of assuring the anonymity of the respondents are to supply plain envelopes in which the questionnaires can be sealed, or have them folded and dropped into sealed containers similar to secret ballot boxes.

The consumer buying habits survey can be aided considerably by explaining at a meeting of the general assembly just before the survey is due to begin, its importance to the development effort, how and when it is to be conducted, the fact that none of the respondents will be identified, and the need for candid and complete answers. This public announcement can be accompanied by appropriate publicity, including reminders of the survey date and requests for community-wide cooperation. The suggested survey form is as follows:

CONSUMER BUYING HABITS SURVEY

(In duplicating this form be sure to leave enough space for full and complete answers.)

Introduction: This survey is being taken as a part of the community development program to help determine how our local business district could be made more attractive, and in that way improve our community's economy. The overall results of this survey will be tabulated and reported for discussion in a meeting of the general assembly. *But each questionnaire is anonymous, and the name of the person answering it will not be identified. The survey is not concerned with who or what families the information comes from but only with the collection of information. Your cooperation in giving complete answers to all questions, saying frankly and honestly exactly what you think or feel—knowing your name will not be revealed—will be extremely helpful and very much appreciated.*

1. About how much in each of the shopping categories listed below do you buy in our community and in other communities? Please place an X in the proper columns.

ITEM	IN OUR COMMUNITY				IN OTHER COMMUNITIES			
	All	Most	Some	None	All	Most	Some	None
Food								
Clothes: Men								
Women								
Children								
Shoes: Men								
Women								
Children								
Light appliances								
Heavy appliances								

ITEM	IN OUR COMMUNITY				IN OTHER COMMUNITIES			
	All	Most	Some	None	All	Most	Some	None
Furniture								
Bedding, towels, linen, etc.								
Other household items								
Fabrics and sewing supplies								
Jewelry, watches, etc.								
Drugs and toilet articles								
Hardware								
Luggage								
Stationery goods and office supplies								
Books, magazines, and newspapers								
Miscellaneous gift items								
Musical instruments								
Musical supplies, including records and tape recordings								
Television sets								
Radios								
Record players								
Photographic equipment and supplies								
Liquor								
Tobacco and tobacco supplies								
Sporting goods								
Automobiles								
Gasoline and oil								
Lawn and garden equipment								

ITEM	IN OUR COMMUNITY				IN OTHER COMMUNITIES			
	All	Most	Some	None	All	Most	Some	None
Lawn and garden supplies								
Paint								
Wallpaper								
Lumber and building materials								
Farm implements and repair parts								
Farm supplies								

2. What towns or cities, *other than our community*, do you shop in? Please list the names of these *other* towns or cities beginning with the one you go to most often for shopping, then the one you go to the next most often, and so on down to the one you go to the least often _____

3. About how often do you go shopping in towns or cities *other than* our community? Per month _____ Per year _____

4. About how much money would you estimate you spend for shopping in towns or cities *other than* our community?
Average amount per month $ _____
Average amount per year $ _____

5. What are the various reasons why you go to these *other* towns or cities to shop?
_____

6. In your private and frank opinion, how do the business districts in these *other* towns or cities compare with the business district in our community? _____

7. About how many times a year do you take trips away from our community for recreational or entertainment purposes? _____

8. Do you do any shopping while you are on these trips for recreational or entertainment purposes? Always _____ Most of the time _____ Once in a while _____ Never _____

9. About how often do you go out to eat in restaurants just for the pleasure of going out? _____

10. When you go out to eat in restaurants just for the pleasure of going out, about how often do you go to restaurants that are located in places *outside* our community? Always _____ Most of the time _____ Once in a while _____ Never _____

11. What are the various reasons why you go out to eat just for pleasure in restaurants that are located in places *outside* our community? _____

12. What is your private and frank opinion of the restaurants in our community?

_____

13. Do you do any buying by mail order, either directly by mail or through a catalogue office? Yes _____ No _____

14. If yes, what kinds of things do you buy by mail order?
_____ Food
_____ Men's clothes
_____ Women's clothes
_____ Children's clothes
_____ Men's shoes
_____ Women's shoes
_____ Children's shoes
_____ Light appliances
_____ Heavy appliances
_____ Furniture
_____ Bedding, towels, linens, etc.
_____ Other household items
_____ Fabrics and sewing supplies
_____ Jewelry, watches, etc.
_____ Drugs and toilet articles
_____ Hardware
_____ Luggage
_____ Stationery goods and office supplies
_____ Books, magazines, and newspapers
_____ Miscellaneous gift items
_____ Musical instruments
_____ Musical supplies, including records and tape recordings
_____ Television sets
_____ Radios
_____ Record players
_____ Photographic equipment and supplies
_____ Tobacco supplies
_____ Sporting goods
_____ Oil for automobiles or other uses
_____ Lawn and garden equipment
_____ Lawn and garden supplies
_____ Paint
_____ Wallpaper
_____ Farm implements and repair parts
_____ Farm supplies
_____ Other items: Please list in spaces below _____

_____

15. About how often do you buy things by mail order? Average number of times per month _____ Average number of times per year _____

16. About how much would you estimate you spend shopping by mail order? Average amount per month $ _____ Average amount per year $ _____

17. What are the various reasons you shop by mail order? _____
_____
_____
_____

18. Thinking it over, about how much would you estimate you spent for Christmas shopping this past year in mail orders, plus going shopping in towns or cities *other than* our community? $ _____

19. Do you have any of the following business services performed by workers or businesses that are located in towns or cities *other than* our community? Please place an X in the proper columns after each service listed below.

	All	Most	Some	None
Barber shop				
Hair dresser				
Laundry				
Dry cleaning				
Plumbing				
Heating repairs				
Air conditioning repairs				
Other home repairs				
Interior home decoration				
Exterior home decoration				
Television repairs				
Radio repairs				
Record player repairs				
Light appliance repairs				
Heavy appliance repairs				
Automobile repairs				
Lawn and garden equipment repairs				
Insurance				
Banking				

20. Please try to estimate about how much on the average you spend per year for these services you get from workers or businesses located in towns or cities *other than* our community? $_____

21. What are the various reasons why you obtain these services from workers or businesses located in towns or cities *other than* our community? _____

22. Do you go to towns or cities *other than* our community for any of the following professional services? Please place an X in the proper columns after each service listed below.

	All	Most	Some	None
Doctor				
Dentist				
Optometrist				
Hospital care				
Nursing care other than hospital				
Veterinarian				
Lawyer				

23. Please try to estimate about how much on the average you spend for these professional services in towns or cities *other than* our community?
$ _____

24. What are the various reasons why you go to towns or cities *other than* our community for these professional services? _____
_____

25. When you go to towns or cities *other than* our community for any of the business or professional services listed above, do you usually do some shopping for various other items while you are on the trip? Yes ____ No ____

26. Speaking now of the stores in our community, what do you *like most* about them? _____

27. What do you *dislike most* about stores in our community? _____
_____
_____

28. What improvements do you think ought to be made in the stores in our community?
____ Cleanliness of stores
____ Modernization of stores
____ Appearance of displays
____ Variety of merchandise
____ Quality of merchandise

_____ Arrangement of merchandise
_____ Price of merchandise
_____ More special sales events
_____ Service and attitude of sales people
_____ Other improvements: Please list in spaces below

29. Speaking now of our community's business district as a whole, what is your honest private opinion of its overall appearance?
_____ Very attractive
_____ Only fairly attractive
_____ Not very attractive
_____ Pretty bad
Please state in your own words what you think of the overall appearance of our community's business district. _____

30. What would you suggest to improve the overall business district in our community?
_____ New store fronts
_____ More attractive window displays
_____ Fix up the physical conditions of buildings
_____ Provide better parking facilities
_____ Provide cleaner and better public rest rooms
_____ Paint and general clean up
_____ Other improvements: Please list in spaces below

31. Does the overall condition and appearance of a business district make any difference to you when you go shopping? Yes _____ No _____

32. If yes, how and in what ways? _____

33. What items or services do you buy that you can't get in our community? In round figures, about how much do you spend for these items or services over the course of a year?

Items or Services	Approximate Average Amount Spent Per Year
_____	$ _____

34. What kinds of new stores and services do you think our community needs and could probably support? _____

35. When do you most like to do your shopping? Days of the week _____
Time of the day: Morning _____ Noon _____ Afternoon _____ Night _____

36. What nights of the week would you most like for the stores in our community to stay open late? _____

37. If changes and improvements were made in our local business district along the lines indicated by your answers to this questionnaire, would you do more shopping in our community than you do now? A whole lot more ___ Quite a bit more ___ Enough more to make a real difference in where I spend my shopping dollars ___ Not very much more ___ No more at all ___

This survey should provide a reasonably good estimate of the amount of money your community is losing each month and year to other towns and cities and the major causes for the loss. As we have indicated, it would be unrealistic to expect to keep all of this money in local circulation. Many of the causes of the loss are quite obviously irreversible. However, other causes will be revealed that imaginative and determined local initiative *can* change. These are the problems which present opportunities for action that could improve the competitive position of your community. It is therefore of utmost importance that the replies to the survey questions be compiled and reported in ways that point up as sharply as possible the amount of shopping dollars being lost, the causes for the loss, and opportunities for profitable action. This can be done by presentations of statistics both in percentages and dollars, by written interpretations that help drive home the problems and opportunities for improvement, and by including in the report selected quotations from the questionnaires showing what people said about why money is being drained out of your community and what they said about your local business district. These quotations will add extra punch to the committee's report, but in listing them care should be taken to avoid references of a personal nature that could motivate anger instead of action. Additional suggestions for fact-finding in the field of retail trade and services are as follows:

1. Obtain data showing the gross retail sales in your community during each of the past five years and presenting the breakdown according to types of retail or service businesses from which this total was derived. Using population data and the total retail sales figures, compute the per capita retail sales during each of the past five years. If possible, obtain similar data for selected neighboring communities. Then prepare statistical tables and graphs, accompanied by written interpretations, showing comparative rates of growth or decline from year to year. If your state has a sales tax or a retail occupation tax, the basic retail sales data for these purposes can be obtained from the tax collection office of your state

government. Other sources would be the business census of the U.S. Department of Commerce regional office for your area, banks, utilities, and trade associations. Also, data of this kind is compiled by various other business research organizations and can be obtained by making inquiries through your state university or cooperative extension service.

This data, together with the results of the consumer buying habits survey and other information suggested below, will provide the basis for objective analyses that can help your local merchants and other business services gauge the effectiveness of their efforts to obtain their share of the market in your trading area; it will also open new ideas and opportunities for planning and action aimed at attracting more shopping dollars to your community.

2. Obtain data showing the total effective buying power in your community for each of the past five years and compare these figures with your community's total retail sales for those years. (The term "effective buying power" refers to the total spendable income of your community's population after deducting an amount which allows for taxes, insurance, utilities, mortage payments, rent, and other fixed costs.) If, for example, your community's effective buying power last year was, let's say, $10 million and your total retail sales were only $6 million, the implication is that your community lost approximately $4 million in trade in that year alone. The results from the consumer buying habits survey will explain some of the major reasons for this loss. This information will further indicate the currently unrealized potential of your community as a trading center, and help focus attention on the need for planning and action to go as far as possible toward realizing that potential.

Possible sources of data on the effective buying power of your community include "Survey of Buying Power" in *Sales Management* magazine, your state government, the regional office of the U.S. Department of Commerce, and your state university or cooperative extension service. If your community is smaller than those for which such data is broken down, you can obtain the data for your county, then arrive at a reasonable estimate for your particular community by conferring with the financial institutions and utilities that serve your community.

3. Prepare a list of all retail business and service establishments in your community arranged according to types of trade or service categories, including communications, such as newspapers and radio and

television stations; eating and drinking places, such as restaurants and cocktail lounges; and overnight accommodations, such as motels and hotels.

(a) Taking all of these retail and business service establishments together, what is the total number of persons they employ (including owners or managers), and what is their total aggregate annual payroll?

(b) Considering each trading category separately, list all needed improvements and opportunities for expansion the committee's research indicates would be possible and economically feasible.

(c) List any retail or business service enterprises your community does *not* have for which the committee's research indicates there are profitable opportunities.

(d) List any professional services such as medical, dental, and the like, your community does *not* have for which the committee's research indicates there are profitable opportunities.

4. Questions 27 through 30 in the consumer buying habits survey sought public opinions concerning the overall appearance and desirability of your community's business district and suggestions for its improvement. Related questions were raised in the fact-finding outline suggested for the environmental improvement committee. Further questions along this line were implied in connection with the government committee and were also raised in the suggestions for the industrial development committee. If your community's business district needs improving, these fact-finding activities from varying points of view should go a long way toward pinpointing what improvements are needed. However, the retail trade and services committee should examine these findings in still further depth, adding any other needs for improvement it may discover, and exploring such matters as:

(a) How these needed improvements could be accomplished.

(b) Costs.

(c) Sources of financing and possible arrangements for amortization.

(d) Economic feasibility and possible economic benefits to the community.

(e) The advisability of holding special adult education classes or seminars on modern merchandising practices, sales techniques, and related subjects that would be of practical value to local proprietors or employees engaged in retail trade and services. Such classes or seminars led by highly qualified personnel could be arranged in your community through a community college, your state university, or your cooperative extension service.

(f) The possibility of stocking special library materials designed to serve the technical needs of people in the field of retail trade and services.

(g) The feasibility of developing a comprehensive plan for downtown physical renewal and beautification. This plan could be accompanied by schematic drawings to help illustrate various ideas. It could include architectural designs to provide a distinctive appearance and decor for which your community would become widely known. It could include special plantings of trees and other greenery, perhaps a downtown mall, renovation or removal of old buildings, new or restored store fronts, and other features that would cause your community to be not only more interesting to its local residents, but a special attraction for people from other places as well. In short, what imaginative and creative action could be taken to give your community a reputation as a unique and desirable place in which to shop, go out to eat, and spend extra time visiting and poking around its business district?

6. One of the major business enterprises in the nation today is tourism. Even if your community is not located in a resort area, tourists still have to stop somewhere to eat and stay overnight. If through creative action you have built an interesting and attractive business district they will probably stay long enough to do some shopping. Tourism is therefore another aspect of retail trade and services that should receive the committee's attention.

(a) Looking again at the list of eating and drinking places and of hotels and motels included in the overall list of retail and business service establishments called for above, just how well does your community stack up from the standpoint of tourist accommodations? Does it have all the accommodations of this kind it can support? Are they interesting, attractive, and inviting? Or are they uninteresting, unattractive, and uninviting? In what respects are they adequate or inadequate? Does this suggest any practical opportunities for improvement, or for economic expansion? If yes, how might this be accomplished?

(b) List all existing points of interest, historic sites, possibilities for outdoor recreation, and other attractions that might help draw tourists to your community. What has been done, if anything, to develop and advertise these attractions? Has this development been sufficient, or is there room for more action in this respect?

(c) Again, using your imagination and vision, are there any promising opportunities for new tourist developments in your community or surrounding area, such as camping grounds, artificial lakes, summer cottage sites, sporting activities, or various special events?

(d) In summary, are there any prospects or potentials for increasing your community's tourist trade that are being overlooked or allowed to go undeveloped?

Having sought out every shortcoming or inhibiting factor that stands in the way of building up your community as a trading center, and having ferreted out all potential and realistic opportunities for expansion, the retail trade and services committee is ready to write its report and prepare its presentation for discussion in the general assembly—giving specific recommendations for action. After the assembly discussions have been completed, and all recommendations for action have been publicly aired and approved or amended, special additional meetings on the committee's report and the secretary's reports on the assembly discussions should be held with the community's business people to get all feasible action firmly set in motion. Close cooperation for this purpose should be cultivated with the chamber of commerce, the municipal government, architects and designers, decorators, bankers, builders, construction material suppliers, and all agencies or institutions—local, state, or federal—that are in a position to help bring this essential part of your development effort to fruition.

22

The Housing Committee

ONE of the most important measures of a community's well-being is its residential housing. The quality of available housing affects virtually every aspect of the human condition. It can influence standards of morality, levels of emotional stability, the solidarity of family life. It can be a major determinant of human behavior, of civic responsibility or irresponsibility, of the presence or absence of personal pride and self-respect.

Traditionally, the task of providing essential housing has been an individual or family responsibility, and in general this principle still holds. But in the context of modern times, the production of adequate housing whether in the form of new construction or rehabilitation has also become a major public concern and an integral part of comprehensive community development. The environmental improvement committee will be interested in housing conditions from the standpoint of the community's physical appearance and the overall quality of the environment. The government committee will be concerned for similar reasons, though from a somewhat more legalistic point of view. The industrial development committee will be looking at housing conditions as an important element in the community's ability to attract and hold industry, and other committees will be interested in housing in connection with their roles in the development operation.

The housing committee will add still another dimension concerning this component of the community's makeup. In preparing for their research all members of this committee should first review section 6, "Procedures and Responsibilities of the Fact-Finding Committees," then as the committee's work goes along, all information relative to housing conditions collected by other committees should be examined, along with the secretary's reports on meetings of the general assembly. This will strengthen the housing committee's work, and enable it to coordinate its activities with the development operation as a whole. Suggested fact-finding is set forth below.

Supply and Demand

1. Categorize the prevailing monthly price ranges for rental housing in your community. Less than $_____ per month. More than $_____, but not more than $_____. More than $_____, but not more than $_____. More than $_____, but not more than $_____. Over $_____ per month. How many units suitable for occupancy are available for rent in your community in these various price ranges? How many families or individuals need or are looking for rental housing in these various price ranges? How does the need or demand for rental housing in these various price ranges compare with the supply? Do these facts pose any problems

in regard to the existing housing situation in your community? If yes, describe the nature and extent of these problems.

2. Categorize the prevailing price ranges for housing for sale in your community. For less than $_____. For more than $_____, but not more than $_____. For more than $_____, but not more than $_____. For more than $_____, but not more than $_____. For more than $_____. How many units suitable for occupancy are available for purchase in your community in these various price ranges? How many families or individuals need or are looking for housing to buy in these various price ranges? How does the need or demand for housing to buy in these various price ranges compare with the supply? Do these facts pose any problems in regard to the existing housing situation in your community? If yes, describe the nature and extent of these problems.

3. Summing up, does the supply and demand situation suggest a need for any of the following actions? New construction of private housing for rent? If yes, in what price ranges? New construction of private housing for sale? If yes, in what price ranges? Rehabilitation of existing housing, either for rent or for sale? If yes, in what price ranges? New real estate subdivisions by private developers? If yes, in what price ranges? Public housing construction for low-income families who are not financially able to obtain decent housing in the private market? If yes, give the number of families in your community that would be eligible for public housing and would occupy such housing if it were available. If the demand for housing either to rent or buy, or both, outstrips the supply in any of the price ranges indicated above, what actions would the committee recommend? To what extent are these various actions economically feasible? If none is economically feasible either in terms of private or public investment, and housing needs still exist, what then would the committee recommend be done?

Condition of Existing Housing

1. How many housing units in your community, if any, are dilapidated to the point of being unfit for human habitation, are economically unfeasible to rehabilitate, and should be torn down? What percentage of the total housing in your community falls into this category? Give the location of each of these housing units and plot them on a map. To further point up the problems, a series of photographs would be helpful. How

many of these housing units are vacant? How many are occupied? If any
of these units are occupied, how many are renter occupied? How many
are owner occupied? Compile lists of these dilapidated housing units
according to vacancy and occupancy, including the names and addresses
of owners. What is the attitude of the owner of each of these units toward
their being torn down? What acceptable actions could be taken to make
satisfactory alternative housing available to the occupants of these dilapidated units? Describe the problems and ramifications concerning this
dilapidated housing, and the committee's recommendations as to what
actions would be the most feasible means of eliminating this form of
blight.

2. How many housing units in your community, if any, are now in
process of deterioration which if unchecked will lead to dilapidation,
though are still sufficiently sound structurally to make rehabilitation
economically feasible? What percentage of the total housing supply in
your community falls into this category? Give the location of each of
these units and plot them on a map. To further point up the problems these
deteriorating housing units represent, a series of photographs would be
helpful. How many of these housing units are vacant? How many are
occupied? If any of these units are occupied, how many are renter
occupied? How many are owner occupied? Compile lists of these deteriorating housing units according to vacancy and occupancy, including
the names and addresses of owners. What is the attitude of the owner of
each of these units toward getting them remodeled or rehabilitated? What
would be the estimated cost of restoring each of these units to acceptable
condition? Can the respective owners handle this cost? If not, what
possibilities are open or could be opened to deal with this practical
matter?

3. How many housing units in your community are currently in good
condition? This type of housing is an important asset, but there is always
a need for public emphasis on the importance of continued maintenance
and conservation to avoid the beginnings of deterioration. This concerns
the need for preventive action, by far the least expensive, to which
community-wide attention can lend invaluable support. What percentage
of the total housing supply in your community falls into this category?
Give the location of these housing units and plot them on a map. To
further point up the positive value of this housing, a series of photographs
could encourage continued maintenance and help stimulate remedial
action concerning the community's "problem housing."

4. Housing maintenance is influenced to a considerable extent by the social and physical conditions of the neighborhood or community as a whole. In the fact-finding suggested for the environmental improvement and government committees, as well as for other committees, considerable attention has been focused on these conditions from varying points of view, including community attitudes, zoning, building codes, the upkeep of community facilities such as streets and public properties, commercial operations, habits toward littering, regularity and frequency of trash pickup, and so on.

Dividing your community into neighborhoods or sections, which ones seem to be such as to contribute toward adequate housing maintenance, and why? Which ones seem to be such as to contribute to the decline of adequate housing maintenance, or to deterioration and ultimate dilapidation? Why?

What corrective measures are needed to eliminate the negative conditions of the "problem sections"? What recommendations for action would the committee make in this regard? How do these recommendations relate to recommendations being made by other committees in the development operation?

For example, what about your local government in connection with the upkeep of neighborhood areas and public facilities that influence the maintenance of individual housing units? Is your local government adequately meeting its responsibilities in this connection, and if not, what are the committee's recommendations in this respect? Or, what about any commercial operations that may influence the overall conditions of a residential neighborhood? If there are such operations, are they fulfilling their part of the responsibility for neighborhood upkeep, and if not what recommendations would the committee make in this regard?

Citizen Responsibility
for Housing Conditions

1. What are the proper responsibilities of tenants for the maintenance of rental housing? To what extent and in what ways are these responsibilities being met? To what extent and in what ways are these responsibilities not being met? What community actions could be taken to help cause these responsibilities to be met more adequately? What recommendations would the committee make in this respect?

2. What are the proper responsibilities of owners or landlords for the maintenance of rental housing? To what extent and in what ways are

these responsibilities being met? To what extent and in what ways are these responsibilities not being met? What community actions could be taken to help cause these responsibilities to be met more adequately? What recommendations would the committee make in this respect?

3. What are the proper responsibilities of owners to their community for the maintenance and appearance of the housing in which they reside? To what extent and in what ways are these responsibilities being met? To what extent and in what ways are these responsibilities not being met? What community actions could be taken to cause these responsibilities to be met more adequately? What recommendations would the committee make in this respect?

4. Are there any significant differences in your community between the maintenance and appearance of renter-occupied housing and owner-occupied housing? If yes, why? If no, why? Does this influence housing conditions in your community? In favorable ways? In unfavorable ways? If in unfavorable ways, what corrective actions would the committee recommend?

5. What are the proper responsibilities of all citizens, renters and owners alike, for keeping up the appearance and overall conditions of neighborhood areas and the public facilities that comprise so important a part of the general housing environment? To what extent and in what ways are these civic responsibilities being met? To what extent and in what ways are these responsibilities not being met? What possible community actions could be taken to cause these responsibilities to be met more adequately? What recommendations would the committee make in this respect?

6. Are there any specific examples of housing and neighborhood rehabilitation in your community that could serve as models to encourage more efforts in this direction? If yes, how could these examples be given maximum public visibility as a means of demonstrating what can be done when people really get together and make up their minds to do it? If no, what plans could be organized and carried out, and in what sections of your community, for the purpose of creating such model demonstrations?

NOTE: In a town of about five thousand population in which a comprehensive community development effort was organized, the residents of a badly deteriorated neighborhood got together and selected one square block to convert into a model block, their idea being that this would demonstrate both to themselves and to their entire community what could be accomplished through voluntary cooperative action. With the help of an architect who donated his services they worked out a master design for the entire block, including renovation, landscaping, and the like. On a strictly voluntary basis, residents of the entire neighborhood with prior approval from both owners and tenants went to work and did a complete cleanup of this block, demolished four two-story dilapidated houses that were vacant and hazardous, removed all unnecessary outbuildings, rehabilitated and painted twenty-one homes, built a small neighborhood park, and did a complete job of landscaping. Building suppliers made paint and other materials available at cost. The block became so attractive that four families bought the lots that had been cleared of the dilapidated houses and later built new homes there. Following this demonstration similar improvements spread through the rest of the neighborhood, then the community at large, and became contagious over the entire county—all a result of local initiative, determination, and pride. This is another example of the kind of civic action we discussed in section 17, "From Study to Action," which can be accomplished in any community where there is a determined citizenry. From a business standpoint there could have been no better advertising for home improvement materials—a side effect clearly reflected in increased retail sales throughout the area.

The Role of Private Enterprise
in Improved Housing Conditions

1. Have private builders and suppliers made any organized drives to promote housing repairs and new home construction in your community? If yes, how effective have these drives been? Could more be done in this respect, or could a more concerted selling job be mounted by private industry to develop increased interest in housing repairs, rehabilitation, and new construction? What recommendations for action would the committee make in these respects?

2. What should be the responsibility of real estate dealers in promoting increased attention toward housing repairs, rehabilitation, and new construction in your community? To what extent is this responsibility being exercised? What recommendations for action would the committee make in this respect?

3. What private financial institutions are available in your community or in other towns nearby from which funds may be borrowed on reasonable terms to help meet the cost requirements for housing rehabilitation and for new home construction in the price ranges your community most

needs? Is a concerted effort being made by these financial institutions in cooperation with other private firms connected with the building industry to promote better housing conditions in your community? Could greater and more intensive efforts be mounted in this respect? If yes, what would such action achieve in terms of enhancing your local economy? What recommendations would the committee make in this respect?

4. Are there any other private sources available to your community, such as individuals, from which suitable loans for home improvements and construction could be obtained?

5. What practical means could be devised to promote the flow of private capital into neighborhoods or sections of your community that are most in need of better housing? Is as much being done in this respect as could be done? What are the practical limitations of private capital for this purpose? Are there any practical recommendations for action the committee should make in this respect? Does the formation of housing cooperatives suggest a practical means of dealing with needed home repairs and new home construction in your community? If yes, how and in what ways could the housing committee and the development operation as a whole generate local initiative and leadership for this purpose?

The Role of Trade Unions in
Improved Housing Conditions

1. Have trade unions made any organized drives to promote housing repairs and new home construction? If yes, how effective have these drives been? Could more be done in this respect, or could a more concerted selling job be mounted by trade unions to develop increased interest in housing repairs, rehabilitation, and new construction? To what extent do trade unions and private enterprise cooperate for this purpose? What recommendations for action would the committee make in these respects?

Public Resources for
Improved Housing Conditions

1. What financial aids are available from governmental sources to supplement private capital or to ensure essential loans for needed home repairs and new construction that would not otherwise be possible? What requirements would have to be met to make these governmental aids available? Could such aids be obtained on a basis acceptable to the

community and the families or individuals most directly concerned? What would be the committee's recommendations in this respect?

Benefits of Improved Housing Conditions

1. What will be the benefit of home repairs, rehabilitation, and new construction on property values in your community?

2. What will be the effect of such improvements on the occupancy rate of rental housing?

3. What will be the effect of such improvements on the relationships between owners and tenants as regards rental housing?

4. What will be the benefits of such improvements in regard to the health and safety of your community's residents, including the reduction of fire and other hazards?

5. What influences will such improvements have on the vitality of community spirit, better human relations, local civic pride, and citizen interest in maintaining the overall physical environment—including neighborhood cleanliness and sanitation?

6. What influences will such improvements have on child care and the ability of children to function in school and grow into responsible citizens?

7. What influences will such improvements have on your community and its overall attractiveness as a place in which to live and work and enjoy life?

23

The Education Committee

THERE is a common tendency to think of education and going to school as the same thing, though in reality they very definitely are not the same. The most powerful educator of man is not the school but the community in which he has his being. This is simply to say that education goes on whether school keeps or not, and that going to school is only one aspect of education.

Formal schooling should provide an opportunity to acquire certain basic skills and information; sharpen students' abilities to think, analyze, and deal with problems; improve their capacities to get along with others; form constructive attitudes of mind, gain a sense of history, and understand their cultural heritage. It should help them acquire practical insights into the workaday world, select useful and satisfying careers, and help develop essential attributes of responsibile citizenship. But these and other desired human qualities cannot be expected to come entirely from going to school.

Beginning in early childhood and continuing through life everything that happens to an individual, everything he hears and experiences —whether in school or out of school—becomes a part of his education, and for better or worse influences his personal behavior. In his childhood years he is educated by his parents and his relationships with other members of his family. He is educated by his playmates and by every other person with whom he has significant contact. He is educated by the quarters in which he is housed, by his neighborhood surroundings, and by all the human activities and events to which he is exposed.

His education comes from the whole process of living. It is in the streets, in parks and vacant lots, in the homes he visits, in stores, in places he works, in his travels, in places where he finds entertainment or recreation. It is in the church and organizations he joins. It is in the beliefs, customs, and actions of his associates. It is in everywhere he goes and in all he does. It is in everything that becomes a part of his community, including the whole array of influencing forces that emanate from society at large—not the least of which is the unending stream of words and pictures which flows daily into his community through the mass media.

This does not mean that the community or the individuals who inhabit it are without choice. But it does raise this basic question: Are the people making the best use of their own inner resources, plus available external resources, to build a community in which an educative life of positive human values is most likely to flourish? This gets back to the broad goal of community development we discussed, in section 2, and the influence of human attitudes on the people's ability to realize that goal. It is within this comprehensive development context that the citizenry should look at its public school system, not as the sole purveyor of education, but as an important institutional resource that can help enrich the educational impact of the community on its people.

Thus, as an effort to improve all aspects of community life and upgrade the general level of civic performance, this entire development operation is essentially an enterprise in education. But the specific fact-finding and recommendations for discussion in the general assembly concerning the public school system will be the responsibility of the education committee.

Due to school consolidations and unit districts, many small communities today are served by schools that also serve all other communities in the area. In this situation much of the fact-finding and formulation of recommendations can best be accomplished as a joint endeavor by education committees in all communities the school system serves. During the transition from phase one to phase two of the development operation, this cooperative arrangement may culminate in a single area education committee consisting of representatives from each community in the area. However, in keeping with earlier recommendations in this guide concerning the importance of building a solid foundation of local participation upon which to construct an effective area development effort, an education committee in each individual community is the most effective means of beginning.

Variations in school district organization and geography, communities in which local schools have been replaced by huge area schools often remote both in distance and outlook from many of the localities from which they draw their students, conflicting demands and expectations from varying local constituencies—these are only a few of the conditions of modern life that influence the public schools. But despite all the changes modern times have brought, at least one basic fact remains. Although the public school system is under the general authority of the state and in various ways is regulated by federal authority, essentially it still belongs to the community or communities it serves. Thus, in a very real sense the problems of the school are not the school's problems but the community's problems. This means the school can go no further and be no better than the community will permit, and within legal and fiscal limitations the community may utilize this institutional resource as little or as much as it wishes.

In preparation for its work the education committee should carefully review section 6, "Procedures and Responsibilities of the Fact-Finding Committees," and look for items brought out by other committees and by the general assembly that may call for further inquiry related to the schools. Starting with schooling up to and through the secondary level, suggested fact-finding is set forth below.

The School District and School Financing

1. Prepare a map with appropriate written descriptions showing the boundaries of the public school district that serves your community. Plot the location of all schools in the district, indicating what communities they serve in addition to yours. If your elementary school district is separate from your secondary school district, prepare separate maps and descriptions for each.

NOTE: In many localities elementary and secondary school districts have been merged into a single unit, though separate elementary and secondary districts are still common. For purposes of convenience this suggested fact-finding outline will refer simply to the school "district," and the committee should tailor its work in whatever ways may be necessary to fit your specific situation.

2. What is your community's current elementary school enrollment? Its secondary school enrollment?

3. Compare these enrollments with previous years and give estimated future projections. Are these enrollments increasing, decreasing, or remaining about the same? Does this pose any problems? If yes, describe these problems and their implications. What recommendations would the committee make to deal with these problems?

4. If other communities are included in the school district serving your community, obtain comparable enrollment statistics for them. In comparison with the other communities served by your district, where does your community stand in terms of current total enrollments? In past and probable future trends? At the elementary level? At the secondary level? Does this pose any problems? If yes, what are these problems, and does the committee have any recommendations in this regard?

5. What is the racial or ethnic composition of the student population in your school district? At the elementary level? At the secondary level? Does this pose any problems? If yes, describe the nature and extent of these problems, and what solutions the committee would recommend.

6. Is bussing necessary for student transportation in your school dis-

trict? Does this pose any problems? If yes, what problems, and what would be the committee's recommendations?

7. Does the committee feel the present school district is too large, too small, or about as it should be? Why? If the high school in your community has been closed as a result of consolidation or merger, or if your community no longer has an operating school, what advantages and disadvantages has this brought? To the school? To the students? To the community? On balance, which outweighs the other—the advantages or disadvantages? If your community is the center of a large consolidated school, drawing students from other communities, what advantages and disadvantages has this brought? To the school? To the students? To the community? To the district as a whole? On balance, which outweighs the other—the advantages or disadvantages? If the committee feels any changes should be made in these respects, what changes would it recommend and why? As a practical matter, could such changes be brought about? How?

8. How many members are there on the school board in your district? List them by name. What are their terms of office? If your school district serves communities in addition to yours, indicate which community each board member is from. Does this pose any problems? For the school? For the community? If yes in either case, what are these problems, and what would the committee recommend be done about them?

9. What are the chief functions and responsibilities of the school board? From the point of view of the board members, what are the advantages and disadvantages of serving on the board? Is there a need in your district for more cooperation or understanding between the citizenry and the members of the board? If yes, in what ways? What would the committee recommend in these respects?

10. Based on a sampling of public opinion, are there any problems in regard to the school board's handling of its responsibilities? If any problems appear to exist in this respect, what are they, and what are the chief reasons for them? Do the board members agree with these conclusions? Why, or why not? Upon what do the people sampled base their opinions? Upon what do the board members base their opinions?

11. What is the total assessed valuation of your school district?

12. What is the present school tax rate? Is this too high, too low, or about right?

13. What is the annual school tax revenue?

14. What is the present legal tax limit for school purposes in your district?

15. For how long a period may special local levies for school purposes be voted? Is this as it should be? If yes, why? If no, why?

16. What are the legal bonding limits for school purposes in your district?

17. What is the present indebtedness of your school district? At what rate is this indebtedness being decreased? When will it be paid off?

18. How much more, if any, could be raised in your school district for bonding purposes at the present time, assuming the voters would approve?

19. By what procedures are special levies or bond issues for school purposes accomplished in your district?

20. Are property taxes the sole source of school revenue collected from your school district? If not, what are the other local sources? Is this fair to all local taxpayers? If yes, why? If no, why?

21. How much revenue does your school district receive from state and federal sources? On what basis is the amount of this revenue determined? Is this as it should be? If yes, why? If not, why?

22. Draw up charts showing the present school budget at both elementary and secondary levels and how these budgets are distributed within the schools. Also indicate probable future needs and trends. Draw up companion charts showing the various sources from which these school budgets are derived and indicate what percentage of the total comes from each source. Based on current conditions and future projections, are revenue increases needed? If yes, why? If not, why? Is it realistic to expect that substantial increases, or any increases, can be obtained? From what source or sources?

23. Do these matters concerning school financing pose any problems? If yes, describe the nature and extent of these problems, and what recommendations the committee would make to help resolve them.

24. One of the long accepted assumptions in our society has been that increased revenue for public schools will necessarily result in better schools, thus lifting the general level of achievement which in turn will create a more competent citizenry. However, in recent years many people have begun to question this assumption, and they are now saying that such factors as family background and aspirations, individual aptitudes, value patterns, life styles, personal motivation, community at-

titudes, plus other human attributes are the major determinants of an individual's attainments, and that beyond a certain point, continued increases in school budgets will have no appreciable effect one way or the other. Does this raise any important questions for inquiry and discussion concerning school revenues? Does the education committee feel that your school district is yielding the best possible return in individual and community benefits from each dollar the district is now spending? If yes, why? If not, why? Would the committee recommend any changes concerning current school district revenue and its allocation within the system? If so, why and in what ways?

Policies and Objectives of the Public School System

1. Conduct separate individual interviews with members of your school board, with school administrators, and with a sampling of teachers and other citizens in your community as to what they feel should be the policies and objectives of your public schools, then draw up a composite statement of these opinions. Also, have each member of the committee write out a statement of what he or she feels should be the policies and objectives of your public schools, then draw up a composite statement of these opinions.

2. If there are any differences of opinion concerning school policies and objectives, what are these differences? Why?

3. Do these opinions as to what school policies and objectives should be differ in any way from the policies and objectives that actually exist at the present time? If yes, in what ways? Why?

4. Do existing school policies and objectives differ in any ways from actual school practices? If yes, how? For what reasons?

5. Does the committee feel that present school policies, objectives, and practices are sufficiently attuned to the needs of your community and its youth? Are any changes or improvements needed? If yes, why? What changes would the committee recommend? How would it suggest these changes be accomplished?

School Program

1. Describe the overall program now being provided by your school district at elementary and secondary levels, both curricular and extracurricular. This description need not list every course and activity, but it

should be sufficiently comprehensive to provide a clear understanding by the general citizenry of the program your school district is offering.

2. Does the school program place less emphasis than it should, too much emphasis, or about the right amount of emphasis on academic matters? If yes, why? If not, why?

3. Does the committee feel enough emphasis is being given to vocational matters? If yes, why? If not, why?

4. Considering the percentage of high school graduates in your district who enter college, the percentage who enter vocational schools, and the percentage who terminate formal schooling upon completing high school, does your school program offer a proper balance between academic teachings and vocational teachings? If yes, why? If not, why? Does the committee have any recommendations in this regard?

5. Is a sufficient effort being made to help students determine whether they should point themselves in the direction of going to a university and on into higher education or plan to go in a more specific vocational direction? Is equal status given in your school system from the standpoint of social standing to these two possible directions? Does the committee have any recommendations in this regard?

6. Does your school district provide adequate counseling and testing services? For career purposes? For help with psychological or emotional problems? Does the committee have any recommendations in these respects?

7. Does the school program include any specific effort to help its students increase their awareness and understanding of the responsibilities of marriage and parenthood? Should this subject receive attention in your public school program? Why, or why not? If this subject is included in your school program, is it being given too much emphasis, not enough emphasis, or about the right amount of emphasis? Does the committee have any recommendations in this connection?

8. How and in what ways does the school program help young people in your community to develop a constructive sense of civic responsibility?

9. Is sufficient emphasis placed on the origin, development, and workings of the major institutions of our American society with adequate attention to both strengths and weaknesses? Does the school maintain an objective stance toward these matters in terms of philosophical bias or partisan politics?

10. In helping young people increase their awareness of today's public problems and issues, how effective are your schools in teaching students to recognize and analyze propaganda and objectively weigh possible alternatives?

11. To what extent are young people in your community encouraged to participate in the community development operation? How can the work of the fact-finding committees and the meetings of the general assembly help enrich the teachings students receive in school?

12. Are there any provisions in the school program for students to visit industrial plants, retail business enterprises, and public offices as aids in learning the realities of the workaday world? Through school-community cooperation are there any arrangements for students accompanied by their instructors to visit your state capital to help gain insight into the workings of state government? How about the national capital and the workings of the federal government?

13. What about other practical training for responsible citizenship? For example, driver education? Special projects designed to stimulate leadership ability, creative imagination, resourcefulness, self-confidence?

14. How about relationships between teachers and parents? Do most of the parents really know what is going on in the schools, how well their children are performing, and the extent to which they may be encountering or causing problems? To what extent do the teachers know about family or neighborhood problems that influence the performance of students? How often do parents and teachers get together for individual conferences about students' problems either inside or outside school? From talks with parents, teachers, counselors, school administrators, and students, does the committee see any problems in these respects? If yes, what are these problems, and how might they be resolved?

15. Are there any parts of the school program, curricular or extra-curricular, the committee feels are not necessary and should be eliminated? If yes, what are they? Why are they regarded as unnecessary? What corrective actions would the committee recommend? Do your school officials agree? If yes, why? If not, why?

16. Are there any courses or activities not now included in the school program the committee feels should be included? What are they? Why should they be added? What actions would the committee recommend in this regard? Do your school officials agree? If yes, why? If not, why?

17. What is your high school dropout rate? Is it increasing, decreasing, or remaining about the same? How does this compare with other high schools in your state? What are the major reasons for dropouts from your high school? What actions could help prevent these dropouts? What recommendations would the committee make in this regard?

18. Should all dropouts be encouraged to return to high school? If yes, why? If not, why? Are there alternatives that would be preferable, and if so, under what circumstances? Would on-the-job training be a practical alternative, and if so under what circumstances? What recommendations would the committee make in these respects?

19. Is your school district confronted by drug problems? Underage drinking? Promiscuous sex? Vandalism? Theft? Other forms of delinquency? If yes, why and to what extent? What action, if any, is being taken to deal with these problems? How effective is this action? Does the committee have any recommendations for further actions?

Preelementary Schooling

1. Does your school system provide for public kindergartens, or a preelementary program? If yes, to what extent does this contribute to the preparation of children for the beginning of regular schoolwork? Does it have the general endorsement of the community? If no, should such a preelementary program be established? Why or why not? What would it cost? If such a program is regarded as desirable and financially feasible, what should it include? What recommendations would the committee have in this regard?

School Personnel

1. List the educational institutions in which the teachers and administrators in your public school district obtained most of their professional training. How many of the staff members in your school district think these institutions enabled them to acquire the skills they need for the work they are now doing? What parts of their professional studies do they think benefited them most? What parts do they think benefited them least? What changes, if any, would they recommend in preparatory programs for today's schoolteachers and administrators?

2. How many staff members in your school district have found the skills they need most have come from on-the-job experience? Why? What are these skills? How many of these staff members feel the acquisition of higher degrees makes any real difference in their ability to do the

work they are now doing? Does this reflect any problems in your school system, in state certification requirements, in obtaining the most able teachers and administrators, in the training of school personnel?

3. How many staff members in your school district have had less than one year experience in their profession? One to four years? Five to ten years? More than ten years?

4. How many staff members in your school district are very well satisfied with their current working conditions? Fairly well satisfied? Somewhat dissatisfied? Very much dissatisfied?

5. List the major reasons for the answers given concerning the state of satisfaction or dissatisfaction indicated under question 4. What, if anything, can be done to eliminate any causes for dissatisfaction? What would the school personnel recommend? What would the committee recommend? Do the members of your school board agree? If yes, why? If not, why? If the education committee feels certain changes are clearly needed, what actions would it recommend to the general assembly?

6. Does your school district have a definite personnel salary schedule? If yes, is it the same for both sexes? If not, why? If there is a definite salary schedule, is it adequate? If there is not a definite salary schedule should one be established? Does this pose any problems, financial or otherwise? If so, what are these problems, and what recommendations would the committee make for practical solutions?

7. What has been the rate of turnover of teachers and administrators in your school district during the past five years? Is this rate of turnover sufficient to suggest any significant problems? If yes, what are these problems, what are their major causes, and what can be done to correct them?

8. To what extent do the staff members in your school district feel they are a definite part of the community in which they work? Is improvement needed in this respect? If yes, what would the committee recommend to achieve that improvement?

9. Do all staff members in your school district take an active part in the community development operation? If not, why? What recommendations would the committee make in this regard?

10. What is the ratio of students to teachers in your school district? On the average, are the classes in your public schools too large, too small, or about right? Does this pose any problems? If yes, what would the committee recommend in this respect?

11. Through private consultations with members of the school board

and a sampling of other citizens, including parents, how would the education committee rate the effectiveness of the staff members in your school district? (In the committee's report the answers to this question should be given in statistical form only, individual names being withheld.) Excellent ＿＿ Good ＿＿ Fair ＿＿ Poor ＿＿ Does this pose any significant problems? If yes, what recommendations would the committee make in this connection?

School Buildings and Equipment

1. How many buildings are currently in use in your school district?

2. Make an inspection tour of these buildings and determine the extent to which they are satisfactory or unsatisfactory for their current purposes: Age, physical condition and upkeep, including landscaping and sidewalks. Space for today's needs, and for estimated future needs. Heat. Ventilation. Sanitation. Light. Safety. Auditorium. Gymnasium. Health examination and treatment rooms for emergency first aid. Library facilities. Laboratory facilities. Vocational shops. Teachers' lounges. Storage facilities. Cafeteria facilities. Furnishings and interior decoration. Lavatories. Office space. Supplies and teaching equipment. Playgrounds and athletic fields. Adult meeting rooms. Other points.

3. List all needed improvements and estimated costs. What efforts, if any, are being made to effect these improvements? Can the school district afford all these improvements at present? Which of these improvements appear to be absolutely essential, and which ones could just as well be postponed or done without? Are there any limitations beyond which "extras" would not justify the cost? Considering the entire list of physical improvements that would be desirable, together with probable costs, what are the committee's recommendations? Could any of these improvements be accomplished as community projects with volunteer labor or at least partly volunteer labor? With materials the community or communities in your district could obtain through donations or at cost? The importance of this kind of civic action has been discussed in section 17, "From Study to Action," and in other sections. Action such as this would provide further ideal opportunities to build closer ties between school and community, thus creating a better community and a better school. Such action could form the basis for constructive local and area initiative in which adults and young people could work together for their common good. This in itself would be an important exercise in community education and would further in significant ways the basic goal we

discussed in section 2. Indeed, these intangible benefits would far out-weigh the physical improvements themselves, thereby making these improvements instrumental in creating an increasingly active, problem-solving citizenry. What specific recommendations might the education committee make in this respect?

The Community's Attitude toward the Schools

1. To what extent do the people in your community turn out for school events to which the public is invited—not only sports events but school plays, class demonstrations, open house, and such? Check attendance figures over the past few years and compare these figures with your community's total population above high school age. What are the various types of school events in your locale to which the public is invited? List these events in their order of popularity based on public attendance, beginning with those which draw the largest attendance down to those that draw the least attendance. What does this seem to indicate in terms of general public interest in the school system? Does this suggest any problems concerning community attitudes toward its schools? If yes, indicate the nature and cause of these problems. What does the committee think will be necessary to improve this situation?

2. On the average, how many people in your community attend meetings of the school board from time to time to keep themselves informed on the problems and decisions with which the board is con-fronted? Is there any significant increase in public attendance at school board meetings when a controversial issue is coming up? On such occasions do most of those who attend do so only to protest, or do they attend for the purpose of rational exploration and discussion in an attempt to help find workable solutions? Are there any advantages to be gained from citizen participation in school board meetings, or is it just as well to let the board go it alone?

3. Is there any substantial friction between the community and its schools? If yes, describe the nature of this friction and the reasons for it. Are these reasons valid, or are they due chiefly to rumors and mis-information? What actions can be taken to reduce any friction that may exist? From what source or sources should this action be initiated?

4. Is the school thought of as a real community center that serves not only the educational needs of children and youth but is also used for special community events and activities?

In many places public school buildings are being used as centers for evening classes in adult education. These adult offerings may include hobbies and other forms of recreational activity. They may include virtually any subject in which a sufficient number of people are interested, and for which competent instructors can be found, often through the extension service of state universities, or nearby community colleges. This extra usage of school facilities provides added outlets for personal pleasure and lifelong learning, makes for a greater return on tax investments in the public school system, and has the effect of generating closer community-school relations.

5. What is the record over the past several years of community support or lack of support for school bond elections or special levies? Why?

6. Is a bond election or special school levy being proposed at the present time, or in the near future? If yes, for what reasons? Is this a popular or unpopular issue in the community as a whole? Why?

7. How long has it been since the last major school improvements were made as a result of public referendum? What were these improvements and how difficult was it to pass the referendum?

8. To what extent do citizens in the community assist the school in providing supplemental instruction when needed and when they are qualified to do so?

9. To what extent do the community's business firms make an effort to provide part-time employment for students seeking work? Summer employment? Employment for graduates?

10. Is there a PTA in your community or school district? If yes, what percentage of the parents in your community belong, and what percentage do not? What is the total PTA membership? Over the past year, what has been the average attendance at PTA meetings? How does this compare with previous years? Is the attendance at PTA meetings increasing, decreasing, or remaining about the same? What have been the major PTA achievements over the past year? Could this record of achievement be called impressive, fairly impressive, not impressive, or fairly poor? Why? How does this past year's record compare with that of previous years? Why? Is the present PTA program one that could be called vital, lively, urgent, and concerned with important matters, or would it be more accurately described as mild, routine, or dull? If program improvements are needed, what are they, and how could they be accomplished? Do all persons who attend PTA meetings have an adequate opportunity to

express themselves? For newcomers, is it easy, fairly easy, fairly difficult, or very difficult to get acquainted? To what extent is the overall PTA membership really informed on important problems pertaining to the school? On laws and regulations to which the school is subject from higher levels of government? On school administration, teaching, organization, program content, finance?

11. In summarizing the community's attitude toward its public school system, to what extent would the committee say it could be called a high degree of interest, a fairly high degree of interest, a fairly low degree of interest, or not very much interest at all? Why?

The Schools' Attitude toward the Community

1. To what extent do the members of your school board, your school administrators, and your schoolteachers welcome sincere inquiry, suggestions, and advice from parents and other citizens in regard to problems and activities pertaining to school operations? Does the school system willingly open itself to public scrutiny, recognizing that it is not a closed private entity, but a public service owned by the people and accountable to the people? Are there any problems in this connection? If yes, what actions would the committee recommend to correct them?

2. To what extent does your school system as a public institution cooperate freely and willingly with other community agencies and organizations when called upon to assist in community improvement projects? Is the school system genuinely active and supportive of your community development effort? Do these questions pose any problems?

3. Does the school system work effectively with local business firms in connection with student employment by helping to match applicants with available jobs to the best advantage, and by coordinating classroom teaching with on-the-job training?

4. To what extent does your school system seek out and make an effort to use in its instructional program people in the community who have special information or experiences to offer?

5. Do your schools make sufficient efforts to plan school events in which parents and students may be involved together?

6. In summarizing the attitude of your school system toward the community, how would the education committee characterize this attitude: Highly cooperative, only fairly cooperative, just mildly coopera-

tive, or defensive and grudgingly cooperative? Why? Does your school system's attitude toward the community pose any problems? If yes, describe these problems and the recommendations the committee would offer to resolve them. Family, church, school, community—these are some of the basic institutions essential to constructive youth development. To accomplish this task with the greatest possible success, these institutions must work with each other, not against each other.

Other Items of Concern

If there are matters of interest concerning your community and its schools not covered in this outline, the education committee should add these matters to its fact-finding.

24

The Library Committee

WE have thought of the public school system as an important educational resource which the community may or may not be using as fully as it could. Another important educational service is the public library, the value of which also depends not only upon the quality of the institution itself but upon the extent to which the community makes use of it.

People of all ages may obtain books from the public library for their individual reading pleasure, for self-enlightenment, or for enhancing their aesthetic appreciation. Thus, the library can make a significant contribution to lifelong learning, and provide a means of individual recreation which in itself is a part of the learning process, thereby enriching the overall quality of the community as a place in which to live. By assessing the range of needs and interests in the locality it serves, the library may therefore become a major center of community service. The materials it offers may help citizens gain deeper insights into the currents and meanings of changing times and provide technical information that contributes to family living, to the varied activities of the community's organizations, to the operations of local government, and to businesses and occupational pursuits.

These materials may be provided in the form of fiction and nonfiction books, pamphlets, directories and specialized reference volumes, newspapers, magazines, and other printed matter. They may also be provided in the form of documentary films and recordings, suitable for individual entertainment and education, or for discussion groups which meet periodically for recreation or any number of educational purposes.

By supplying materials that deal with community problems and what has been done about such problems in other places, the public library may also become a major instrument for community problem-solving. For example, special reference materials may be stocked that will be of practical use to the various fact-finding committees engaged in the community development effort.

In recent years there has been a significant move in many parts of the nation toward the development of regional library systems and centralization of acquisitions and accounting as means of supplying library services to communities that cannot afford to maintain library services independently. The distribution of library materials through these systems is done through local libraries that are a part of the regional system, and through what essentially are "traveling libraries," or bookmobiles. Systems such as this provide considerably more financing than would otherwise be available, making it possible for even the smallest rural communities to obtain library materials that would not be accessible to them on a strictly local basis.

The fact-finding and recommendations concerning the needs for, and the maximum possible use of, library resources in your community will be the responsibility of the library committee. All members of the committee should first review section 6, "Procedures and Responsibilities of the Fact-Finding Committees," and take careful note of items brought out in other committee reports and in the assembly discussions that may call for further attention in preparing the library committee's report. Suggested fact-finding is as follows:

1. List and describe all library services and programs currently available to your community: Fiction for reading pleasure and informative

purposes. Nonfiction of both general and specialized interest. Reference and technical volumes. Magazines and newspapers. Book reviews. Films and recordings suitable for entertainment or informational programs, or for discussion groups on various topics of interest. Adult education activities that contribute to lifelong learning. Materials that provide information useful to business and occupational pursuits. Materials providing practical information and ideas pertaining to community problems and possible means of resolving them. Other items that may occur to the committee.

2. Does your community have a library building currently in use, or is such a building available within easy access to your community? If yes, is this building adequate as a center of community service? If it is not adequate, in what ways is it in need of improvement? From the standpoint of space for the storage and arrangement of library materials? From the standpoint of space for reading and studying? From the standpoint of meetings and discussion groups? From the standpoint of equipment? From the standpoint of personnel? From the standpoint of budget and operating costs? If no, should a library building be constructed? How large a building? How should it be designed? What would it cost? How could the cost be met? Can your community afford the cost? If not, what practical alternatives might be considered?

3. Does your community get bookmobile services? If not, are such services needed, and how might they be obtained? If yes, are these services adequate?

4. To what extent are available library services being used by your community? Does the committee feel that greater use of these services is needed? If these services are not being used to the extent the committee feels they could be, why aren't they? What could be done to cause these services to be used more fully?

5. If your community has no library service, what steps should be taken to obtain such services?

6. What agencies, such as your state library or a regional library system, could be consulted for professional advice concerning your community's needs for improved library services? Members of the committee should be designated to make personal contact with these agencies and obtain the benefit of their knowledge and suggestions.

7. What recommendations for action should the library committee include in its report for discussion in the general assembly?

25

The Health Committee

SHORTLY after the founding of the World Health Organization in 1948, health was said to be a state of complete physical, mental, and social well-being, not merely the absence of disease or infirmity. Clearly, this is an extremely ambitious goal, calling for continuing research in laboratories and medical centers around the world and free exchange of knowledge and new discoveries among researchers and practitioners. It also calls for special efforts by each of us individually to protect our own health, and for cooperative efforts by whole communities along with numbers of communities working together on an area or regional basis to provide the health services and facilities which must be available to all of us. Indeed, the entire thrust of the comprehensive development work with which this guide is concerned is the minimum operational requirement if all people are to benefit from the offerings of medical science and achieve to any major degree this far-reaching concept of health.

Soaring costs, current shortages in various categories of health personnel, and many other factors have combined to virtually deny adequate medical care to numerous communities, a situation that makes access to needed health services even in America a problem of nationwide proportions. This further points up the fact that in the field of health people and the communities in which they live cannot afford to resign themselves to inaction and simply wait for solutions to be handed down from above. For as this guide has repeatedly emphasized, regardless of what may be done at the higher levels, no community is likely to get very far with any needed improvement in the absence of concerted local initiative.

Also, particularly from the standpoint of rural communities, it should be stressed that although many obstacles must be overcome in finding solutions to today's health needs, the current situation is by no means entirely negative. Considering the enormous progress the health sciences are making, the positive aspects of the situation may well outweigh the negative. A long list of diseases that not more than a generation ago were major killers are virtually unheard of today, and rapid progress is being made toward eliminating many of today's most potent killers. Recent breakthroughs in medical science, along with new methods by which modern health services may be distributed to remote areas are making it increasingly possible for communities throughout rural America to have at their disposal a range and quality of health care that only a few years back were not even dreamed about.

For example, recent experimentation in the use of helicopters for emergency ambulance service has opened a whole new field of potentialities. This form of transportation for emergency treatment has been most dramatically demonstrated by the military services, but which on a limited scale is now being successfully adapted to civilian use, with still more adaptions looming on the horizon. Centrally based hospitals linked to small outlying diagnostic facilities by computers and other electronic equipment is a newly developing system that holds promise of bringing specialized expertise into communities where such expertise could not previously have been even anticipated.

These and other innovations are being discovered at an ever-increasing rate by the nation's medical schools, private health organizations, commercial laboratories, insurance companies, the National Institutes of Health of the U.S. Public Health Service, municipal and state health agencies, and other institutions devoted to research and development. Advanced methods of rehabilitation for numerous conditions once looked upon as hopeless are making rapid strides. Newly developed training programs are making it possible to turn out doctors and nurses in substantially less time than was previously considered possible. Modern nursing homes coupled with improved health insurance are being developed to bring comforts to the elderly, infant mortality rates are being drastically reduced, and new methods are being introduced to ensure better care for expectant mothers. New technology is also being developed for preventive measures to help avoid illness—greatly increased knowledge in nutrition being only one of many examples.

New discoveries, new methods, new knowledge, and new ideas still to come are offering a wealth of opportunities to explore. But many communities are not likely to realize these opportunities unless there is a local willingness to systematically assess and catalogue their health-service needs as a beginning step in carefully organized planning and action. From this listing and analysis of needs, determinations can be made as to what plans and what actions will be required to realistically meet those needs. Through this kind of effort the community can discover what it is capable of doing for itself, and it will be better able to determine which of its health needs can be satisfied only by working with its neighboring communities for the development of cooperative efforts on an area-wide scale.

To an ever-increasing extent adequate modern health services can be developed in rural America only if all communities in a given geographical area are willing to think, plan, and act collectively for their mutual benefit. Indeed, it may well be that the mere recognition of the inability of individual communities to provide independently all the health services they could obtain through area-wide efforts may in itself be one of the major health discoveries of the modern era.

Just how large a given area should be to comprise an effective health-planning unit will depend upon such considerations as distance, the number of communities involved, the size of their combined population, available financial resources, and the degree of capability that must be mustered to support the needed health services. Thus, the extent of the area to be selected as a feasible unit for developing these services may be an entire county. It may embrace several counties, or depending on terrain, local attitudes, route of transportation and patterns of mobility, it could be an area that doesn't fully coincide with county lines or any other established political boundaries.

The fact-finding and recommendations for action, which will form the basis for discussion and decision-making in the general assembly concerning this aspect of community development, will be the responsibility of the health committee. In preparation for this work all members of the committee should carefully review section 6, "Procedures and Responsibilities of the Fact-Finding Committees," look for health-related items brought out in other committee reports, and check through the secretary's reports for any such items that may call for additional inquiry. A suggested fact-finding outline is set forth below, but the committee should not hesitate to expand or alter this outline to fit specific local conditions.

Health Agencies and/or Institutions

1. Public.
   A. Prepare a list of all public health agencies or institutions that serve your community. Then confer with the officials of these

agencies or institutions to obtain information that will aid the committee in determining the community's health needs and possible actions that may be appropriate and workable. Some of this information may be as follows: A detailed listing of the services each of these facilities provides. What do each of these agencies or institutions see as their major problems and limitations, both internal and external? What do they feel could be done to correct these problems or limitations? Under what conditions or on what basis are these services available to your community? How frequently does your community receive these services? Are these services adequate? If not, why? What actions would be required to make them adequate? What do the officials of these agencies or institutions regard as the major health problems of your community? In the professional opinion of the officials of these agencies or institutions, are there any health facilities or services your community needs to which it does not now have access? If so, what facilities or services do they feel are lacking and what actions would they recommend to make these services available? How far from your community are each of these agencies or institutions located? How large an area, how many other communities, and how large a population do they cover? Does this pose any problems? If yes, what are these problems, and what actions would be required to resolve them? In terms of services offered and services used are there any problems? That is, is there any friction, lack of mutual cooperation or understanding between any of these agencies or institutions and your community? If so, why? What is the nature of the problems in this regard, and what can be done to improve the situation? Are there any other points of information the committee should obtain from the officials of these agencies or institutions that would help identify the health needs of your community?

B. Having conferred with these officials and obtained the facts and opinions they have provided, the committee should make inquiries from a sampling of people in the community itself to obtain their thoughts, ideas, and experiences to further help determine the community's health needs and possible actions that might be taken to deal with them. These inquiries in the community itself should parallel the line of inquiry indicated above, but may suggest still more questions that ought to be looked into.

2. Private.

    A. List all private health agencies or institutions that serve your community, including hospitals, clinics, nursing homes, and any other professional sources of health service.

    B. Make similar inquiries from these private sources, and within the community, as have been suggested above concerning public health agencies or institutions.

3. Facilities Summary.

    A. Having conducted the fact-finding indicated above, list in detail all existing problems your community faces in regard to health agencies or institutions, both public and private.

    B. Draw up a comprehensive plan of possible action for dealing with these problems. In putting this plan together the committee should seek the aid of whatever expertise it may need.

Health Personnel

1. Do the people in your community have satisfactory access to sufficient numbers of health personnel in the following categories: Doctors, general practioners. Doctors, specialists. Registered or professional nurses, including public health nurses. Practical nurses and nurses' aides. Dentists. Dental hygienists. Other essential health personnel.

2. What is the relationship between the supply of health personnel in these various categories and the availability of health-services agencies or institutions?

3. If there are shortages in any of these categories of health personnel, what possible actions could be taken to resolve this problem?

Mother and Infant Care

1. Does your community have adequate access to prenatal care services and advice? If yes, are these services always utilized by persons who need them? This portion of the fact-finding concerns not only the availability of a critical health service, but also an aspect of health education aimed at cultivating an awareness on the part of expectant mothers that will motivate them to take full advantage of these services.

2. What is the infant mortality rate in your community? The mortality rate of women resulting from pregnancy and childbirth? How do these

rates compare with those of your county? Your state? The committee should confer with appropriate practitioners or county or state health officials to help determine what problems, if any, may exist in this regard and what actions are needed to deal with them.

3. A continuation of the inquiry concerning prenatal care concerns postnatal care for new mothers and babies. Are adequate services for these purposes available? Are these services effectively utilized in all cases. Here again is the dual need for available services and for essential health education.

4. If adequate services for prenatal care and advice and for mother and baby care are not within ready access to your community, or if such services are ignored or not effectively used, what actions would the committee recommend to help remedy this?

School Health Programs

1. The committee should consult with appropriate health and school officials, even if it means a visit to the state capital, to help determine what components and services a modern school health program should include.

2. With this information as background, what health services are now being offered in the public schools serving your community? Are these services adequate? Do they ensure proper examinations and care when needed? Does it enable school personnel to detect needs for referral of students for appropriate medical or dental attention that might otherwise go unnoticed?

3. Compile a list of any deficiencies that may exist in your school health program, and in cooperation with your school administrators, teachers, and board members, prepare recommendations for correcting these deficiencies.

4. Examine in this connection the adequacy of the school curriculum in the fields of health instruction and physical education. This may be done in cooperation with the education committee.

The Elderly

1. What are the major problems of elderly people in your community?

2. Are there any programs in your community or within easy access specifically designed to serve the elderly—programs of adult education, hobbies, arts and crafts, or other group activities elderly people would enjoy?

3. Are there any practical ways in which elderly people in your community could turn various hobbies and recreational activities into full- or part-time occupations?

4. Do the employers who hire people in or from your community recognize the special assets of older people as employees? Is there any effort to adjust retirement policies to enable older people to contribute their experience and skills in gainful employment as long as they wish and are physically able to do so, rather than forcing them into retirement at some arbitrarily determined age whether or not they are still qualified and would like to keep on working? Many companies in the United States have helped solve the problems that often result from forced idleness due to premature retirement by finding other jobs older people can do with a high level of efficiency, even though it is unduly difficult for them to continue in the same position they have held over the years.

5. What about volunteer community service programs in which elderly people can participate and supply their individual talents or the benefits of experience and wisdom? Are the capabilities of elderly people being utilized to the greatest possible extent in your community's overall development effort?

6. Elderly people, just as people at any age, obviously do not all enjoy the same things. Any program designed to help them occupy their time in healthful and productive ways should therefore include a wide range of varied activities and opportunities. In keeping with the central thrust of the entire development operation, the best way to develop programs and activities elderly people will enjoy is for them to do it themselves. The important thing is that the elderly not be ignored, that no one is left to live out his or her old age in loneliness or idle frustration. This is a matter that really comes to grips with the concept of physical, mental, and social well-being to which the committee should address itself and devise recommendations for effective action.

7. What institutional facilities and special care are accessible to the elderly people in your community who are in various stages of being no longer able to care for themselves? Are these facilities and services satisfactory? If not, what possible actions can be taken to improve them? If there are no such facilities or services readily accessible to your community, what possible actions can be taken to remedy this situation? Through exploring questions such as these with various people in your community, with experts on the subject of aging who may be found in your county or state health departments, or in your state universities or

community colleges, and through the exercise of creative imagination, the committee should be able to discover many potentials for dealing with the problems of the elderly.

Mental Health

1. Make whatever inquiries may be necessary to determine what problems confront your community from the standpoint of mental hygiene.

2. Is drug abuse a problem in your community?

3. Do people in your community have satisfactory access to professional counseling for whatever reasons they may need and desire such services?

4. What is the divorce rate in your community? How does this compare with the divorce rate in your county? In your state? In the nation? If the breakdown of family life or marital partnership is a serious problem in your community, what is there about the community itself the committee can identify as possible contributing factors? If child desertion or child abuse or neglect are problems of serious proportions in your community, what possible conditions are there in your community life that may be contributing to these problems? If factors can be identified in the life of your community that contribute to these expressions of poor mental hygiene, how might these factors be remedied or eliminated?

5. Prepare a description of conditions in your community with respect to vice, crime, delinquency, and other manifestations of antisocial behavior. What problems, if any, does your community have in this respect? What actions would the committee recommend to deal with these problems?

6. What agencies or institutions are available to your community to help resolve these kinds of problems? Are the services provided by these agencies or institutions as effective as they should be? If not, in what ways are they deficient? What actions are needed to make these services more effective?

Sanitation

The health committee should consult with the committees on environmental improvement, government, and industrial development concerning water supply and distribution, sewage disposal, trash and garbage pickup and disposal, and any nuisances that could be put under the heading of health hazards. All four of these committees will be interested in these particular matters, though from varying points of view. The health committee may wish to look into these matters from a somewhat different frame of reference than those of the other committees mentioned above. However, by conferring with these other committees, many parallel interests will be discovered and unnecessary duplication may be avoided. Further, on the basis of the findings and recommendations of these other committees, the health committee can more effectively determine what additional fact-finding, if any, it should conduct in regard to sanitation. Perhaps it will be sufficient merely to summarize the findings and recommendations of these other committees for inclusion in the health committee's report. This would fortify and give added impetus for action to improve conditions of sanitation which are having adverse effects on the community's environmental health.

Summary

Earlier in this section it was pointed out that the health needs of many communities in rural America can be met only through cooperative planning and action by numbers of communities working on an area-wide basis. If this applies to any of your community's health problems, the committee should make recommendations as to what other communities and what area should be involved for purposes of the most feasible and realistic health planning and action.

26

The Recreation Committee

ONE of the most important aspects of the quality of community life is sufficient opportunity for the people to express themselves through varied forms of recreation. This calls for facilities and activities that enable people to exercise their intellectual, emotional, and physical energies for the sheer enjoyment of doing, thus finding a pervading sense of freedom from their daily work routines.

In many respects the community development effort itself is a form of recreation. For in the process of carrying out this effort countless opportunities are opened for voicing ideas, thinking creatively, exchanging expressions of feeling and opinion in a direct and dynamic way, and experiencing the satisfaction that comes with identifying and resolving community problems. This contributes not only to the well-being of the community as a whole, it also contributes to the well-being of the people individually.

The lack of healthy self-expression through wholesome recreation has become commonplace in many communities partly because of the modern tendency to depend on others to do our entertaining for us while we sit by and watch. As people have increasingly allowed themselves to be captured by television and other forms of spectator entertainment there has been a marked acceleration of the notion that unless professional standards are attained a thing isn't worth doing. This is part of the phenomenon of social change which has come with the decline of the small community, the expansion of urbanization, and of a kind of sophistication coupled with an underlying restlessness that has contributed to the current state of boredom with which so many people are afflicted. There is a tendency to discard traditional ways whether they have enduring values or not. Life in America has always been far from perfect. But even today when a great deal of innovation is needed to deal with rapidly changing conditions, there is no need to keep reinventing the wheel. Just because an activity is old does not necessarily make it irrelevant to current needs.

The tendency to judge literature, music, painting, drama, and other art forms by the finished product rather than by the creative and emotional energy released in the process of doing is one of the modern dangers to self-expression.

Recreation created by individual or local community initiative, the opportunity to play, participate in avocations from which we derive pleasure and fulfillment, to provide ourselves with physical exercise we find exhilarating and helpful in keeping fit are as important to human happiness and a vigorous community life as the opportunity to work and earn a living.

"There's nothing to do in this town," is not literally true, but is a remark people make almost every day in communities throughout the nation. The mere fact that people are alive means that every minute they will be doing something. It may be sleeping or just sitting and worrying. But whatever it is—good, bad, or of no consequence—everybody of every age does something every minute. The feeling so many people have that there is nothing to do for recreation probably means there is nothing that interests them, or if there is they haven't found it. It may also mean that those who say this are too tired or too indifferent, perhaps too lazy, to get out and look for recreational activity or to use their imaginative powers to create activities that would appeal to them either individually or in company with others.

This lack of either finding or creating opportunities for satisfying recreation is attested to each year by the increasing need for mental institutions, rising crime rates, inner fears and warped personalities, increasing divorce rates, the breakdown of family life, and the premature wearing out of millions. There is nothing like active play to relax tense nervous systems and overworked minds and bodies, provide a tonic for the idle, or supply a form of therapy for the emotionally distraught. For children and young people constructive recreation can be a positive substitute for negative attitudes that often lead to rebellion and trouble. And when whole families participate with other whole families in mutually interesting recreation, then the full meaning of enriched community life gets a personal application.

Disunity, intergroup hostility, a lack of community spirit and local pride usually can be reversed when people join together in recreational activities of their own making. Indeed, active and creative recreation properly organized and carried out can be one of the most effective means of engendering a social climate that enables communities to rise to their full capacity for development in all fields of concern.

The best programs of community recreation are sufficiently diversified to serve all who wish to take part regardless of age or individual limitations. Comprehensive recreational planning should therefore be such as to appeal to the old, the young, and the in-between. It should include outlets for all interests, and if enough imagination and thought go into the planning, it should stimulate new interests. This kind of planning may be projected to cover all seasons of the year and designed in ways that will make recreation an integral part of the community's ongoing life activities.

Such diversified year-round recreation is possible in every community where the people are willing to recognize its importance and sufficiently apply themselves to make it a reality. Much of the value of planning effective community recreational programs, then setting them in motion, comes from the very process of creating them. Professional advice brought in from outside may provide a useful boost in thinking through the initial problems of getting started and enlarging the community's vision of what is possible. But as in all other aspects of community development, if programs of recreation are to take root and grow, the initiative and support necessary to create and maintain them must come from within.

In many communities there are recreation centers standing idle largely because they were set up by a few well-intended leaders, but without adequate consideration for the kind of recreation that would have broad local appeal and without including in the planning a sufficient cross-section of the population. In the case of young people it is virtually axiomatic that recreation centers planned and created for them by adults who in all sincerity think they are being generous and understanding, but provide no opportunity for the youth to assume any real responsibility in the planning, almost always go defunct. Failures such as this are often a shock to the adults who did the planning and leave them feeling unappreciated for reasons they often find difficult to comprehend. And if the centers are vandalized by the very youths the adults thought they were helping, the shock becomes even greater. Regardless of good intentions, this may only widen the gap between generations, and actually do more harm than good.

In contrast to this situation a group of young people in a small town decided for themselves that life in their community was dead and offered them nothing to do. They could have turned to a variety of debilitating activities, which many youths had already done, thus creating still other community problems. Then with the guidance of a wise adult leader who had just the right touch for working with youth groups, and who understood the negative drift that had started, the young people formed a committee to see what they might find as constructive alternatives. Ideas began to flow and it wasn't long before they were talking about creating recreational programs of their own in accordance with a more healthful life-style. Within a few weeks they had evolved a comprehensive plan for year-round activities and a recreation center with the necessary facilities and equipment. With proper leadership the youths had discovered for themselves the constructive alternatives they were seeking. At a community-wide youth meeting the young people decided what they could do for themselves to make their new ideas come true, then began contacting adult organizations. The young people made it known they were willing to do as much fund raising as possible by performing services such as car washing, lawn mowing, and other useful jobs. They were also willing to do the work of cleaning out an old firehall, no longer being used, and convert it into the recreation center they had included in their planning. All they wanted from the adults was help with matters the young people couldn't handle alone.

The adults were so impressed by this showing of initiative, no one could resist. In a short time the project grew into a general community enterprise, with people of all ages working together to renovate the building and equip it as a recreation center. Nobody worked any harder than the young people themselves, and the program became an established part of the community. Said the high school principal, "Those kids learned more about practical organization and responsibility than we could teach them in a year at school."

In another community the merchants got together and converted portions of their window displays into an art gallery where arts and crafts made by local residents were exhibited. The exhibits were changed from time to time, and in a spirit of healthy competition the merchants vied with each other to make the most attractive arrangements of the things being shown. One week they would feature photography, another it would be ceramics, another things made of wood, and another week floral arrangements. Then the program began featuring local organizations: Boy Scouts, Girl Scouts, 4-H Club, and adult groups. Widespread community interest was stimulated in creative activities and more and more people began taking part. As news of what was being done got around, people started coming from other localities to see the displays, did some shopping, and as a by-product, local retail trade increased.

Another idea with recreational appeal is creative writing groups, which can function in any of a variety of ways. For example, anyone interested may join without worrying about literary standards, the only qualification being a desire to write or the urge to try. The writing can be fiction or nonfiction. Considerable interest may develop in local and regional history, or in other material concerning your community and area. Once a month the group may hold an all-day meeting, including a potluck lunch, with people taking turns reading aloud pieces of writing other members of the group have produced. Then after reading a given work, members of the group may turn over to the author suggestions they have noted down as the reading went along. This may be followed by a general discussion about each work, pointing out its strengths and weaknesses, and in this way the participants help each other become more skillful writers. In time, members of the group may be selling to commercial publishers, thus not only getting paid but enjoying the supreme satisfaction all writers get from seeing their work in print.

In one community a group of people who enjoyed creative writing put out a local magazine four times a year consisting entirely of pieces written by "homegrown" authors, much of the material being drawn from incidents, events, and real characters in the community itself. And they had no difficulty selling enough copies and obtaining enough local advertising to break even.

Community recreational programs have included music groups, both choral and instrumental. And here again people need not be professional musicians or singers to enjoy themselves. A Beethoven concert provides the audience with a great spiritual lift and is a priceless part of our cultural heritage. But the prime purpose of community music groups is to provide outlets for creative expression and the fun of participating. Over time, such groups will increase their skill, and the more proficient people become in any recreational activity the more fun it will be. Still, the essential ingredient in community recreation is in the doing, and to obtain this intrinsic value a person does not have to be a master artist.

Community drama can yield rich returns in recreation. This may be in the form of huge pageant dramas containing a series of episodes, a cast of several hundred, produced in outdoor amphitheaters in which local people build their own stage, and thus create a medium through which to tell themselves the true story of their community. Local committees may write the script, compose the music, do the costuming, and in one way or another virtually all residents of the community may become engaged in this means of telling themselves who they are as a people, how they came to be as they are, how their problems have evolved, and project their potential future as a community. Productions such as these have been done in many communities, drawing audiences from miles around, in some instances even larger than the local population.

However, community drama does not need to be on this large a scale. All communities, just as all individuals, have their limitations, and to attempt dramatic productions that overtax local energies and resources can result in serious frustration which could damage the entire development effort. But dramatic productions organized and tailored to your community's ability and interests can offer fruitful opportunities for highly creative and enjoyable forms of recreation. And if you wish to use this as a means of pointing up local problems and possible solutions, this can be a learning experience of great meaning, thus supplying a powerful form of motivation for constructive action. But community drama doesn't have to deal with real-life problems. It can be just for fun. In any event, this form of recreation can add luster and vitality to the spirit of your community.

Square dancing is popular in many community recreational programs, and special performances by such groups can be extremely attractive. Some communities have found it worthwhile to plan a series of recreational events appropriate to each month of the year, thus providing special monthly events in which varying interests can be expressed and large numbers of people of all ages can participate.

One community came up with the novel idea of an annual "hometown holiday" over the Labor Day weekend which featured a wide range of gala events beginning in the morning and running late into the evening as a means of making it attractive for people to stay in town instead of driving to some distant point for recreational purposes during this high-risk weekend. Special committees functioned throughout the year to do the necessary planning, and most local residents turned out for the fun—at home.

In almost all communities, some start has been made toward recreational programs, yet much remains to be done. In checking your community for facilities that could be used for recreational purposes, the best way to begin is to think of facilities already available. Almost everywhere there is space which is idle most of the time. School buildings and grounds may be used only five days a week, nine months a year, and even this much usage is usually confined to a relatively small portion of the day. Church buildings and other facilities may get even less use. And there may be vacant or abandoned buildings that with voluntary work could be made suitable for recreational purposes. These are community resources. The basic question is a matter of determining how all local resources can be fully utilized for the people's benefit. This applies to vacant lots, streams, lakes, and other outdoor areas, as well as to indoor areas. Many communities have found feasible ways to develop new lakes and outdoor picnic and camping areas, which not only provide additional opportunities for recreation but also stimulate economic growth.

Leadership is the first essential in starting community recreation programs, or in expanding and diversifying those that may already exist, and again, the best place to look for this leadership is in the community itself. It would be ideal, of course, if the community could afford to hire a full-time professional recreation director to work as a coordinator of volunteer leaders. But good community recreation programs are possible even without a full-time paid director. In your community there are undoubtedly people whose hobbies or professions have given them expertise that could be used to help develop recreational activities, and who would enjoy teaching these activities to others. These are merely a few examples of the numerous possibilities for community recreation and may suggest ideas for the recreation committee.

All members of the recreation committee should review section 6, "Procedures and Responsibilities of the Fact-Finding Committees," note any items concerning recreation that may have been brought out in other committee reports or in the discussions of the general assembly. A suggested outline for the committee's fact-finding and recommendations is as follows:

Recreational Facilities

1. Prepare a list of all facilities in the community and its surrounding area that are now being used for recreational purposes—buildings, play yards, parks, streams, lakes, and such—and describe each facility. Name and type of facility, and its location. Age groups being served. Equipment available for use. Programs or activities now being offered at this facility. Capacity of the facility. Hours and frequency of use. Is this facility being used to full capacity? If not, why? For what additional activities might it be suited? Is the facility overcrowded or being used to more than full capacity? If it is what could be done to remedy this situation, or expand the facility's capacity? Sponsorship and ownership. Cost of upkeep and operation. What sources supply these costs? Are additional funds needed? If yes, from what sources might these funds be provided? Are there any existing problems or inadequacies concerning each facility? If yes, what actions should be taken to bring about needed improvements? Other pertinent factors the committee feels should be included in the description of the facility.

2. Prepare a list of all facilities in the community and its surrounding area that could be useful for recreational activities, but which are not now being used for such purposes. Name and type of facility and its location. Kinds of activities for which it might be suited. What actions, equipment, and improvements would be necessary to put this facility to use for such activities? How much cost would this involve? Would it be economically feasible? Ownership. Age groups the facility might serve. Capacity. Hours and frequency it would be available. Leadership needed. Possible sources of this leadership.

Human Resources

1. Compile a directory of all persons in the community who would be willing to serve as voluntary leaders for recreational activities, or who have special skills they would be willing to teach for such activities. This directory should also include all organizations in the community and its surrounding area that would be willing to act as sponsors for recreational activities.

2. Does your community have a full-time recreation director? If so, does this person have sufficient help to do all that is needed? If this person does not have sufficient help how might additional help be recruited?

Recreational Needs and Interests

To help determine what recreational activities would be of most interest in your community and obtain other information asked for above, lists of questions are suggested below which the committee may use in conducting surveys.

QUESTIONS FOR THE COMMUNITY AT LARGE

(In preparing survey forms be sure to leave enough space for full and complete answers.)

1. Name and address of person being interviewed _____
   Age ____ Sex ____

2. What are your favorite recreational activities in the:
   Spring _____
   Summer _____
   Fall _____
   Winter _____

3. Are there sufficient opportunities in our community area for you to take part in these activities? Yes ____ No ____ If not, do you have any suggestions as to how

such opportunities might be created? _____
_____

4. What recreational activities other than those given above do you think you might become interested in, but have no way of doing so because they are not available in our community or area? _____
   A. In your opinion, what feasible actions could be taken to make these activities possible? _____
   B. What costs do you think might be involved? _____
   C. What suggestions do you have as to how these costs might be covered?
   _____
   _____

5. For what recreational activities do you go away from our community or area?
   _____
   About how often? _____

6. Which of the following recreational activities would you or members of your family like most if they were included in a recreation program in our community or area?
   Note: For this part of the survey the committee should compile as comprehensive a list of activities as it can think of that people in the community might enjoy, then ask the persons being interviewed to check those activities they think would be of greatest interest to them.

7. In our community and its surrounding area, do you think the recreational and cultural needs of the people are being met as well as they should? Check for each group listed below.
   A. Preschool children: Yes ____ No ____ If no, what do you think is most needed? _____
   B. Grade-school children: Yes ____ No ____ If no, what do you think is most needed? _____
   C. High-school-age young people: Yes ____ No ____ If no, what do you think is most needed? _____
   D. Young adults: Yes ____ No ____ If no, what do you think is most needed?
   _____
   E. Adults: Yes ____ No ____ If no, what do you think is most needed and for which adult age groups? _____

8. What would you personally be willing to do to help make more and better recreational activities and facilities available to our community? _____

9. Would you be willing to serve as a volunteer leader for any of these activities? Yes ____ No ____ If yes, which ones? _____

10. What personal skills do you have that could be used in the broad field of recreation? _____

11. Would you be willing to help others learn these skills? Yes ____ No ____

12. Who else in our community do you know of who has personal skills that could be used in the development of various recreational activities? _____
    _____

QUESTIONS FOR TEEN-AGE INTERESTS

(In preparing survey forms be sure to leave enough space for full and complete answers.)

Note: For purposes of making this survey, the committee should engage the active participation of a committee of teen-agers. This committee of teen-agers should conduct the survey among their peers in whatever ways they think will be most productive.

1. Name and address of person being interviewed _____
   Age ___ Sex ___

2. What do you usually do for fun after school?
   On week days _____
   On weekends _____
   In the summer _____

3. What sports do you most like to take part in? _____

4. What other kinds of recreational activities do you like? _____

5. Are there enough opportunities in our community for you to take part in these sports or other activities that you like? Yes ___ No ___ If no, what things do you think are most needed? _____

6. What suggestions do you have as to how these things you think are most needed could be accomplished? _____

7. Would you personally be willing to help get these things accomplished? Yes ___ No ___

8. Who else would you suggest that might be willing to help? _____

9. Do you have any favorite hobbies? Yes ___ No ___ If yes, what are they?

   _____

10. Are there enough opportunities in our community for you to take part in these hobbies as much as you would like? Yes ___ No ___ If not, do you have any suggestions as to how more such opportunities might be created? _____

11. Would you personally be willing to help create these opportunities? Yes ___ No ___

12. Who else would you suggest that might be willing to help? _____

13. What personal skills do you have that could be helpful in developing recreational opportunities in our community? _____

14. In general, do you think there are enough things to do for recreation in our community? Yes ___ No ___ If not, what do you think ought to be done about it? _____

15. Which of the following recreational activities would you and your friends like most if they were included in a recreation program in our community or area?
    Note: For this part of the survey, the teen-age committee in cooperation with some of the adult members of the recreation committee should compile as comprehensive a list of activities as they can think of that young people might enjoy, then ask the persons being interviewed to check those activities they think would be of greatest interest to them.

16. Do you ever go out of town for recreational activities? Yes ＿＿ No ＿＿
    If yes, about how often? ＿＿＿＿＿＿＿＿＿＿＿＿＿＿＿＿＿＿＿＿＿
    For what activities? ＿＿＿＿＿＿＿＿＿＿＿＿＿＿＿＿＿＿＿＿＿＿＿

Summary of Findings and Recommendations

On the basis of the information obtained from the research suggested above, plus any other research the committee feels is necessary, a tentative plan should be drawn up for an all-age, all-season community recreational program for discussion and decision making in the general assembly.

27

The History Committee

AN analysis of your community's history can be an important means of understanding many of its problems of today, for the whole chain of events beginning with its initial founding and settlement up to the present time are some of the primary forces that have made it what it is. And today's thoughts, events, and trends will exert a major impact on what your community will be tomorrow. This is simply to say that your community is to an important extent a product of the past, and that the present is history in the making. Thus, by using the vantage point of hindsight to see what led to various problems of the past and comprehend how past mistakes might have been avoided, the community can enlarge its perspective of current conditions.

A good working knowledge of its own history is also a means of enriching the community's life of today by revealing matters of human interest that might otherwise be lost. Legends, folklore, and songs native to your community or area can add intrinsic values that will contribute to your community's attractiveness as a place in which to live or visit. There are interesting yarns or stories remembered by old-timers that could be preserved in writing, thereby adding touches of color to the community's character. Such ingredients from the past are a part of the community's cultural heritage which if forgotten can leave it less interesting than it could be otherwise.

If your community has been in existence for many years or generations, it will have gone through certain definite periods that can be identified. Events and circumstances that created them can be traced and examined, as can the events and circumstances that led to their decline and gave rise to the periods that followed. This kind of historical review can go a long way toward highlighting the direction your community is moving today and provide the people with a deeper recognition of what they might do to alter this direction if such alteration seems desirable. Change is one thing in the life of every community that is inevitable. But if the people can discover ways to control the direction of change in accordance with their wishes and self-determination, the greater will be their capacity for creating the kind of community in which to find satisfaction for their needs. No community can escape the present or deal realistically with its problems of today by dwelling in the past. But history can be a great teacher.

In the preceding section on recreation, reference was made to various forms of community drama, not only as means of recreation, but also as methods by which people can dramatize their problems—thereby making these problems more vivid for all to see—and provide special opportunities for the community to tell itself who and what it is, how it came to be what it is today, and what actions it must take if it is to become what it would like to be tomorrow. Here, then, is recreation, fruitful entertainment, constructive citizen participation, and community problem-solving all rolled together. The reconstruction and writing of the community's history from this point of view can supply the basic raw materials for the creation of dramatic productions aimed at achieving these purposes.

The fact-finding and recommended actions needed for discussion and decision-making in the general assembly concerning the community's history and the possible benefits of such information for purposes of community improvement today will be the responsibility of the history committee. All members of the committee should first review section 6,

"Procedures and Responsibilities of the Fact-Finding Committees," plus all other reports produced in the course of the development effort that may contain ideas pertaining to possible uses of historical information. Suggested points of inquiry are as follows:

Founding and Settlement

1. When, why, and under what circumstances was your community founded and settled?

2. Describe the nature of the people who founded and settled your community. From what localities, areas, regions, or countries did these early settlers come? What ethnic groups did they include? How did these groups get along with each other? General characteristics of the early population as a whole. Description of community life during the early years of settlement and growth.

3. Causes of the community's early growth and development.

4. What were the major community problems during these earlier years? How did the people go about handling these problems?

5. What were some of the major differences between the community as it used to be and as it is today?

6. What influences, if any, have the various factors concerning the community's early settlement and growth had on the community today?

Historical Periods

1. Beginning with the early years of settlement and coming up to the present, describe in chronological order the various periods through which your community has passed. Factors that brought each period into being. Factors that caused each period to wane and that led to the next.

Special attention should be given to those factors that led to any major periods of economic or population boom in the community's history and to any major periods of decline or depression. For as we have indicated, a thorough examination as to why such periods began and ended could suggest important planning and action for current community development.

For example, there are two communities located within a few miles of each other. According to professional studies made by economic geographers, one of these communities was ideally situated to become a major growth center. Yet it has been the other community with no apparent reasons for major growth that in fact did become the growth center. On careful analysis it was concluded that the chief influencing factor was that the early civic leaders of the growth community were extremely energetic in their promotional and development efforts, while the community with all the natural advantages lagged in such efforts.

2. Prepare a descriptive list of all current community problems, if any, whose origin can be traced to various periods in the community's history beginning from the early days of settlement to the present.

3. Write a brief historical description of various aspects of your community: Its economy. Its school system. Its churches. Its civic organizations. Its civic development enterprises. Its news media. Its voting patterns in local, state, and national elections. Other aspects of historical importance.

4. What influences have these aspects of history had on your community as it is today?

5. Collect and write up anecdotes, incidents, events, and personalities taken out of your community's history that have contributed to its human interest and vitality.

6. In what ways, if any, are the past and present influencing your community's future? Short range? Long range?

7. What possibilities are offered by this study and analysis of your community's history for purposes of creative writing? Music? Dramatic productions? Other forms of self-expression? Again, drawing attention to the possibilities of historical drama, would the history committee or other community groups be interested in writing and dramatizing the chain of historical events, periods, and matters of human interest that have been so integral a part of your community? As we have emphasized, this could provide your community with a powerful means—both educational and entertaining—of gaining additional insights into itself, and what it can do to build a better tomorrow.

If the history committee is interested in such a production, what recommendations and project description should be prepared as the basis for consideration and decision making in the general assembly?

28

Transition from Phase One
to Phase Two

AS the intensive first phase of the development effort comes to a close, much should have been accomplished. If the general assembly with its fact-finding and administrative committees is in smooth working order, actively supported by the sponsoring consortium formed during the early stages of getting started, your community should now have a powerful instrument for self-improvement. The citizenry should have become a more cohesive self-confident people. It should have gained new insights into the nature and causes of its problems and should have acquired increased skill in dealing with them. It should know realistically its potential for civic performance and what must be done to achieve that potential. It should have recognized with increasing clarity what it can do only for itself, and what it can do only in cooperation with its neighboring communities on an area basis.

It should also be clear that much more yet remains to be accomplished, that if community development is to really count, this is a form of development that never really ends, and that the transition to the second and more permanent phase of operations is now at hand.

Actually, this transition does not represent a sudden change, but a growing and maturing system of local and area development which in reality has been occurring all along—in the work of the committees, in the deliberations of the general assembly, in the mutual cooperation among the organizations and institutions in the sponsoring consortium, in the actions already taken, and in further actions now being planned or envisioned.

Thus, with the broad base of citizen participation which has been established, the community should now be well prepared to move forward with the more formal organizational machinery that will be needed for increasingly larger and more complex improvements. And it should be much more able to determine with precision what outside financial assistance it can effectively use and for what purpose.

In summary, the community should now be ready to handle the formalities of needed development tools such as incorporated entities and governmental aid programs without getting bogged down in needless conflict and red tape. It should be prepared to function as an effective partner with its neighboring communities in an area development effort, and it should have achieved a solid effort of its own to which needed federal aid programs can effectively respond.

For example, in economic development the essential role of an incorporated entity, or a commission attached to municipal or county government empowered to deal in real estate, develop plant sites, build industrial parks, install whatever physical facilities may be required, enter into legal contracts, handle the business of industrial plant location and other aspects of economic resource development, should now be recognized by the citizenry as a whole and have broad public support. This again brings into focus the importance of area-wide cooperation instead of the inter-community jealousy and petty bickering that so often become an extremely serious impediment to effective economic development. Moreover, the point brought out earlier in the guide that an expanding area economy helps all communities in the area should now be well understood and publicly accepted.

Therefore, if all communities in your area have initiated and are carrying out the first phase of the development effort insofar as it applies to each individual community, you now have a solid foundation upon which to build the long-range second phase of operations at both local and area levels. Suggestions and procedures for the transition from phase one to phase two are given below. With variations tailored to specific local and area situations, these procedures have been eminently successful under widely differing conditions.

Beginning at the local level, it is recommended that each community in the area convert its phase-one development organization into a nonprofit incorporated membership association. This will provide a more lasting arrangement and could include not only individual memberships but institutional memberships as well. This is not just another organization but a community-wide coordinating body capable of bringing together all segments of the community and providing necessary planning and action for projects started by the development association itself or any of its affiliated organizations or institutions, including municipal and county government.

The prime requisite is to maintain community-wide solidarity and avoid the fragmentation that can so easily occur by unwittingly falling into piecemeal action or "projectitis"—a condition now commonplace throughout America in which assorted groups work along parallel tracks, rarely if ever getting together in any united effort. A condition such as this would weaken the community as a problem-solving social body and undo much of the comprehensive community-wide pulling together developed during the first phase of operations.

Also, in phase two, the committee structure may be changed if this seems desirable, while other committees may be kept intact and continue as before. But here again a basic principle should be observed. No committee should be allowed to "run out of steam" or become "deadwood." Either it functions as an effective force for fact-finding, planning, and action, or it should be changed in personnel or discontinued —its members moving into other committees where they feel they can make a greater contribution. Any facet of the operation that ceases to be effective or that becomes counterproductive can be a drag on the effort as a whole. This must not be allowed to happen.

It is further suggested that in phase two of the operation, meetings of the general assembly be held less frequently—monthly, quarterly, or at whatever intervals seem to best fit your community. This is in accordance with a principle pointed out earlier in the guide that no effort in community development can be maintained at peak levels of intensity over more than limited periods of time. However, whatever intervals are adopted for assembly meetings during phase two, the schedule should be regular, just as it was in phase one. This will help make it a community habit, and if an emergency or urgent situation should arise calling for a special assembly meeting, such a meeting can be convened. Following are some of the items to consider.

A simple constitution and bylaws should be prepared for phase two of the operation, care being taken to comply with laws applicable in your state to incorporated nonprofit membership associations. Some of the items to be considered in the constitution would include:

1. The name of the incorporated body, which could be simply (the name of your community) Community Development Association, Inc.

2. Closely tied to this association a special incorporated entity may be set up for purposes of economic development, or if such an organization already exists, close relationships should be established between it and

the overall development association so that major civic action for a given project concerning economic development can be quickly mobilized. Also, if you have a local chamber of commerce close cooperation should be maintained between it and the economic development agency. This agency may be an outgrowth of the industrial development committee that functioned during the first phase of the operation and may include the same personnel. Several communities in your area may have such agencies, but all of them should maintain close coordination with each other and with any economic development agency established at the area level.

3. Eligibility for membership in the community development association, as in phase one, should be open to all interested citizens in the community, plus all interested organizations or institutions—both private and public.

4. The advisory council may be changed to a board of directors, the number of directors and their terms of office to be determined.

5. Leadership positions such as president, vice-president, secretary, treasurer, and their terms of office should be determined. It is recommended that persons holding these positions be members of the board, with the president serving as the board chairman.

6. Standing committees should be listed, and provision made for discussion leaders, recorders, and block captains as in phase one.

7. For all elective offices it is strongly recommended that provision be made for appointing a nominating committee to select a slate of nominees prior to each election to be submitted for voting in the general assembly, ample opportunity being provided for additional nominations from the floor. This will make it possible to obtain in advance of each election the acceptance of all persons chosen as nominees, thus making for a much smoother election procedure and helping to ensure nominees who will really work. The first nominating committee may be appointed by the general chairman of the phase-one organization, succeeding nominating committees being appointed by the president of the phase-two organization. Voting in the general assembly should be by secret ballot.

8. Sources of outside financial assistance from government agencies or foundations to help support projects that require such assistance should be sought out, and a special committee for this purpose should be provided. This committee, perhaps called the finance committee could also be responsible for planning fund-raising drives within the community as may be necessary.

These are some of the decisions to be made locally in accordance with local needs and desires in each individual community as the development effort is shifted into the more formal ongoing phase of operations.

To reach these decisions, along with numerous others that will undoubtedly arise, in as definite and public a manner as possible it is suggested that shortly before the phase-one series of general assembly meetings is due to be completed, the general chairman announce that the time of transition to the second phase of the operation is approaching and a special meeting of the advisory council is being called to draw up a tentative plan on permanent organization to be submitted for discussion in the general assembly.

It should be pointed out that such a plan will enable all citizens and existing organizations or institutions to pool their combined energies for concerted community-wide action on a continuing basis after the first phase of the operation is completed. In general this will concern actions that no one group can handle alone, or actions for which community-wide support is essential.

The announcement of this special advisory council meeting, along with an explanation of its purpose, is essential for two reasons: First, to initiate the advance planning needed for phase two; second, to make certain that the same opportunity is provided for active participation by all interested citizens and organizations or institutions in the second phase of operations as was provided during the first phase. It should be made known in this regard that ideas and suggestions are welcome from everyone, and the subject of permanent organization for the continuing phase of the development effort should become a major topic of conversation throughout the community—so everybody is in on it, everybody is aware, everybody's views may be expressed, and nobody is taken by surprise. Otherwise some people may not feel comfortable with the new arrangement. Some could even feel left out, thus introducing a needless sour note.

The same announcement concerning the permanent organization needed for the ongoing operation in your community should also include the importance of an appropriate development organization at the area level in cooperation with your neighboring communities, suggestions and procedures for which will be dealt with after we have completed our discussion for the phase-two organization at the local level—in your community and in your neighboring communities.

By making certain there is general awareness that advance planning is under way for the long-range phase of the development operation, and that all citizens, organizations, or institutions wishing to offer suggestions for this purpose have ample opportunity to do so, it will be possible to blend phase one into phase two with community-wide understanding and acceptance—another basic principle of community development.

As soon as the advisory council has devised a tentative plan of organization, embracing all details mentioned above, plus any others applicable in your community, this tentative plan should be put into a written report, including the proposed constitution and bylaws, and submitted to the general assembly for discussion and adoption or amendment. This assembly meeting should proceed in the same manner as the others—all persons receiving a copy of the report as they enter the meeting hall, the advisory council giving a highlight presentation of the content and objectives of the report, the assembly breaking into small discussion groups so all persons may have full opportunity to express themselves, then reconvening in the general assembly for reporting from the respective groups, followed by final action. This gives the community a development guide of its own making with which to work as it moves into the second phase of the operation.

After the plan for permanent organization has been finally adopted and the phase-one series of assembly meetings is completed, it is suggested that to mark this as a historic moment, a special public meeting be called with as nearly as possible all citizens in the community attending. This meeting should be planned as a gala occasion—as a time to celebrate the work of the first phase of the development operation and the formal opening of the ongoing second phase. This will be a means of reporting to the entire community what has been accomplished thus far, and pointing the way to the unfinished development tasks that lie ahead.

The meeting hall should be decorated with American flags, banks of flowers, streamers, colored lighting effects, and other items according to all the creative imagination that can be mustered. There should be a band and chorus. There should be whatever will make this meeting a memorable occasion and reinforce the determination to move forward.

The general chairman, assistant general chairman, secretary, treasurer, and all committee chairmen and other members of the advisory council should be seated at a long table at the front of the meeting hall—preferably on an elevated platform or stage.

The agenda for this special meeting marking the transition from phase one to phase two may be somewhat as follows:

1. The band provides spirited music as the crowd arrives, and copies of a summary report of accomplishments and plans for the future are distributed.

2. The general chairman calls the meeting to order.

3. A local clergyman give the invocation.

4. The general chairman, or someone else designated for this purpose, gives a short inspirational speech congratulating the community on its performance through phase one of the development effort, and issues a challenge for continued performance as the work moves into the long-range second phase.

5. The general chairman reads the list of all community actions and achievements accomplished thus far, then outlines briefly the permanent organization as approved, pointing out its significance to the community and what is being done to get it activated.

6. Each committee chairman gives a summary of his or her committee's work, the recommendations on which action has already been completed and on which action is currently in process, plus recommendations now in the planning stage or which represent challenges yet to be met.

7. The general chairman calls the roll of all existing organizations and institutions in the community, the entire membership of each rising as its name is called. A spokesman signifies the readiness of that group to affiliate with the permanent community development association and pledges full cooperation and support.

8. After the roll call of organizations and institutions, the band plays, the chorus sings, and at the appropriate point the crowd joins in the singing.

9. The general chairman announces the date and time for the first regular meeting of the new permanent community development association, at which the nominating committee will be ready with its report and the election will be held. That first meeting of the new development association might well be a special banquet with an inspirational outside speaker, which could lead to an annual community event.

10. If at all possible, it is recommended that prior to this public meeting the advisory council select a special community-wide action project along the lines discussed in section 17, "From Study to Action," that can be presented with a date set not more than two weeks later for the action to begin. The day set for this action to begin could be declared by the mayor and city council as a local holiday—not to celebrate an event

from the past, but to celebrate tomorrow—with all citizens turning out to join in the action. A project such as this, if settled on and agreed to in advance, scheduled as an immediate follow-up to this special public meeting, will give a tremendous psychological boost to the second phase of operations.

11. With the band playing softly and with appropriate lighting effects, the chorus sings an inspiring closing number, and as the music fades a clergyman pronounces the benediction.

12. The general chairman declares the meeting adjourned. The house-lights return to full illumination, and as the crowd moves toward the exits, the band plays an appropriate goodnight. The first phase of the development effort is now completed, and the long-range second phase is ready to begin.

In principle the formation of the area development association is little different from the formation of the development associations in the area's individual communities. At the appropriate point in time when the transition from phase one to phase two is being worked out, the general chairman in your community and the general chairmen in your neighboring communities arrange a series of joint meetings of all local advisory councils.

Matters calling for attention at these joint intercommunity meetings will include all items suggested above for consideration in devising the plan of organization for the second phase of operations in your individual community. However, other items will also come in for consideration in planning and putting together the area development effort. Some of these will be:

1. What geographical territory is to be regarded as your area? Is it your county, or two or more counties? It could be a territory that cuts across county lines, but this could have certain political disadvantages, and if at all feasible it is recommended that the area be limited to adjacent counties that are regarded as a natural geogrpahical area. Another question to be considered is whether or not this is an area within which there are sufficient resources, including one or more towns or cities that could be considered growth centers or potential growth centers, to make it viable from the standpoint of social and economic development. In short, before an area development association or other area corporate entities, such as an economic development commission, can be formed, it is first necessary to determine the geographical and political boundaries of the territory to be regarded as "your area."

2. How is each community in the area to be represented in the leadership and committee structure of the area development association? Membership in the area association, as in the local development associations, should be open to all interested area residents and existing organizations or institutions.

3. How is the area development association to be structured? In considering this question it is recommended that it be structured along the same lines as the development operation for phase two in each individual community—a nonprofit incorporated membership association with a general assembly, an appropriate group of elected directors and officers, and a series of committees for fact-finding, planning, and action in applicable fields of interest.

4. If some of the communities in your area have not yet undergone the phase-one development effort, they should be encouraged to do so with the help of people from communities in which this effort has been carried out.

5. As in the individual communities, a name needs to be chosen for the area development association, a constitution and bylaws need to be written, positions and terms of office determined, a nominating committee established, and the legal procedures applicable in your state to the formation of nonprofit membership corporations must be followed.

6. The frequency of area meetings should be determined—general area membership meetings probably not more than once a year, which could be a dinner meeting. Committees and other such groups within the association or related to it in various ways—for example, an economic development commission—would meet much more frequently.

7. Consideration needs to be given as to what committees the area association should include, and how these committees are to relate to and coordinate with committees included in the development effort in the individual communities.

8. We have mentioned the probable need for a separate incorporated entity at the area level for economic development. What about other fields of interest? Should there be other separate area corporate entities, and if so in what fields? For example, a council of local governments would be extremely useful, particularly for purposes of federal funding. How are special corporate entities at the area level to relate to their counterparts at the local community level, and to the area development association as a whole?

9. What will be the operating costs of the area development association and of any separate corporate entities it may include? What revenues are available to cover these costs? To what extent will outside financial assistance be needed, and from what sources might this assistance be obtained? Should there be a paid staff for the area development operations? If so how large? Should provision be made to bring in outside professional consultants from time to time? If so, this too should be taken into account in determining probable costs and sources of financing.

These are some of the questions the representatives of the cooperating communities must look into and for which answers must be found in devising a plan for the area development association that will be needed during the long-range second phase of operations. Certainly there will be many other serious questions to consider, but the basic principle to keep in mind is that this is an area development effort evolved from the bottom up, not from the top down, and for that reason the answers to these questions are for you—the people—to think through. This will give your area development effort more meaning, and in the long run you will get more done. By reporting the tentative plan of area organization back to each individual community for discussion, amendment, and approval, it will become the people's plan. And as the area effort goes into operation it will do so with broad public understanding and support from all area communities. It will be truly a partnership effort, among communities, and between all communities and the total area of which they are a part.

As in all aspects of community development, there is no one right way of structuring the area organization. But there are these guiding principles: That it be built by the people themselves, drawing on whatever outside professional consultation may be needed; that an effective two-way flow of communications be maintained between the area operation and the operations in all individual communities; and that all of these operations be mutually supportive and conducted in accordance with local and area needs as determined by the people in cooperation with their civic leaders and elected officials. If these basic principles are carefully observed, effective local and area development will be achieved. The importance of the many decisions that go into this effort cannot be overemphasized. For when the kind of local and area development to which this guide is committed is truly activated across the nation, American democracy will be strengthened, and the community problems that have accompanied the modern age will become less resistant to solution.

Index